# The Potlatch Papers

# THE
# POTLATCH

Christopher Bracken

# PAPERS

### A Colonial
### Case History

The University of Chicago Press
Chicago and London

CHRISTOPHER BRACKEN is assistant professor of
English at the University of Alberta.

The University of Chicago Press, Chicago 60637
The University of Chicago Press, Ltd., London
© 1997 by The University of Chicago
All rights reserved. Published 1997
Printed in the United States of America

06 05 04 03 02 01 00 99 98 97   1 2 3 4 5


ISBN: 0-226-06986-9 (cloth)
ISBN: 0-226-06987-7 (paper)

Title page illustration: Alert Bay (detail),
courtesy of Vancouver Public Library,
photograph no. 9896

Library of Congress Cataloging-in-Publication Data

Bracken, Christopher.
    The potlatch papers : a colonial case history /
Christopher Bracken.
        p.   cm.
    Includes bibliographical references and index.
    ISBN 0-226-06986-9 (cloth : alk. paper).—ISBN 0-226-06987-7
(paper : alk. paper)
        1. Potlatch—Canada—History—Sources.   2. Indians of North
America—Canada—Social life and customs.   3. Indians of
North America—Canada—Government relations.   4. Indians of
North America —Legal status, laws, etc.—Canada.   5. Canada—
Politics and government.   6. Canada—Race relations.   I. Title.
    E78.C2B78   1997
    971'.000497—dc21                                          97-9829
                                                                  CIP

*You there, what do you say about what you
are, while you are saying what I am?*

ROBIN BLASER (CITING MICHEL DE CERTEAU),
*THE HOLY FOREST*

CONTENTS

ACKNOWLEDGMENTS

It was Dara Culhane who first suggested that I look at the potlatch papers. "The what?" I said. Her seemingly casual remark changed everything. Erin Soros remains my first, best, and most terrifying reader, but it would have been impossible to write this book if I hadn't known that Lorraine Weir was going to read it next. John Borrows offered insightful and timely comments on the first final draft. Charlotte Coté corrected my misunderstanding of the word "Aht." And I could not have brought this book to publication without the support and encouragement of Daniel Boyarin, Judith Butler, J. C. Smith, and Gerald Vizenor. Thanks also to Alan Thomas for being the first editor to really understand what I was trying to do. The support of the Social Sciences and Humanities Research Council of Canada was indispensable to the realization of this project and is gratefully acknowledged.

Map 1: Canoe nations of the northwest coast
Map by Eric Leinberger from *The Great Canoes: Reviving a Northwest Coast Tradition* by David Neel. Reprinted with permission of Douglas and McIntyre and University of Washington Press.

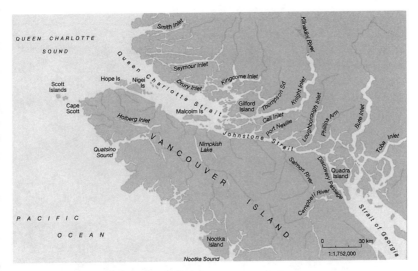

Map 2: Kwakwa̲ka'wakw territory

From *Kwakwa̲ka'wakw Settlements, 1775–1920: A Geographical Analysis and Gazeteer* by Robert Galois. © UBC Press 1994. Reprinted with permission. All rights reserved.

# SEND-OFF

SEND-OFF

If it began anywhere, it began in the mail. In 1884 the Parliament of Canada passed a law banning the performance of potlatches and tamanawas dances among the First Nations of British Columbia. The new statute took its place in a long series of letters, reports, memoranda, and petitions that had circulated between Ottawa and British Columbia, and between Ottawa and itself, since at least 1872. As it shuttled from post to post, this correspondence had knitted traders, missionaries, settlers, government officials, and aboriginal people into an immense web of communication. After the statute came into force on 1 January 1885, writing gathered around it with increased intensity. Most of the correspondence aimed to define, to regulate, and ultimately to destroy the social systems of the British Columbia First Nations. But many texts were delivered in their defense, usually in self-defense. Over the years these potlatch papers gathered to form an archive of postal literature—from the first missives of the 1860s to the last reports of the 1930s, when the mail finally stopped coming and this file, at least, was closed.

What was sent in the potlatch papers? It would be correct to say that they transmit the arguments and counter-arguments, the errors and corrections, the recommendations, hatreds, and resistances of a whole canon of minor authors. But something else was sent, something that left its mark in every dispatch yet resided nowhere. For the correspondence gives us access to the postal principle that in the late nineteenth and early twentieth centuries sent Canada out to its western limit, delivering it to the very edge of itself on the west coast of British Columbia, where it immediately overlapped itself and returned to sender.

*Opposite:* A potlatch given in nineteenth-century Victoria, British Columbia. The sheer number of onlookers makes it impossible to see exactly what they are watching. Courtesy of The Field Museum, neg. no. 17526, Chicago.

And behind Canada came Europe, traveling to its west-ernmost boundary via the same system of posts. In the northwest, Europe was to discover not only its geographi-cal border, but its conceptual limit, the line where Western European metaphysics confronted the beyond of its own restricted enclosure. But Europe had also *preceded* Canada to the northwest coast. It was already there when Canada arrived, already there where Canada would come to be— as if Europe were Canada's past sent to meet it from the future. When I say that Europe arrived on the coast be-fore Canada, however, I do not simply mean that Euro-pean explorers had scouted the Pacific Northwest in the 1770s, almost a century before the Dominion of Canada came into being and only a few years after Britain had seized control of New France. Nor do I point to the fur trade that had brought British, Russian, Spanish, and Euro-American traders to coastal waters from the 1780s to the 1850s. Nor do I merely acknowledge that Vancouver Island had become a British colony in 1849. Or that Brit-ain's Colonial Office had entrusted the administration of the colony to the Hudson's Bay Company until 1858— the year the mainland colony of British Columbia was established—and had overseen the union of the two colo-nies in 1866. Nor, finally, do I allude to the missionaries from Europe and elsewhere who had begun circulating through the northwest in the 1840s. In putting Canada behind Europe I do not just confirm that Europe's repre-sentatives had arrived on the coast long before 1871, when British Columbia passed out of Britain's supervision and became the sixth province in the Canadian confedera-tion.

Although these events all have a place in the historical record, they do not belong to the "already-thereness" that I wish to evoke here. What I want to underline instead is that, when Canada finally delivered itself to its western border, it found Europe already embodied in a group of cultures that white Canadians wished to define themselves against. Europe was already there among the very First Nations that European Canada, Europe-in-Canada, con-sidered absolutely different from itself. Since Canada failed to distinguish itself conclusively from the people it encoun-tered at its limit, an uncertainty about whiteness has not ceased to haunt the settler society that grew up in British

Columbia. It was as if from the moment that society found itself reflected back to itself by the local First Nations, it could no longer lay claim to its own identity—as if white settlers arrived in British Columbia only to discover they were somehow unequal to themselves.

# FOLDING
FOLDING

*If there were no fold, or if the fold had a limit somewhere—a limit other than itself as a mark, margin, or march (threshold, limit, or border)—there would be no text. But if the text does not, to the letter, exist, then* there is [il y a, es gibt] *perhaps a text. A text one must make tracks with.*

DERRIDA, "THE DOUBLE SESSION"

## THREE ZONES

In what follows I want to locate the law against the potlatch and tamanawas within three intertwining zones of textual contradiction. I have already identified two of them. First, there is the limit. In the colonial text the limit marks the line, or set of lines, where Europe attempts to trace a clean boundary between itself and its exterior. Yet the limit inevitably fails to establish itself because it is crossed by the very movement that draws it. The limit occupies a textual zone where the marking of limits is impossible.

The fold is the second zone of contradiction. It draws together everything that the limit sets apart. The fold is a bend in the colonial text where Europe brings itself back into an intimate encounter with all that it situates outside its outermost rim. It is where Europe overlaps itself with what it defines as its own beyond. Considered as a rhetorical structure, the fold is perhaps a mode of irony: it makes contradictory terms interact.

Then there is the gift, though it cannot be thought without the limit and the fold. In the colonial text the gift lo-

*Opposite:* Gunboat diplomacy. Sailors from *H.M.S. Boxer* pose against the backdrop of Tsawatti in Knight Inlet on 2 June 1873, while members of the Kwakwaka'wakw First Nation pose with a group of white sailors. Photographer Richard Maynard accompanied Israel Wood Powell, the Superintendent of Indian Affairs for British Columbia, as he toured the coast in 1873 and 1874. Courtesy of The Field Museum, neg. no. 17523, Chicago.

cates itself on both sides of Europe's self-imposed limit. It occupies the zone where what Europe identifies as its outside bends back over its interior. In the vicinity of the gift, Europe returns to itself even as it tries to remain at an absolute distance from itself.

I call the limit, the fold, and the gift intertwining "zones" to distinguish them from concepts. They are not ideas that inhere in a human subject, nor do they represent objects that exist in the world outside the mind. They are instead the evanescent yet violent effects of writing. And they set to work within the postal literature that delivered Europe-in-Canada to British Columbia in the nineteenth and twentieth centuries. Together they make up a region in the colonial text where an author's discourse consistently fails to do what it says it is doing. To map the three zones, therefore, is to show how a given text diverges from itself.

## LIMIT

In his 1889 report to the Geographical Society of Berlin, Franz Boas interprets the northwest coast of British Columbia as Europe's outer edge, the westernmost border of the West. It traces the conceptual and geographic limit of European civilization. Yet the traveler who arrives there hoping to study the region's aboriginal, non-European cultures quickly finds that Europe's "influence" (*Einfluss*) has infiltrated almost every corner of the province. In British Columbia, Europe defines its limits only to find that it has already exceeded them.

Published under the title "Herr Dr. F. Boas: Über seine Reisen in Britisch Columbien," the report is a postcard sent home by an observant tourist-ethnographer. Boas describes the sights he saw and the people he met during his first two research expeditions to British Columbia: the privately funded voyage of 1886 and the 1888 voyage that began his work for the British Association for the Advancement of Science (BAAS) Committee for Investigating and Publishing Reports on the Physical Characters, Languages, and Industrial and Social Condition of the North-Western Tribes of the Dominion of Canada. Curiously, Boas prefaces his geographic and ethnographic remarks by suggesting that it would be just as easy for his readers to go and look for themselves. Boas's British Columbia is a place where everything remains to be seen. Now that the Canadian Pacific Railroad is complete, he says, "every year the beauty of the country attracts a stream of tourists [*Vergnügungsreisenden*] who visit the accessible parts of the Rocky Mountains, the Selkirks, or the picturesque coast," and since neither the topography, nor the geology, nor the plants and animals, nor the original inhabitants of "this vast mountainous chain are sufficiently known" to Europe, the province "remains wide open" to the gaze of the tourist-explorer (*Forscher*) (Rohner 1969, 3). British Columbia lies at the outer boundary of European knowledge.

If the province as a whole is situated on the rim of Western thinking, then the mountainous coast forms the rim of this rim, its "outermost line" (*der äufserste Rand*). Boas reports that "there are only four routes" that pass through the Coast Mountains to connect "the long drawn-out coast with the interior." In the south the Fraser River serves as "an old traffic artery," while a difficult and dangerous trail winds through "the dark gorge of the Bute Inlet." Further north the Bella Coola river joins the upper Fraser Valley to the coast, and the Skeena and Stikine rivers trace a final pass through the mountains. Bound tightly within its borders "the coast forms, geographically and economically, a closed-off piece of territory [*ein in sich geschlossenes Gebiet*] which has little in common with the interior of the country" (4).

What distinguishes coast from interior, for Boas, is not just a geography but a whole economy of closure. On this "closed-off" strip of land Europe ceases to have an exchange with itself. Not only does Western knowledge have no currency here, but Europe, conceived as a distinct body of territory, comes to its end. The West posts itself only as far as this coastal boundary and does not circulate beyond it.

The western limit takes the form of a quadrangle anchored at four terminal points. Just as four overland routes tie the coast to the interior, so four cities mark out the liminal zone where British Columbia gives way to the Pacific Ocean. On the Fraser River delta, New Westminster is home to agriculture and salmon fisheries. Victoria, the provincial capital and seat of trade, lies at the south end of Vancouver Island, with the coal-mining town of Nanaimo to the north. The city of Vancouver, "built after the Pacific Railroad was finished," sits on the mainland at the mouth of the Fraser. Boas observes that "[s]teamboat lines to east Asia originate there and the planned cable to Australia will start from there" (5).

Newly tacked to the edge of the edge of North America, the port of Vancouver marks the point where Europe comes to its end and gives way to something called "Asia." But just when it has arrived at its limit and begins to rub against the borders of the "East," the West folds back to find that even at its end it is still contiguous with itself. The British Columbia coast is soon to be tied to Australia, a once Eastern space that, like Canada, has been forced into the orbit of the Western world. At the terminus of the new railway, Vancouver binds together a set of contradictory movements: it points away from Europe by pointing directly back to it. Here the West brings itself to a close only on the condition that it simultaneously begin again.

It is at this paradoxical limit-without-limit, where West and East join only to part again, that Boas situates the objects that he wants most to study. After describing British Columbia's landscape he devotes the rest of his postcard-report to a discussion of the people living on the coast: the people he names "Indians" (*die Indianer*). What he suggests is that, despite the efforts of settlers to make the province into a prosthesis of Europe, the whiteness of this "outermost line" remains precarious. "The total number of Indians in British Columbia is estimated at 38,000," he says, "the majority of whom live on the coast; there they outnumber the white inhabitants" (5).

"The stranger coming for the first time to Victoria," observes Boas, "is startled by the great number of Indians living in this town." Tourists and explorers "meet them everywhere," though he notes that "[t]hey dress mostly in European fashion [*meist nach europäischer Sitte gekleidet*]" (5). No matter where the European ethnographer looks, he confronts his own doubles. "Totally other and yet the same," the aboriginal people of Victoria reflect the observer's Europeanness back to him while changing it utterly.[1] They adopt a code of dress that signifies their proximity to Western civilization, yet by repeating that code they render it different from itself and distance it irretrievably from all things Western. Boas's encounter with Victoria's aboriginal residents is therefore an instance of what Homi K. Bhabha names "colonial specularity." It sets up a screen where in a single glance Boas sees himself *as* an "Indian": "colonial specularity, doubly inscribed, does not produce a mirror where the self apprehends itself," says Bhabha, "it is always the split screen of the self and its doubling, the hybrid" (1994, 114).

Yet Boas hints that Victoria's aboriginal citizens are bound to Europe only insofar as they pass beyond it and attach themselves instead to Asia and to Japan. As he describes their clothes and their faces—"the color of their skin is very light; they have prominent cheekbones, straight, short-cut hair, and dark eyes"—he notes that "[t]hey remind us so strongly of the east Asiatic peoples [*ostasiatischer Völker*] that throughout British Columbia there is the indisputable opinion that they are descendants of Japanese sailors [*japanischer Schiffer*]" (6).

Boas avoids discussing the complex identity of these figures who, in their singular being, simultaneously tie and untie West and East. He merely asserts that they are not sufficiently authentic to be proper objects for serious ethnographic inquiry. "Victoria," he confides, "is not the place to learn much about the Indian." To his gaze the aboriginal people of Victoria have deprived themselves of their proper identity by imitating Europe and reflecting it back to itself. But why does their adoption of European dress not deprive Boas of his own identity? If the Native people of Victoria render their aboriginality less aboriginal by acting more European, surely their mimicry also makes Europe less European, and more aboriginal, than it was before encountering them. For Boas, though, the Europeanness of these non-Europeans is just an obstacle to research and does not give pause for reflection.

Instead he advises his readers that, to understand the people of the northwest coast, it is necessary to move beyond Europe's edge and shift closer to Asia. "We have to seek [the Indian] out in his own country," he says, "where he lives according to his old customs, not influenced by European civilization [*europäischer Zivilisation*]." The best way to slip beyond Europe's grip is to seek out "the northern parts of the coast," where the economy of closure restricts the traffic of European "influence" (6).

Still, even the northern section of the coast does not surpass the bounds of Western civilization. A few "trading posts" and "missions" have been established there, and the region is strewn with "salmon fisheries" and "canning plants"—"all situated in the larger Indian villages because the Indians do the fishing." Boas insists that the impact of these European outposts on the most remote First Nations is both pervasive and negligible. He says the fisheries "exercise a much greater influence on the Indians than the missionaries do," but in the next sentence he affirms the opposite: "A number of tribes, however, have even escaped this influence, as for example, the Kwakiutl of northern Vancouver Island" (6).

To find a culture uncontaminated by European influence—because situated outside Europe's outermost limit—Boas directs his audience ever northward to the region where the tip of Vancouver Island angles toward Japan. He names the people who live here the "Kwakiutl," though Europeans have also called them Quackewlth, Quackuli, Quackerewhs, Quoquolth, Kwakiool, Kwawkewlth. In Boas's lexicon the name "Kwakiutl" refers not only to the so-called Southern Kwakiutl, but also to the Heiltsuk and the Haisla. The Southern Kwakiutl now tend to call themselves Kwagiulth in communities lying to the south of their territory and in the north Kwakwaka'wakw, which means "speakers of the Kwakwala language."[2] For Boas, the Kwakwaka'wakw are not "totally different yet the same" with regard to European civilization. They are instead absolutely other. But other to whom?

## FOLD

When positioning the Kwakwaka'wakw Boas presupposes that he already understands who they are, though that is what he has traveled to the coast to find out. According to a precomprehension that he knows without knowing it, the Kwakwaka'wakw are a people and a culture who live just beyond the westernmost limit of the West. Yet this definition presupposes another presupposition, assumes another assumption. To make the Kwakwaka'wakw into the absolute other of Europe suggests that Boas already understands what Europe is. It assumes that, if called upon to do so, he could define the West that he defines the Kwakwaka'wakw against, as if somewhere in his store of knowledge, he held the very essence of the West, Westness itself.

But what is this thing that places every "non-Western"

and "non-European" culture at a clear distance from itself by pushing them, if necessary, toward Japan? One might say that Europe is a geopolitical body, a particular volume of territory. But this body cannot be clearly delimited because it constantly adds members to itself, strapping on prostheses like British Columbia, Canada, and Australia. Besides, the Europe sketched by Boas is not a place so much as a force, an "influence," which is rapidly and violently imprinting itself onto every region of northwestern North America. This force arrives in excess, moreover, for it is constantly overflowing itself. Forever edging closer to Japan while turning away from it, Europe puts limits on itself only to discover that it has already slipped past them.

Yet the Europe under discussion here is really not a thing at all but rather a fold in certain texts that locate the limit of the West in British Columbia. The signifier "European" marks the place where the structure of these texts subverts, in advance, their own efforts to determine what Europe-in-British-Columbia is. For Europe *is* not. Rather, Europe folds. It binds together themes that desire to remain at an uncrossable distance from each other and inexorably situates Europe there where, by its own calculations, it cannot and must not be, placing it amid everything it holds to be most *un*-European.

As it folds, Europe doubles itself. It lays itself alongside itself and renders itself different from itself. And the irreducible spacing that divides Europe from itself clears the way for an uncertainty over the Euro-Canadian identity. Since Europe holds itself apart from itself, it finds its own reflection in the most un-European regions of Canada, and there intervenes the possibility not simply that Europe-in-Canada has ceased to be itself but that it has never been itself. The Euro-Canadian identity takes form only on the condition that it remain unequal to itself. It produces itself by destroying itself, and the play of production-destruction is generated within the folds of the colonial text.

The fold and the uncertainty it creates implicate not only Europe and Europe-in-Canada, but all the substitutes that tend to stand in for them in the literature to be considered here. The series of Europe's substitutes includes civilization, the West, Christianity, improvement, progress, elevation, the settler, the colonist, and, inevitably, "the white man." In texts dealing with a former British colony like

11

*folding*

British Columbia, though, a sustained synecdoche tends to substitute England for the whole of Europe and its "influence."

Gilbert Malcolm Sproat's *Scenes and Studies of Savage Life*, published in 1868, exemplifies each of these rhetorical turns: both the synecdoche that takes England for all of European civilization and the fold that destroys Europe-in-Canada by making it overlap a region that it defines as absolutely different from itself. Perhaps because *Scenes* interlaces autobiography with ethnography, it is a text that has as much to say about itself as about the culture it claims to describe. It is an autobiography of itself in that it constantly draws its reader's attention to the foldings that govern its structure—as if the narrative were more concerned with its own life than with the life of its author. As an ethnography *Scenes* records not the customs of other cultures but the ways in which the author's discourse becomes other to itself. For the reasoning that Sproat delivered to the shores of Vancouver Island did not fail to fold back on itself when it encountered the people who live to the south and west of the Kwakwaka'wakw.

Sproat arrived on the island more than fifteen years before Boas. And if Boas was a student come to study the region's aboriginal cultures—a task that drove him to seek a region of authentic "old customs" somewhere beyond Europe's limits—then Sproat was a colonial post-officer sent to deliver the West to its westernmost edge. It was his task to disseminate the civilizing influence that Boas tried to circumvent.

When Sproat sailed into Barkley Sound in 1860, his mission was not just to oversee the operation of a sawmill and the construction of a company town in what is now Port Alberni. As he passed through the sound and continued up Alberni Inlet, heading far into the southern portion of the island, he planned to set up Europe: to Europeanize not only a landscape, but its inhabitants as well. Alberni was not to be just another colonial outpost; it was to become a part of England, an appendage sewn to the empire's flank.

Sproat observes elsewhere that in his view Vancouver Island, British Columbia, and Canada itself were not English colonies. They were England's equivalents. And so thirteen years after his arrival at Alberni, in a speech entitled "Canada and the Empire," he proposes Canada as a substitute for England. By 1873 Sproat was the agent general for British Columbia in London, at the seat of English government. Noting that he shares the desires of "the younger political men of Canada," he advises Great Britain to adopt the Canadian political system and transform Canada, England, Scotland, and Ireland into "provinces" joined under one imperial parliament—"a change that would make Vancouver Island essentially an outlying English county" (1873, 7, 2, 13). Sproat assures his audience that "[t]he Canadian political system is the natural development of the English; it would not, therefore, be a foreign, or incongruous excrescence" (7). Canada is not a parasite upon the body of the empire. Rather it lies at the empire's heart—a legitimate child who expects to inherit the privileges that belong to its parent. If for Sproat the English are "a dominant race" among dominant races, the most European of European nations, then Canada is more English than England itself (8). Just as the Native people of Victoria offer a double of Europe to Boas's gaze, so Canada offers itself as England's double and sends back to the English an improved image of themselves. But this is 1873.

In 1860 Canada was still taking shape as a nation, and Sproat situated himself in the vanguard of the colonization of its northwest coast. He recalls in the preface to *Scenes* that (unlike Boas) he did not arrive on Vancouver Island to collect ethnographic data. His book was an accident, a by-product of the five years he spent as "a colonial magistrate, and also a proprietor of the settlement at the head of Alberni Inlet." "I did not intend, originally, to publish these observations," he says, "and have made no attempt, now, at literary ornament in producing them" (1987, xxiii). He did, however, append epigraphs by various English poets to each of his book's twenty-eight chapters, and several short poems of his own "ornament" the original 1868 edition. What is more, the problem of literary style poses itself in every sentence of his book.

In the first scene of *Scenes* Sproat makes himself a character in his own story and recalls that "[i]n August 1860, I entered Barkley Sound, on the outside, or western, coast of Vancouver Island, with the two armed vessels, *Woodpecker* and *Meg Merrilies*, manned by about fifty men, who accompanied me for the purpose of taking possession of the district now called Alberni" (3). However, according

13

*folding*

to Charles Lillard, who edited the 1987 Sono Nis edition of *Scenes,* Sproat was not there to supervise the seizure of this territory. At least one work party had landed in June 1860, more than two months before Sproat arrived to take up his post as overseer of the settlement.

While the opening sentence foregrounds the role story-telling plays in Sproat's ethnography, Lillard insists that "[t]his statement is Sproat's only excursion from fact to fiction in the pages that follow" (xvii). It is as if Lillard, like Sproat, wants to defend the text against a reading that examines how the author's discourse fails to offer a true account of its world. But there are many more occasions when Sproat's constative assertions turn against themselves and the demands of literary ornamentation add a trace of "fiction" to his supposed statements of "fact."

When Sproat lands at Alberni, he informs the people who already live there that he and his companions have "bought all the surrounding land from the Queen of England, and [wish] to occupy the site of the village for a particular purpose." Later, he will name these people the Aht, though today they are widely known in the surrounding world as the Nootka and call themselves Nuu'-chah'nulth. Since Sproat's description of them has more to do with "literary ornament" and the textual fold than with everyday life in a nineteenth-century Nuu'chah'nulth community, one must take care not to assume that the name Aht, as he deploys it, has any relation to the same name as it is used today among the Nuu'chah'nulth. What is certain, though, is that at the start of his narrative Sproat resorts to the threat of violence—"being provided, fortunately, in both vessels with cannon"—to drive the Aht from their ancestral village (4).[3]

Like Boas after him, Sproat identifies the fringe of British Columbia as the western limit of Western knowledge. "These were the first savages that I had ever seen," he confides, "and they were probably at that time less known than any aboriginal people under British dominion" (5). A double synecdoche establishes itself here: Sproat is the agent who stands in for the whole of "British dominion," while Britain's boundaries in turn substitute themselves for the borders of Western science. At this limit Britain and the West mark themselves off from a community of so-called savages who embody all that the European intruders insist they themselves are not. But as soon as Sproat distances Europe from its beyond, the distinction between them begins to collapse, and all the thematic strands that signify "civilization" become intertwined with those signifying "savagery."

A few days after his arrival Sproat talks with the "Chiefs" of the "Sheshaht," the people he claims to have driven from their homes. An elder tells him, "We do not wish to sell our land nor our water; let your friends stay in their own country." From the start of his narrative, then, Sproat puts the Nuu'chah'nulth on stage in an act of protest against the arrival of the colonizers, but because he is the author of these "scenes," he controls both the direction and the outcome of the debate. Though it is staged, however, his encounter with this unnamed Nuu'chah'nulth elder establishes a pattern that will repeat itself for years to come in the discourse on the potlatch, for one of the defining qualities of that discourse, particularly after 1914, will be the attempt by the First Nations of coastal British Columbia to seize control of the techniques of representation in order to substitute their own accounts of who they are for the stories that European Canada tells itself about them. The problem, though, is that the discourse on the potlatch will exceed the concept of representation altogether. It will occur, to borrow Gerald Vizenor's phrase, in "the ruins of representation."

Meanwhile, speaking as a character in his own story, Sproat replies to the Nuu'chah'nulth elder by assuring him that he and his people will soon become white just like the European intruders: "the white men will come," says Sproat. "All your people know that they are your superiors; they make the things which you value. You cannot make muskets, blankets, or bread. The white men will teach your children to read printing, and *to be like* themselves." The elder responds that the Aht have no desire to be eaten by Europe: "We do not want the white man. He steals what we have. We wish to live as we are" (4–5, emphasis added).

What Sproat shows, though, is that even before contact the Aht already resembled the Europeans, were already "like" them. The similarity that is to spring up between the two cultures in the future is already coming toward them from the past, for just when the Aht are said to be most different from the Europeans, the text folds back on itself and brings the two groups into an intimate proximity.

15

*folding*

And Sproat fails to put a racially "pure" Europe into writing. I limit myself to two examples.

In chapter 4 Sproat describes the "physical appearance" of the "Aht." He argues in the fourth paragraph that the "Haida and other natives to the north are fairer in complexion than the Aht"—indeed so fair that "[t]heir young women's skins are as clear and white as those of Englishwomen." Yet if for Sproat the Haida sometimes resemble Englishwomen, the appearance of the Aht sets them at an unbridgeable distance from all northern Europeans. "Cook and Meares probably mentioned exceptional cases," he assures us, "in stating that the natives of Nootka had the fair complexions of the north of Europe," and he insists that "[t]he prevailing colour of the people in Vancouver Island is unmistakably, as here described, a sort of dull brown" (21).

But Sproat's discourse has already overlapped itself with an equal and opposite counterassertion. The same "dull brown" complexion that divides the Aht from northern Europeans in paragraph 4 draws them near to the English in paragraph 3. Says Sproat, "Their complexion is a dull brown, just about, perhaps, what the English complexion would be if the people were in a savage instead of a civilized condition—the difference being explained by the habits of life of the Aht, by their frequent exposure, and by the effect of their food of blubber, oil, and fish" (21).

Though at one instant Sproat is careful to separate the two cultures, at another he says that the difference between the Aht and the English is a difference neither between two stages of human evolution nor between two races but between two diets and two "habits of life." What he suggests, just before he affirms the opposite, is that the Aht are well-tanned English people who spend much of their time outdoors and eat a lot of fish, while the English are pale-skinned Aht who tend to stay indoors and, perhaps, eat too much bread. In his discourse the Aht are no longer simply brown, and the English, and indeed all "northern Europeans," are no longer simply white. The two groups were "like" each other before they even met. To the colonizing gaze, however, the mingling of races is unbearable.

Sproat tells the elder of the "Sheshaht" band that the white skin of the European settlers makes them superior to the Aht. However, his commentary on racial difference shows that whiteness cannot be put into discourse without immediately becoming tangled up in its opposite—and ceasing to be white. The text assigns "white" and "brown" the task of holding the "civilized condition" apart from the "savage," yet these words serve only to draw "civilization" and "savagery" together again. In Sproat's discourse, skin color—which here serves as his privileged signifier of racial and cultural difference—fails to mean what it says it means because it occupies a zone of the text where two opposing themes overlap and cancel each other out. The mark of Europe's superiority crumbles before it can even take shape.

The textual fold recurs in the second to last chapter of *Scenes,* where Sproat shows that civilization is closest to itself precisely when it approaches what it considers most debased and most uncivilized. In the preface Sproat offers his last two chapters as a substitute for the rest of the book, as if the entire narrative had been folded up and lodged at the end. "I have stated in the two concluding chapters the opinions which I have formed from my observation and experience of these savages," he says, and he predicts that "[s]ome, perhaps, will read these chapters, who have not time to read the whole book" (xxiii).

The next-to-last chapter offers "some remarks . . . on the subject of intercourse between civilized and uncivilized races" (183). It is here that Sproat foresees the death of the Aht. He recalls that, when he first arrived in Alberni, he did not see a change in his neighbors—but only because he had failed to observe "the gradual process" of their decline. Then suddenly he read the first signs of doom: "I seemed all at once to perceive that a few sharp-witted young natives had become what I can only call *offensively European,* and that the mass of the Indians no longer visited the settlement in their former free independent way, but lived listlessly in the villages, brooding seemingly over heavy thoughts" (186, emphasis added). Why should the narrator be offended to find Native people reflecting an image of Europe back to him as they edge toward extinction? The offense lies in the fact that their imitations actively destroy Europeanness by rendering it different from itself. For no matter what is happening to the Aht, it seems that Europe is already dead.

The act of mimicry presents European civilization with

17

its own likeness, but the production of that likeness is possible only if Europe was from the start never itself. Europeanness can be repeated by the Aht only because it was already a repetition. It is divided from itself when it is imitated, but if Europeanness did not already and by definition stand apart from itself, within itself, then it could not be taken away from Sproat and sent back to him by the "sharp-witted young natives" of Alberni. A Europe that maintained a unified and unruptured self-sameness could not be separated from itself and confronted with its own image. Europe is already dead because it is haunted by its own ghost, which doubles it in effigy. Europeanness exists only on the condition that it has, in advance, failed to exist.

Though it is Europe that confronts its own death here, Sproat insists the reason the Aht have become too European is that they, and not Europe, are passing into oblivion. He attributes the "decay" of their culture neither to the disease nor the alcohol nor the social upheaval that European settlement has brought with it. The disaster is instead the result of a change in the light. "The steady brightness of civilised life seemed," he says, "to dim and extinguish the flickering light of savageism, as the rays of the sun put out a common fire" (187). The binary opposition that contrasts the brightness of civilization with the "dull" flicker of barbarism can only mean the death of barbarity. Unless it means the text cannot keep the two apart.

Sproat says the Aht responded to the construction of the settlement at Alberni by stepping off the path of human progress and regressing toward sheer bestiality. "The effect is this," he says:

18

> the Indian loses the motives for exertion that he had, and gets no new ones in their place. The harpoon, bow, canoe chisel, and whatever other simple instruments he may possess, are laid aside, and he no longer seeks praise among his own people for their skilful use. Without inclination or inducement to work, or to seek personal distinction—having given up, and being now averse to his old life—bewildered and *dulled* by the new life around him for which he is unfitted—the unfortunate savage becomes

more than ever a creature of instinct, and approaches the condition of an animal. (190, emphasis added)

But just when the Aht have stripped themselves of whatever marks of civilization they once possessed and have
reached the absolute limit separating humans from animals—at the point where it would be impossible to de-
scend any farther—at this same point they find European
civilization rising from the depths to join them. While they
wilt under the glare of Europe's white light, Europe itself
turns in its upward path of social evolution, folds back,
and begins to sink.

Sproat's rhetoric places Europe simultaneously at the
height of human attainment and below the line dividing
humanity from bestiality. Here is the next sentence: "He
frequently lays aside his blanket and wears coat and trou-
sers, acquires perhaps a word or two of English, assumes
a quickness of speech and gesture which, *in him,* is unbe-
coming, and imitates generally the habits and acts of the
colonists. The attempt to improve the Indian is most beset
with difficulty at this stage of his change from barbarism;
for it is a change not to civilization, but to that abased
civilization which is, in reality, worse than barbarism itself" (190–91, emphasis added). The most bestial, most
barbaric thing an aboriginal person can do is to imitate
the white colonist. Every code that signifies Europeanness,
including the codes of dress and of speech, of gesture and
of habit, every symbolic act said to denote the racial superiority of settler society is transformed into its opposite the
moment it is repeated by an aboriginal mimic. But why?
Sproat insists these codes harbor no barbarism within
themselves. Their debasement inheres only "in him": in
the aboriginal figure who takes them up and doubles them.
But why? What he finds most abhorrent in the mimic is
nothing less than civilization itself. Civilization, "abased"
within its own enclosure, is "worse than barbarism itself,"
and improvement itself blocks every "attempt to improve
the Indian."

When faced with a specular image that brings otherness
to bear on Europe's dream of its unruptured sameness to
itself, Sproat, like Boas, calls for a return to absolute difference. To become a European in his eyes it is not enough

19

*folding*

for "the Indian" to imitate European codes. What is required is a total "change" to "civilization": one must become flawlessly white. The mimic who overlaps the civilized with the uncivilized, sameness with difference, is intolerable. "He is a vain, idle, offensive creature," says Sproat, "from whom one turns away with a preference for the thorough savage in his isolated condition" (191). He desires either an "Indian" who is exactly equal to himself or one who can be held at an absolute—"thorough"—distance.

Sproat's ambivalence confirms an argument that Bhabha has made in another colonial context—one that concerns Indians rather than "Indians." What Bhabha suggests is that the "post-Enlightenment English Colonialism" that brought its civilizing mission to India in the eighteenth and nineteenth centuries was driven by a "desire" for "colonial mimicry," and this desire was, by definition, ambivalent. It generated folds. Bhabha (1994, 86–87) cites the example of Charles Grant, who advocated reforming Indian manners and morals through Christian education. Grant's "dream" was twofold: to make the people of India more English by subjecting them to missionary schooling and at the same time to prevent them from becoming too English lest they demand freedom from British rule. The term "colonial mimicry" underlines the contradictory nature of a project to make the colonized subject similar but not too similar to the colonizer. Elsewhere Bhabha attaches the adjective "uncanny" to the mimic who imports an element of difference—and also unease—into the colonizing culture by repeating its codes (136–37). To mimic the colonizing society is to confront it with its own double, and, as Freud argues, the encounter with the double invariably evokes, as part of its structure, a sudden and involuntary flood of anxiety.

But Sproat has another reason to voice anxiety here, for the act of doubling undermines the logic he deploys in order to seize the land around Alberni. He insists that his identity as a European and particularly as a British European justifies his occupation of the territory of the Aht and the slow extermination of their culture. "My own notion," he declares in chapter 2, "is that the particular circumstances which make the deliberate intrusion of *a superior people* into another country lawful or expedient are connected to some extent with the use which the dispossessed

20

*folding*

or conquered people have made of the soil, *and* with their general behaviour as a nation" (8, emphasis added). Sproat's "own notion" bears an uncanny resemblance to a notion elaborated by John Locke in chapter 5 of *The Second Treatise of Government*, published in 1690. Locke says that in the state of nature—which is ruled by God's gift to "man," the law of natural reason—humanity holds the world in common, and every person has an equal claim to the fruits of nature. However, you have a right to own a portion of nature if you add something of your own to it: namely your labor. Property is that share of the common that you have mingled with what is proper to yourself. Locke says the main form of property is land, and if you work it, you may own it without seeking anyone's consent. To cultivate is therefore to dominate: "As much land as a man tills, plants, improves, cultivates, and can use the product of, so much is his property" (20). By owning a parcel of land you are not depriving anyone else of property, Locke insists, because there is enough for everyone. Almost the whole of America lies unused, he notes, and so is open to cultivation. One has only to seize it from the "Indians" who, according to Locke, have no right to it because they do not work it. All they own, he suggests, are the acorns they gather and the deer they kill. He places only one restriction on the right to private property: you may own as much as you can use before it spoils. What limits the right to own what is one's own, then, is the act of waste.

If Sproat does add a "notion" of his "own" to Locke's notion of property, it is his sense of his own superiority to the Aht, though strictly speaking the sense of cultural superiority is also proper to Locke. Sproat gives himself the right to seize "the soil" around Alberni because the Aht do not "use" it *and* because "their general behaviour as a nation" annuls their claim to it. Labor, for Sproat, is more than the source of the right to private property. It is a sign of what he considers to be a "superior" culture— his own. He claims the land since he means to work it, and he means to work it, he says, since he belongs to a "superior people": a people that "makes things" and, pre- cisely because it makes things, stands above a "nation" that, he alleges, has no use for the notion of use. Yet the episode where the Aht redouble so-called civilization and render it offensive to itself destroys Europeanness along with its assurance of its own superiority and transforms Europe into a place where nobody can ever be at home again. The mimics of Alberni simultaneously have the European identity and lack it, and they tell the white man who looks upon them that he has lost it forever because he never had it to begin with. Without his Europeanness, moreover, he is deprived of his chief means of justifying the appropriation of aboriginal land.

Though the colonist rejects the fold that catches up his writing in its movement—stating that he cannot bear to see an image of European Canada that is not equal to itself, a Europe-in-Canada that does not reflect itself back to itself point for point—nevertheless it is his own discourse that divides Europeanness within itself. The distance between civilization and savagery collapses along a fold line that hinges opposing themes together. Since a European Canada distinct from barbarism cannot be put into writing, Sproat's discourse establishes sameness at the very place where it situates difference. When it arrives at its western limit, Europe-in-Canada can only articulate itself within a zone of contradiction and inevitably bends back to find it is unequal to itself. The scene of mimicry underscores the impossibility of tracing an unbreachable limit between Europeanness and its beyond.

## GIFT

Sproat begins his literary ethnography by stating that the Aht lie beyond the range of Western European knowledge, but he claims to know them nonetheless. His observations assume it is possible for Western European knowledge to surpass the limits it sets for itself without undermining the certainty of its findings. At the same time, though, the folds in his discourse show that it is impossible for Europe to delimit itself at all. Europe defines itself in opposition to cultures that it considers wholly other to itself, yet as Sproat's writing suggests, there is no stable distinction between what is the West and what is not.

Perhaps an uncertainty necessarily afflicts any text that assumes itself to be Western but leaves Westness unthought. Indeed, the undecidability at the core of the West imposes a singular responsibility upon the Western observer of the non-Western world: can one discuss aboriginal cultures without simultaneously asking what Europe's limits are, and whether it ends where it says it does? Yet even to pose this question assumes that others have already been answered. What is it to be "Western" or "European" for instance? Or, more important, what is it to be "non-Western"? The inquiry into Westness as such, and into the Westness of the northwest coast, reveals that Europe neither discovers nor investigates the cultures it endeavors to know. Rather, in its will to ethnographic understanding, Europe gives non-European cultures to itself. By adding others to itself, moreover, Europe extends its limits in the very act of trying to see past them. But what is a gift, and what does "giving" mean? Above all, what is the relation, or nonrelation, between the gift, the other, and the limits of the thing that gives itself the name of a direction—the West?

In his later essays Heidegger situates the gift at the outer limit of Western European philosophy. It marks the origin of philosophy as well as its end. Since Boas locates Europe's limit somewhere between Germany and Japan, perhaps it is more than a coincidence that Heidegger stages his "Dialogue on Language," published in the early 1950s, as a conversation between a German Inquirer and a Japanese Scholar. "Dialogue" does not deal directly with the gift but nevertheless makes a place for it on the border between Europe and Asia—as if some necessity were insistently driving European discourse to set Europe's outermost boundary in the vicinity of the Pacific Northwest.

The two voices that speak this "Dialogue" stand in for Heidegger himself: the Inquirer (*der Fragenden*) claims authorship of all of Heidegger's previous work, while the Japanese Scholar (*der Japaner*) acts as a discursive mirror that reflects the Inquirer's ideas back to him. Their discussion begins under the shadow of death. The Scholar reports that his teacher, Count Shuzo Kuki, who wrote a book that applies European aesthetics to the study of Japanese art, has died "too early" (Heidegger 1971, 1). The count had once studied with the Inquirer, but when told of his student's death, the Inquirer does not pause long to mourn him. He points instead to the danger (*die Gefahr*) that attends the meeting of European thought and Japanese art. He argues that European aesthetics, and indeed the whole of "European thinking" (*europäischen Denken*)—which Heidegger elsewhere calls "philosophy," "Western metaphysics," and "ontotheology"[4]—"must ultimately remain alien to Eastasian thinking [*ostasiatischen Denken*]" (2). Since Europe and Asia are said to be absolutely other to each other, the two speakers ask if a dialogue of West with East is even possible. They talk and yet question whether there can be any talking between them. Moreover, this is precisely the question raised by the discourse on the potlatch: it is a system of utterances that Canada will endlessly recite to itself in order to put limits on the actions of indigenous societies, but it will be impossible for the purveyors of this discourse to listen to the voices of those same societies when they speak eloquently in defense of their own social practices.

The Inquirer insists that the mutual otherness of West and East raises "a controversial question," namely, whether it is "necessary and rightful" for Asian thinkers "to chase after European conceptual systems." He says that the language of Western philosophy tends to dominate whatever it attempts to know, for when it sets out to understand things, philosophy reconfigures them, making them strange even to themselves. The Scholar answers that the "modern technicalization and industrialization of every continent" makes it impossible for thinkers in Asia and beyond to avoid engaging Western concepts. Though there lurks a danger that such concepts might lead Asian thinkers "astray" in their research, one cannot wish away what the Inquirer calls the "complete Europeanization" of the earth and its inhabitants (*die Europäisierung des Menschen und der Erde*) (3, 15). If the world is becoming Europe's intellectual colony, then it is up to Asian intellectuals to reclaim the European tradition for their own purposes.

The Inquirer notes that "the danger" confronts not only Asian thinkers who borrow from European philosophy but also European thinkers conducting research on Asian cultures. Because the danger inheres within the fabric of language, the translation of non-European matters into European terms makes it difficult, perhaps impossible, for European thinkers to speak about Asia. If language is the house of Being, then Europe and Asia occupy "entirely different" houses, and communication between them verges on sheer noise (4–5).[5] Yet "the danger" also threatens to make Europe incapable of entering into a dialogue with *itself*, for the speakers agree that Europe has always overlooked what is nearest to it. It has forgotten its own essence, forgotten what it is. As it extends its domination over non-European lands and peoples, Europe remains a stranger to Europe.

The Scholar points out that the Europeanization of the world is normally thought of as the triumphal march of a European reason that asserts its dominance through its technological achievements (13–14). According to the Inquirer, though, the essence of Europe is not to be found in its technology and its industries. Indeed, its essence has yet to be thought. The influence of the Western "technical world" spans the globe, but "a true encounter with European existence" has failed to occur—"in spite of all assimilations and intermixtures" (3). Since the Europeanization of the world "attacks at the source everything that is of an essential nature," Europe's essence may well be that it cannot know its essence (16).

Ironically, if Europe finds itself nowhere, it still knows where it is not. Since it insists that it is not in Japan (and that it ends just short of the "Kwakiutl"), the European's Europe consistently hesitates to merge with any of the cultures that it has tried to swallow. Hence in "Dialogue" the two voices speaks of the Europeanization of Asia rather than the Asianification of Europe. Europe is always assumed to dominate its others, but it is anxious to remain pure of them.

The speakers agree that Europe cannot enter into dialogue with non-European cultures until it begins talking to itself. Before it can become its own interlocutor, moreover, Europe has to become other to itself. How is its self-alienation to be negotiated? The Inquirer argues that the only way Europe can cease to be other to itself and to its others, the only way it can cease to be both its own other and the other of its others, is to become still more other to itself. By distancing itself ever farther from itself, Europe will return to itself and learn that it never parted from itself. The act of rendering Europe different from itself, and preparing it for a dialogue with other cultures, begins with an effort to initiate the closure of Western philosophy.

The speakers conceive of Europe not as a homogeneous territory nor as a source of political, industrial, and technological dominance but as a logic—a mode of reasoning, a metaphysics—that enacts strategies of conceptual domination. How is this "metaphysics" to be defined? When the late Count Kuki described the experience of Japanese art, he spoke of a "sensuous radiance" that gives its viewers access to "the radiance of something supersensuous." The Inquirer argues that the count's work transforms Japanese art into something European because he makes the mistake of situating it within "the difference between a sensuous and a suprasensuous world." For the Inquirer the distinction between the sensuous and the suprasensuous lies at the base of "what has long been called Western metaphysics" (14). Metaphysics encompasses any Western European conceptual system that opposes the earthly to the transcendent, the real to the ideal, the world to a text, the referent to its sign, an original to its representation, a content to its form. Obeying a postal logic, metaphysics sends the sensuous term in each of these binary pairs to stand in for and "represent" the suprasensuous term. The suprasensuous requires a sensuous substitute because it cannot make itself present to the mind as an object of perception.

To initiate the closure of metaphysics means recalling the limits of this postal logic, this act of sending that exchanges one term for another. What is at stake in "Dialogue," therefore, is a vast "transformation of thinking" in the West (42). The transformation is understood as a "passage" between two sites. The place to be abandoned is Western metaphysics, while the goal to be reached is an unnamed yet uncannily familiar area beyond its boundaries. The goal is "familiar" because a truly antimetaphysical thinking escapes metaphysics only to arrive back inside it: the tradition of Western philosophy reaches its end by folding back on itself and encountering what it has left unthought throughout its history. Since the "unthought" is what has made Western thinking possible since its inception, the closure of metaphysics—a closure conceived as thinking the unthought—takes a step back to its origin. Metaphysics has to become other to itself in order to discover how it has always been self-identical. The transformation of metaphysics makes everything different by leaving everything just where it was.

To illustrate this paradoxical closure the Scholar notes that any philosophy of art that presumes to pass out of metaphysics "also leaves behind the aesthetics that is grounded in metaphysics." An aesthetics beyond aesthetics promises students an entirely new encounter with art, but only by returning to what the old aesthetics forgot. As the Inquirer puts it, the end of philosophy surpasses aesthetics "in such a way that we can only now give thought to the nature of aesthetics, and direct it back within its boundaries" (42). The task of the thinker who leaves the bounds of Western metaphysics is to place limits on metaphysical concepts to keep them from intruding where they do not belong and where, by their intrusion, they destroy the possibility of understanding the matter under consideration.

The work of transforming metaphysics, of rendering it strange yet strangely familiar to itself, begins with an inquiry into the nature of language. The Inquirer says that this question has barely been posed by Western thinkers but promises to return Europe to itself by dividing it from itself. Yet he introduces the problem of language with a note of caution. "The prospect of the thinking that labors to answer to the nature of language," he warns, "is still veiled, in all its vastness." Since there is no easy access to a thinking beyond metaphysics, it is difficult to tell whether the Inquirer's understanding of "the nature of language is *also* adequate for the nature of the Eastasian language." It is possible that "European-Western saying" and "Eastasian saying" might, once the transformation of metaphysics is under way, engage in a dialogue where Europe does not overpower Asia and where there is instead "something that wells up from a single source" (8). However, it is too early to tell if West and East will overcome their otherness to each other and clear a path of mutual understanding outside of Western European domination. The question whether Europe will allow itself to be transformed by Asia goes unmentioned.

But Europe has to learn to speak to itself before it can speak to Asia. Moreover, Europe's dialogue with Europe begins with a step beyond the bounds of the metaphysical understanding of language, for a conversation that would map the end of Western metaphysics cannot rely on the metaphysical notion that words are sensuous signs representing suprasensuous ideas. The dialogue has to occur, rather, in the mode of "saying" (*die Sage*). Saying, as the two speakers define it, is not a form of representation but a way of "letting appear" or even "letting shine." It is "the beginning of that path which takes us back out of merely metaphysical representations" and returns Europe to an encounter with what is essential to itself (47–48). What does it mean, though, to say that saying lets appear or lets shine?

Heidegger's speakers stage their discussion of "saying"

to explain how things arrive before thought. They cannot assume that things are objects existing in the world and that thoughts represent those objects in the minds of human subjects, since this argument draws on the now discredited distinction between sensuous facts and suprasensuous ideas. Instead they have to redefine the way the beings that are present in the world come into the presence of thinking. Their recourse to "saying" allows them to ponder how language gathers things and thinkers together without maintaining—metaphysically—that words represent thoughts and thoughts represent things.

The Inquirer approaches the problem of the being present (*das Anwesen*) of present things (*die Anwesenden*) by distinguishing between the entities that appear in the world (*die Erscheinungen*) and the appearance (*das Erscheinen*) that enables them to become present: between the appearance (*die Erscheinung*) that appears and the appearance (*das Erscheinen*) that allows an appearance to appear (*erscheinen*). However, while he agrees that "to be present itself [*das Anwesen*] is thought of as appearance [*als Erscheinen*]," he cautions that the appearing of appearance (*das Erscheinen*) nevertheless remains to be explained. If "there prevails in being present [*Anwesen*]" an "emergence into openness [*das Hervorkommen ins Lichte*]" that he calls "unconcealedness" (*Unverborgenheit*)—if what is present arrives into presence in an event of unconcealment—then what metaphysics fails to think is precisely the open region where what is present becomes unconcealed, the region where the event of unconcealment occurs (39).

Heidegger says that "what is present," the "present being," can simply be called a thing. A thing is anything that in any way is. Yet when one says that "a thing is," the "is" that allows it to *be* in the world goes unthought. To say a thing is present or absent, that it is or is not, takes the "is" for granted. Thus to inquire into the presence of what is present, or the Being of beings, means asking about the "is" that is presupposed in any discussion of what exists. In "The Nature of Language" (1971) Heidegger poses the problem as follows: "the thing 'is.' Yet, what about this 'is'? The thing is. The 'is' itself—is it also a thing, a step above the other, set on top of it like a cap? The 'is' cannot be found anywhere as a thing attached to a thing" (87). The "is" is a nonthing that permits things to be: Being holds beings in place without being anything itself.

Heidegger identifies the "is"—Being itself—as the un-thought that makes metaphysics possible. But metaphysics has forgotten to think the difference between the beings that are (*Seiendes*) and the Being (*Sein*) that allows beings to be. To bring about the closure of metaphysics, then, is to recall this difference to thought. The end of metaphysics necessarily leads back to its origins, however, because to pose the question of Being is to ask how it has been possible throughout the history of Western European philosophy to say that "there are" beings, entities—indeed, anything at all.

But what gives Being? What sends this mail that carries not things, but the "is-ness" of things? What postal princi-ple can account for such a delivery? Answering these ques-tions leads into the vicinity of the gift because, for Heideg-ger, the thought of Being is tied to a thought of giving. As he notes in "Letter on Humanism," one cannot say that "Being is": this phrasing treats Being as a being and fails to approach the "is" that is itself under investigation. Being is not a being that is. Being *is* not because it is what gives the "is." It is logically prior to the "is" and cannot be un-derstood in terms of it. Heidegger resorts to the idiomatic German phrase *es gibt*—which in English simultaneously means "there is" and "it gives"—to bring Being into lan-guage. He recalls that he once "purposely and cautiously" wrote "*il y a l'Être:* 'there is/it gives' ('*es gibt*') Being," but he notes that "*Il y a* translates 'it gives' [*es gibt*] imprecisely.[6] For the 'it' [*es*] that here 'gives' [*gibt*] is Being itself. The 'gives' names the essence of Being that is giving, granting its truth. The self-giving into the open, along with the open region itself, is Being itself" (1977, 214). Here Being is the open region where, according to the Inquirer, beings come into their unconcealment.

Heidegger calls Being's self-giving activity the "destiny" of Being (*das Geschick des Seins*): "Being comes to destiny," he says, "in that It, Being, gives itself" (215). Yet Being "refuses" itself while giving itself: it goes unthought even as it allows beings themselves to be thought. The history of metaphysics is the history of this self-giving, self-withholding of Being in its various epochs: "The happen-ing of history occurs essentially as the destiny of the truth of Being and from it" (215).

Throughout the history of the West, then, Being has ceaselessly put itself in the mail but has never arrived.

29

*folding*

What sort of postal system sends the self-withholding gift of Being? According to "Letter on Humanism" Being delivers itself to the world through the "saying" of language: "Being comes, lighting itself, to language. It is perpetually under way to language" (239). Being gathers thinkers and things into the "open region" of discourse. Only this "open region," this space of language, permits beings to reveal themselves to thought.

Heidegger modifies his account of the gift in "Time and Being" (1972) by insisting that, although Being is sent to the world, it does not send itself. Here Being arrives without putting itself in the mail. It is delivered in an event of giving, but the gift event is itself prior to Being and indeed is what makes Being possible (8–9). Such an event cannot be thought in terms of Being, for it stands outside of Being and its determinations (20–21). But if Being does not give itself, then how is it given? What is the gift event that Being cannot give to itself?

Heidegger sketches an answer in "The Nature of Language" (1971, 88) when he says that "the word" is what "gives Being" (*gibt das Wort: das Sein*). The gift of the word gives presence to the beings that are present before thought. The word makes a present of presence. "Only where the word for the thing has been found," says Heidegger, "is the thing a thing. Only thus *is* it. Accordingly we must stress as follows: no thing *is* where the word, that is, the name is lacking. The word alone gives being to the thing" (62). A word is a mode of "saying" that holds things and thinkers together in Being. Hence "there are" things to be thought only insofar as "there is" discourse in which to utter them.

30

The word gives access to the unthought that sets Western European metaphysics going but exceeds its boundaries. It is a mode of gift giving that is set at the outermost limits of the West. As a mode of Being, a way of giving the "is" to the thing, the word necessarily belongs to the history of metaphysics, but since the inquiry into the relation between the word and "saying" clears a path to what metaphysics has forgotten—namely Being—the word also plays a role in the transformation that draws metaphysics toward its end, which is also its origin. The word is a gift and the gift a limit.

But what if the word were "potlatch"? If for Heidegger what remains unthought in metaphysics is the way the

*folding*

word—and the name in particular—gives being to the thing, then it follows that words also give the world the things of Western European ethnography. Moreover, if words make a present of whole cultures, then the unthought that lies at the limit of Western thinking is not only the gift of Being but the gift of the other. And the closure of metaphysics requires that thought attend both to the delivery of Being in general and to the precise mechanics that enable words to send Europe the worlds that it tries, always without success, to situate somewhere beyond itself. Especially if the word is "potlatch."

GIVING
GIVING

*The name seems produced, one time only, by an act without a past. There is no purer present, no generosity more inaugural. But a gift of nothing, of no thing, such a gift appropriates itself violently, harpoons, "arraigns" [arraisonne], what it seems to engender, penetrates and paralyses with one stroke [coup] the recipient thus consecrated. Magnified, the recipient becomes somewhat the thing of the one who names or surnames him, above all if this is done with a name of a thing. . . .*

*To give a name is always, like any birth (certificate), to sublimate a singularity and to inform against it, to hand it over to the police.*

DERRIDA, *GLAS*

## NAMELESS DISTRIBUTION

In chapter 14 of *Scenes and Studies of Savage Life,* Sproat affirms that the Aht have a privileged relation to the gift. "The principal use made by the Aht of an accumulation of personal chattels," he says, "is to distribute them periodically among invited guests" (79). The act of distribution keeps the Aht at a marked distance from settler society, moreover, because those who give their "chattels" away continue to clothe themselves in blankets and do not offend the European observer by imitating his dress: "The collection of property for the purpose of distribution is the constant aim of many of the natives who, to the common observer, seems [*sic*] listless and idle. The Indian who stands by your side in a tattered blanket, may have twenty

*Opposite:* Superintendent Powell was careful to distribute "presents" when he visited coastal communities. In 1874, for example, he gave a Nuu'chah'nulth elder "a British Ensign as a distinguishing emblem of law, order, and protection" (Canada, *Sessional Papers*, 1876, no. 9, p. 54). Richard Maynard's portrait shows Powell, seated at center, posing with the Kwakwaka'wakw at Tsawatti in 1873. Courtesy of The Field Museum, neg. no. 17524, Chicago.

new blankets and yards of calico in his box at home. Whatever he acquires beyond immediate necessaries goes to increase this stock, until his high day comes in the winter season, when he spreads his feast and distributes gifts among the guests, according to their rank" (80). While the Aht accumulate property only to give it away, they give all, knowing that every expenditure will eventually be repaid: "The giver does not now consider that he has parted with his property," says Sproat; "he regards it as well invested, for the present recipients of his largess will strive to return to him at their own feasts more than he has bestowed." But how can a gift be called a gift if it has to be given back in excess? This question will haunt Europe's discourse on the gift for years to come.

Sproat offers a standard outsider's description of what came to be known as the potlatch. But he fails to name it. The omission of the name is striking enough to merit a footnote from Lillard in the Sono Nis edition of *Scenes:* "Here the author is describing the potlatch," the editor explains, "the ceremonial distribution of property that established the giver's political or social status." One of the "features of Sproat's description" that is "worth noting," notes Lillard, is that "he never uses the term 'potlatch.'"

It is more than a little ironic that Sproat withholds the gift of the name in this passage. After all, the factor of Alberni is describing a ceremony where gifts are given in the name of the name, for when the Aht distribute property, they receive both a social rank and the title that goes with it: "The person who gives away the most property receives the greatest praise, and in time acquires, almost as a matter of course, but by voice of the tribe, the highest rank obtainable by such means. This rank is not of the highest class. It is only for life, and is different from the ancient hereditary tribal rank. With each step in rank there is usually a change of name. Thus, bearing different names, the industrious or acquisitive native may rise from one honour to another, till finally he reaches a high position." Sproat compares the distribution of property to an election to political office. It gives some individuals a way to improve their rank in the social hierarchy, though for others rank is "ancient" and "hereditary," and therefore not "obtainable by such means" (79–80).

Sproat does not attack the gift-giving ceremony in this 1868 text, but five years later Euro-Canadians will find gift giving so intolerable they will take steps to abolish it forever. How is it that the gift (if it *is* a gift) was a matter of indifference in the 1860s yet became the target of a moral crusade by the 1870s? To answer this question it is necessary to investigate the arrival of the name in the dialogue that the Canadian government held with itself on the subject of "Indian affairs" in nineteenth-century British Columbia, for the shift in the status of the gift is inextricably bound up with the delivery of the gift of the name.

## THE MARK OF EXPENDITURE

When British Columbia joined the Canadian confederation in 1871, the Terms of Union transferred control over Indian affairs from the province to the federal government. In 1872 the Indian Branch of the Department of the Secretary of State appointed Israel Wood Powell as the first Indian superintendent in Victoria.[1] Powell had been trained as a doctor, and though he was hired to manage relations between Canada and the British Columbia First Nations, he continued to practice medicine after taking charge of the new superintendency (Fisher 1977, 180).[2] Douglas Cole and Ira Chaikin note in *An Iron Hand upon the People* (1990) that Powell brought the "baneful aspects of the potlatch" to the attention of the Indian Branch as early as January 1873. According to their account his first annual report to Ottawa claimed "that potlatches, 'quite common' on the coast, retarded civilizing influences and encouraged idleness among the less worthy Indians" (14). Yet this version of Powell's "comments" omits one minor detail: in 1873 he did not yet mention the word "potlatch"—not quite.

His observations are paraphrased by William Spragge, the deputy superintendent of the Indian Branch, in the "Annual Report on Indian Affairs for the Year Ending June 30 1872." Under the heading "The Interior and Coast Indians Compared," Spragge writes: "Superintendent Powell informs us that the interior Indians are far superior in character and general condition to the Indians of the coast." What mark distinguishes the two groups from each other? "Those of the coast retain many of their barbarous customs, among them the great medicine feasts," while in contrast the people of the interior display "a decided capacity for trade, and possess commendable

*giving*

business qualifications" (Canada, *Sessional Papers*, 1873, no. 23, pp. 8–9).

It is already, in the first months of British Columbia's union with Canada, a question of drawing limits. The "medicine feasts" trace a double border. They not only distinguish the First Nations of the interior from those of the coast but also draw an absolute boundary between barbarism and civilization. Powell does not describe the feasts, yet he insists they are a sure sign of moral degradation. They inscribe the coastal First Nations with the mark of savagery. Since the First Nations of the interior do not appear to hold such feasts, Powell locates them toward the pole of civilization. The line dividing coast from interior is not so much a fact of geography as the product of a regulatory gaze that delivers an order of rank to the Pacific Northwest. So far it is the "feast," and not the gift, that marks this division. But the gift is soon to take a leading role in Powell's efforts to range the aboriginal people of British Columbia on a scale of social evolution.

Elsewhere in his report Powell claims (via Spragge, using him as a postal relay) that tyranny is the preferred system of government among the province's First Nations. Each group, he says, is ruled by hereditary "chiefs" who exercise a "despotic power" over their people. Moreover, they shore up their authority by circulating what seem to be gifts: "The chiefs still . . . imply practices peculiar to themselves, in order to maintain as large a share of influence as possible with their people. Some of them donate, *under the name of 'Patlatches,'* to their people, blankets, food, firearms, &c., &c." Here, as in *Scenes and Studies of Savage Life*, gift giving is a means of improving one's rank in a social hierarchy. But by a "strange" paradox, "Patlatches" prove not to be donations at all. "The gifts are dealt out with profusion," writes Powell (via Spragge), "but it is attended with a strange feature; for *an equivalent in return* at a future gathering is expected to be presented" (*Sessional Papers*, 1873, no. 23, p. 10, emphasis added).

From the moment Canada's administrative apparatus arrives on the northwest coast, an undecidability haunts the official inquiry into the truth about "Patlatches." Are they acts of gift giving where no present is ever returned? Or are they a means of exchange where everything that is given away is invariably given back, if not immediately, then "at a future gathering"? In the discourse on "Indian

*giving*

Affairs" the difficulty of deciding whether these practices involve gift giving or exchange is supplemented by the difficulty of naming them. Though Powell calls them "Pat-latches" in 1872, an undecidability never ceases to haunt this word as it circulates through government dispatches. Other versions of both the word and the thing it names were in the mail by 1874.

Powell instructed George Blenkinsop, a former Hudson's Bay Company trader who had found work with the Indian Branch, to visit the Nuu'chah'nulth of Barkley Sound on the west coast of Vancouver Island in May 1874 "for the purpose of acquiring an intimate knowledge of their wishes in regard to lands to be hereafter reserved for them" (*Sessional Papers*, 1876, no. 9, p. 51). According to Cole and Chaikin (1990, 15), Blenkinsop reported "that, until the local Indians were cured of their propensity for potlatching, 'there can be little hope of elevating them from their present state of degradation.' " It is true that Blenkinsop sent back word of gift giving, but the record shows it was not he who put the word "potlatching" into circulation within the government's correspondence.

In a report to Powell dated 23 September 1874 Blenkinsop frames his observations within a set of oppositions between high and low, elevation and degradation, civilization and barbarism. What marks the limit between these contradictory terms is not the "feast" but the notion of expenditure. Blenkinsop writes that the people of Barkley Sound "are a race of people easily controlled" and suggests that "it requires but firm and judicious management to bring them under the sway of civilization as far as is practicable with any of their race" (National Archives of Canada, Record Group 10 [hereafter NA], vol. 3614, file 4105). They are already close to the West and could easily be raised up and swallowed by it. But "two serious obstacles" block their "elevation" out of their allegedly sunken condition and place them at an absolute remove from Western civilization. Blenkinsop declares that "until they are cured of their propensity for gambling and accumulating property, solely for the purpose of giving away to other Indians, there can be but little hope of elevating them from their present state of degradation and bettering the condition and appearance of their wives and families." While Sproat argues that the people of the west coast of Vancouver Island distribute property only on the condition that

37

giving

it be returned later, Blenkinsop informs Powell that on the same coast and among the same people every distribution takes the form of a spending without return. The gift that demands to be given back has given way to the gift that stays with its recipient.

An allegedly pure expenditure marks the people of Barkley Sound with the sign of barbarism and keeps them low in relation to settler society. But what allows expenditure to be endowed with the value and authority of a limit? The assumption that gambling and giving away weigh down the upward pull of civilization finds justification in what Georges Bataille calls "the principle of classical utility." Bataille argues in "The Notion of Expenditure" (1985) that "any general judgement of social activity implies the principle that all individual effort, in order to be valid, must be reducible to the fundamental necessities of production and conservation." What this principle entails is that "humanity [Bataille posits a universal humanity] recognizes the right to acquire, to conserve, and to consume rationally, but it excludes in principle *nonproductive expenditure*." Bataille reserves the term "expenditure" for modes of consumption that contribute nothing to the conservation of life or to the continuation of productive activity within a social formation. Pure expenditures require a loss that "must be as great as possible in order for that activity to take on its true meaning" (117–18). Examples of such a loss include games (like gambling), pleasure, poetry—and the "potlatch." But it is still 1874, and that name has yet to arrive in the post.

It does not appear in the Indian Branch correspondence until 1875 when Powell sends Ottawa an account of a recent voyage to the west coast of Vancouver Island. Whether by chance or by design, Powell's 1875 text is remarkably similar in its logic and phrasing to Blenkinsop's 1874 report. Like Blenkinsop, Powell calls attention to the "paradoxical" fact that "the natives inhabiting the West Coast of Vancouver Island" are "poor" even though they are "the richest of any Indians [he has] met in the Province." And like Blenkinsop, Powell explains this contradiction by noting that, although the Nuu'chah'nulth are wealthy, they spend all their earnings on gambling and giving away property. "They are inveterate gamblers," he says, and they convene "frequent assemblages of the different tribes for the purpose of holding donation feasts ('potlatches'). On such occasions a large amount of property is given away or destroyed" (*Sessional Papers*, 1876, no. 9, pp. 44–45).

When it arrives in Powell's report, the plural of the word "potlatch" is set off from its context by two kinds of marks. First, it is enclosed between parentheses, as if it does not have a legitimate place in his discourse and can appear there only if it brackets itself from its context. The word is doubly enclosed, moreover, since it is also encased in quotation marks—as was "Patlatches," or rather " 'Patlatches,' " in his 1873 report. To explain why Powell says (in parentheses) "potlatches" instead of potlatches, one might recall John Searle's argument that quotation marks are conventionally deployed in written discourse "to mark the fact that the word is not being used normally but is being [mentioned] as a topic of discussion" (75). Powell's use of quotation marks suggests, if inadvertently, that here "potlatches" is itself a problem in need of a solution and does not refer to an event. Though the word has been inserted into his report, it properly belongs to another context where it would itself be the topic of a debate.

What both Powell and Blenkinsop find on the west coast of Vancouver Island, though, is not a word that asks to be discussed but a practice that Western civilization wants above all to exclude from itself: the practice of nonproductive expenditure as it is manifested in gambling and giving away. The gambler spends property in a way that invites a return but cannot guarantee it, while the person who gives property away without hope of getting it back incurs a pure loss, which brings no apparent material benefit. Blenkinsop asserts in his 1874 report that the dominion government has the right to control the lives of any people that gives all. It is as if the principle of classical utility empowers the representatives of European civilization to lay down a regulatory grid to restrict every nonproductive expenditure, no matter where it occurs.

Thus in the postal literature circulated by the Indian Branch in the early 1870s, the northwest coast sits at the very limit of the Western European economy. The gift is the sign of this outer boundary. A pure loss without return, the gift marks the zone where civilization ends and barbarism begins. Or so it seems. For it is also possible that the gift is not a gift at all but rather an exchange that obliges the recipient to make a reciprocal countergift. Neverthe-

*giving*

less, after 1875 Canada's uncertain discourse on the gift continues to focus on the question of pure expenditure, and the question continues to be posed amid the efforts of the British Columbia First Nations to protect their lands from the encroachment of white settlers—because Blenkinsop was not the last reserve agent to pontificate about the evils of giving all.

## PATLACH

The Royal Proclamation of 1763 states that the aboriginal people of what is now Canada retain title to lands that they have not surrendered by treaty to the agents of the Crown. It "is just and reasonable, and essential to our Interest, and the Security of our Colonies," proclaims George III, "that the several Nations or Tribes of Indians with whom We are connected, and who live under our protection, should not be molested or disturbed in the Possession of such Parts of Our Dominions and Territories as, not having been ceded to or purchased by Us, are reserved to them, or any of them, as their Hunting Grounds." The proclamation does not address itself to the First Nations of eastern North America alone. It also says that unless the First Nations of what is now western Canada cede or sell their territory directly to the Crown, they retain title to their share of "the Lands and Territories lying to the Westward of the Sources of the Rivers which fall into the Sea from the West and North West" (Canada 1985b, 4–5; Tennant 1990, 10–11).

James Douglas, the chief factor of the Hudson's Bay Company post at Fort Victoria, was appointed second governor of the colony of Vancouver Island in 1851, and in the first years of his administration, he upheld the principle of aboriginal title. He signed fourteen treaties in the early 1850s, purchasing land from Salish communities near Fort Victoria, Nanaimo, and Fort Rupert and setting aside reserves for their exclusive use.[3] The policy of extinguishing aboriginal title through land purchase came to an end by the late 1850s, however, though Douglas's administration continued to map out reserves on the island. The colonial House of Assembly set aside funds for land purchases in 1862, but the money was never spent. A new policy of allocating reserves without extinguishing title was extended to the mainland after the colony of British Columbia was formed in the wake of the 1857 gold rush (Tennant 1990, 17–38). Since the middle of the nineteenth century, then, settler society has enclosed the First Nations of British Columbia on reserves, but few of them have surrendered their title to their ancestral lands. Only the communities that signed the Douglas treaties and those communities that are located to the west of the Rocky Mountains and were included in Treaty Eight can be said to have formally ceded the territory that the royal proclamation guarantees them.

After Douglas retired in 1864, the principle of aboriginal title continued to be abused as the colonial government, under the impetus of Land and Works Commissioner Joseph Trutch, appropriated reserve lands for the use of white settlers (Tennant 1990, 39–43). The First Nations objected strongly to the infringement upon their land, and when British Columbia joined the Canadian confederation in 1871, their protests received some support from the dominion government, which began a long—and still unfinished—effort to coax the province into increasing the size of reserves (Duff 1964, 67).[4] By 1875 Powell had decided it was "undesirable" to visit aboriginal communities in the interior because "when a question of such vital import to a large proportion of [aboriginal people], as that concerning the quantity of land to be reserved for their benefit and support remains in doubt, an official visit is much more detrimental than useful in . . . promoting confidence and amicable relations between them and the Whites" (*Sessional Papers*, 1876, no. 9, p. 44). Although the dominion government stopped well short of asking British Columbia to recognize the principle of aboriginal title, provincial officials refused to compromise (Tennant 1990, 43–52). At last, in a belated effort to address the land question, the two governments agreed in 1876 to appoint a reserve commission composed of Alexander Anderson, representing Canada, and Archibald McKinlay, representing British Columbia. The joint commissioner, appointed after a delay, was Gilbert Malcolm Sproat.

The commission was dissolved in 1878 because provincial officials claimed it cost too much, but Sproat worked on alone until the hostility of the white community forced him to resign in 1880 (Fisher 1977, 189–99; *Sessional Papers*, 1879, no. 7, p. 15).[5] Some of the First Nations convinced Sproat to increase the size of their reserves, but these gains were clawed back after Trutch's brother-in-law, Peter O'Reilly, took over Sproat's job as reserve commissioner (Tennant 1990, 50–51).

On 6 November 1878 Sproat briefly set aside his work for the reserve commission and wrote the Indian Branch for permission to convene a meeting with "the Nekla-kap-amuk" "people" or "nation" at Lytton. He explained that the Nlaka'pamux wanted to negotiate with federal officials to gain "a clear understanding with the Government as to all matters" (NA, vol. 3669, file 10,691). The meeting was held in the summer of 1879, and Sproat reported that the Nlaka'pamux had outlined a set of community ordinances and agreed to adopt a political system consisting of a chief and thirteen councillors. He advised the dominion to encourage this move toward a municipal form of self-government, noting that "the Government might save money and largely foster self reliance among the Nekla-kap-amuk Indians . . . by encouraging the organisation of these people which they themselves have commenced" (NA, vol. 3669, file 10,691, 26 July 1879). It is likely, how ever, that Sproat tried to impose the municipal system upon the Nlaka'pamux because he opposed their traditional mode of self-government (Tennant 1990, 54–55).[6]

In the 1860s Sproat had taken offense when the people he named the Aht refused to stay beyond the limits of the West and pulled close to their colonizers by imitating European codes of dress, gesture, and speech, but almost twenty years later he encouraged the Nlaka'pamux to set up a local administration patterned after a Euro-Canadian model.[7] There had been a shift in the pattern of substitutions that governed his discourse. Just as he had proposed the Canadian confederation as a stand-in for the existing English parliamentary system in *Canada and the Empire,* so at the end of the 1870s he advocated an elected Nlaka'pamux council as a replacement for the government of Canada. The council was to substitute itself for the system of "Indian superintendents" (like Powell) administered by the Indian Branch—a system that he calls "an expensive farce" (6 November 1878). But why were the Nlaka'pamux not "offensively European" to Sproat when they set about to imitate "the habits and acts of the colonists" by adopting a European form of government? The answer is that they had renounced the gift, and their renunciation brought them over to the "civilised" side of the border between civilization and barbarity.

By the fall of 1879 Sproat had brought his reserve commission to Vancouver Island, and on 27 October, during his stay in the Kwagiulth village of Fort Rupert, he put a name in the mail. In a letter to the superintendent general of Indian affairs (NA, vol. 3669, file 10,691), Sproat recalls the meeting at Lytton and notes that "[a]mong the rules and regulations framed by the Nekla-kap-a-muk Council, now before you for consideration, there is one, namely rule 11, which states that the 'Patlach' is to cease among the Nekla-kap-a-muks." He calls this resolution "[t]he most hopeful Indian fact in the history of the Province."

The word that is lacking in *Scenes* makes its appearance in Ottawa in 1879: "Patlach." It is another version of "potlatch"—the word that Cole and Chaikin add to Blenkinsop's report of 1874, though Blenkinsop himself did not then use it. And it is related both to "patlaches," which surfaces in Powell's 1873 report to Ottawa, and to "('potlatches')," which has only a tenuous place in his report of 1875. Sproat has mailed a present to the discourse on "Indians" in Canada, enclosing his own version of the name as a sort of gift. But will it give the gift of the thing?

Sproat's letter scolds the officials of the Indian Branch for failing to suppress the practice that he names "Patlach" because it "is the parent of numerous vices which eat out the heart of the people." "When I landed in 1860 on the west coast of Vancouver Island," he concludes, "and soon became acquainted with the evils of the 'Patlach,' I would not have thought it probable that 19 years later, I should have to write of the 'Patlach' as I should have written in 1860, and that not in out of the way places but within easy reach of Victoria, and after the management of Indian affairs had been for 8 years in the charge of the Government of Canada which spared no reasonable expenditure." But the outrage he articulates in 1879 contradicts his earlier efforts at west coast ethnography.

For "19 years" earlier, in the 1860s, Sproat did not "write of the 'Patlach.'" He spoke instead of the distribution and destruction of property. And he did not condemn the practice either as a "parent of evil" or as an eater of hearts. Rather, he speculated that "the custom probably is secured by the gratification which the practice affords to two strong propensities in human nature—pride of rank and love of display" (1987, 79). The distribution of property marks just one more place where the narrative of *Scenes* folds over on itself. Distribution is the line where the Aht cease to be absolutely other to settler society and turn to join the Europeans in a "human nature" whose "propensities" are said to be common to people of all cultures.

Strictly speaking, the "Patlach" continues to occupy this same fold in Sproat's discourse. "The habit of the 'Patlach' is based," he writes in 1879, "on the common human desire for distinction which appears to be as strong among uncivilised as among civilised people." The giving of gifts still marks the place where the "uncivilised" aboriginal population overlaps the "civilised" European colonists, and this fold effectively erases the limit that holds "civilization" apart from "barbarism." In 1879, as in 1860, all of humanity shares that "common human desire for distinction" that motivates social life on the northwest coast of British Columbia.

Yet in 1879 the Patlach places aboriginal people and Europeans at an unbridgeable distance from each other even as it gathers them into a universal human nature. Although he collapses the gap between civilization and its exterior, in the next sentence Sproat expels aboriginal cultures beyond the limit of settler society by stripping them of their arts and literature. "Men wish to be talked of among their own and among neighbouring tribes," he argues, "and having no literature, few arts, and no opportunity now of becoming known as tribal warriors, they try to make themselves known by more or less lavish distributions of property among their own, or among other people." It is worth noting that in *Scenes* the Aht are not lacking in literature. Indeed the Sproat of the 1860s insists that "[a]n account of the innumerable original traditions and legends current among the people . . . is sufficient for a large book" (120).

The younger Sproat treated the practice of distributing property in communities on the west coast of Vancouver Island as just another ethnographic object to be recorded but not condemned. By the late 1870s, however, he has given it a name and singled it out as an activity to be regulated and dismantled. Why "19 years later" has the unimpassioned account of distribution offered in *Scenes* given way to a bitter polemic against the "Patlach"?

For the Sproat of 1879 the Patlach is an event of pure

loss, and it violates the principle of classical utility, which according to Bataille forms the basis of bourgeois reasoning. But how has the distribution of property come to be identified as an instance of waste? Sproat makes it clear in *Scenes* that among the Aht property is given away only on the condition that it is to be returned later, yet the nameless distributions described as a means of investment in the 1860s are transformed, in the letter of 1879, into expenditures without return. We have seen that for Locke the waste of property annuls the individual's right to own a share of the common. Bataille argues, in contrast, that the tendency to vilify absolute expenses of property is a defining characteristic of bourgeois discourse.

As Bataille understands it, gift giving does not mark a limit between civilization and barbarity. Rather, it is the demise of the potlatch, the loss of the practice of loss, that signifies the transition from a society dominated by an aristocracy to an industrial society dominated by a bourgeoisie. Bataille (1985, 124–25) defines the bourgeoisie as the class that gives away nothing: "It has distinguished itself from the aristocracy through the fact that it has consented only to *spend for itself,* and within itself—in other words, by hiding its expenditures as much as possible from the eyes of the other classes." Governed by "a reasoning that balances *accounts,*" the bourgeoisie maintains a "sterility in regard to expenditure." It holds itself in an intimate proximity to itself by keeping its wealth close at hand. Hence it is openly hostile toward the possibility of loss: "bourgeois society has only managed to develop a universal meanness," says Bataille, for "the bourgeois are incapable of concealing a sordid face, a face so rapacious and lacking in nobility, so frighteningly small, that all human life, upon seeing it, seems degraded."

Sproat's letter against the Patlach—like the reports by Blenkinsop and Powell on the people of Barkley Sound—suggests that a "meanness" with regard to expenditure rules the life of the professional middle class in late-nineteenth-century Canada. Sproat makes a point of complaining that the Patlach imposes a loss on the dominion government by adding to the cost of Europeanizing the British Columbia First Nations. Canada has, he notes, "spared no reasonable expenditure" in its campaign to make them European but has received no return on "8 years" of investment. His reason for wanting to restrict the expenditures of the coastal First Nations is to decrease the government's own expenses. The government ought to keep its gifts to itself and, in Bataille's words, "only to spend for itself."[8]

But the gift and the people who give it exceed the principle of classical utility altogether because "bourgeois" discourse situates gift giving beyond the borders of European territory—and beyond the bounds of European reason. When Sproat writes to complain about a practice of distribution that he had not criticized in *Scenes*, he is staying at Fort Rupert, at the north end of Vancouver Island: precisely the region that Franz Boas will situate outside Europe's influence, and beyond the limits of European territory, when he submits his postcard-report to the Geographical Society of Berlin almost ten years after Sproat's letter. Sproat sends the gift of the name to Ottawa from an area that the colonial gaze consistently defines as Europe's exterior.

However, his attack on the Patlach coincides not just with his arrival at Europe's geographic limit, but with his experience of the people who live there: the people Boas will define as absolutely other to Europe. By 1879 it was customary for white officials to define the Kwakwaka'-wakw as a group incapable of integrating themselves into Euro-Canadian culture. After Superintendent Powell visited the Nimpkish community of Alert Bay in the spring of 1879, for example, he reported that "like all the Quah-kewlths" the residents of this village "have a decided dislike for anything approaching reform." When he arrived at Fort Rupert (only a few weeks ahead of Sproat), the Anglican missionary Alfred Hall informed him that "the Indians were a most difficult lot to civilize" (*Sessional Papers*, 1880, no. 4, p. 112). If colonial administrators conceive of progress toward civilization as a process of lifting up, then the Kwakwaka'wakw sink like a stone. Sproat therefore composed his Patlach letter at an acknowledged site of resistance to colonization. And the thing called the Patlach is the point where the logic of colonialism comes to crisis.[9]

Like Blenkinsop and Powell, the Sproat of 1879 construes the distinction between civilization and barbarism as an opposition between low and high, heavy and light. He suggests the British Columbia First Nations are poor in culture and can overcome their poverty only by rising to the level that the English have already reached. The reason the Patlach has to be outlawed is that it blocks this upward movement. It is a "great obstacle" holding the First Nations down, for "no material nor social progress among the Indians is possible while the 'patlach' exists." Sproat advises the government to suppress it altogether. "Warning and rebuke from an officer having the great authority of the Government and acting judiciously but decisively," he argues, "would have a remarkable effect in discouraging" the Patlach. The effect will probably not be "remarkable" enough, however, and so Sproat tells the government to be prepared to use coercion to put the Patlach in its grave. "[W]hen the proper time came," he writes, "it might be necessary in some cases to lay an iron hand upon the shoulders of the people in some parts of the country—particularly on the coast."

Sproat complains that the Patlach is a form of aboriginal self-government that stands in the way of the Canadian government and its civilizing mission, arguing as he had years earlier that the Patlach is similar, but not too similar, to an election by ballot. The person who gives away the most property is the one most likely to be appointed "Chief": "Though no direct election as chief follows a [continuously?] large distribution," he says, "the distributor puffs himself up on the strength of it, and has at least the support of numerous friends and the credit readily given to the one who exceeds in what many, if not all, are striving for."

There is no room on the coast for two political systems, though, and the aboriginal mode of government must give way to a European one. Obeying the reversal that has inverted the structure of his discourse, the Sproat who once took offense when aboriginal people mimicked Europeans now vilifies Native communities that refuse to imitate the Euro-Canadian model of municipal government. Instead of criticizing aboriginal people for being too European, he attacks them for not being European enough. Not all aboriginal communities are "fit at present for organization for municipal purposes under the Indian Act," he says, and those who reject the European system by continuing to Patlach "should be rebuked, warned and instructed, and gradually trained for responsible management of their own little affairs."

The fold in Sproat's discourse has shifted since he first landed on Vancouver Island, but he continues to justify his arguments by deploying the metaphor of white light. Though at present the municipal system and the Patlach are in direct competition, he predicts that "[t]he one will quietly and naturally kill off the other as the rays of the sun kills [*sic*] a small coal fire," for "[c]ompared with the 'Queen's chiefs,' the Patlach chief, (under a system condemned moreover by the Queen's officer) would soon be nowhere." In a contest between white sun and dark coal, darkness is fated to die. Settler society gives itself the right to force its civilization upon the aboriginal civilizations of the coast because in the eyes of the colonist whiteness is a stronger shade of color. No other justification is necessary for the suppression of the Patlach than this appeal to a quality of light: whiteness is here an absolute good, and deeds done in its name are above reproach.

Sproat also criticizes the Patlach for producing "indigence, thriftlessness, and a habit of roaming about which prevents home associations and is inconsistent with all progress." In particular he alleges that giving away property encourages the practice of borrowing at interest: "If an Indian impelled by rivalry with another, decides on holding a Patlach, he often has to borrow blankets [which here serve as currency, not clothing] from richer men and they charge him two blankets for one, thus fostering grinding usury." Yet "indigence" and the "thriftlessness" that breeds "grinding usury" endlessly transform themselves into their opposites because the Patlach is an expenditure that requires its practitioners to accumulate wealth. "The poor as well as the rich follow the practice," he notes, "and spend their time and their earnings in accumulating and then in distributing." Governed by a folding he cannot control, Sproat's discourse tangles itself into a web of paradoxes: "It is not possible," he continues, "that Indians can acquire property, or become industrious with any good result, while under the influence of this mania." The accumulation of property prevents the accumulation of property, and the industry that supports accumulation blocks the path to industriousness.

But for Sproat the "worst" effect of the Patlach, and the most urgent reason for laying down an iron hand, is prostitution: "Worst of all, a man will say to his wife, nay to his maiden daughter, that before the spring or other appointed time he must have so many dollars for his proposed 'Patlach'; and they in this way and I believe more

*giving*

in this way than from licentious desire are forced into the prostitution which it has become almost a conventional thing for Indian agents to mention and deplore without seeking to strike down the hideous system which mainly produces it." In the banning of the Patlach, as in the prohibition of *sati* in nineteenth-century India, white men justify colonial legislation by seeking—to borrow a sardonic phrase from Gayatri Spivak (1989, 297)—"to save brown women from brown men." The government administrator's determination to protect aboriginal women from "the hideous system" of prostitution does not arise out of concern for them, since as Sproat hints, whites assume that aboriginal women are by nature prone to "licentious desire" anyway.[10] The allegation that the Patlach fuels the sex trade simply provides a compelling excuse to crush a system of government that competes with the white administration.

By raising the question of prostitution, moreover, Sproat inscribes his opposition to gift giving over a grid of sexual difference. In prostitution a woman sells herself to any taker when what she ought to do, according to him, is give herself freely in marriage to the man of her choice. Women are gifts, he argues, and the Patlach transforms them into commodities that men exchange for profit. The most urgent reason for banning the Patlach, then, is that its gifts discourage women from making gifts of themselves. Deploying a crude logic of penetration, Sproat identifies the figure of the woman as the preferred point where Europe's "civilizing" influence can infiltrate the First Nations and threaten them with Europeanization. He will not be the last chivalric government agent to urge the Indian affairs bureaucracy to rescue aboriginal women by imposing his own version of European civilization upon them.

## ENCOUNTERING LANGUAGE

In "The Nature of Language" (1971) Heidegger argues that in everyday utterances language itself remains unthought, just as in our everyday interactions with beings, we neglect Being itself even though it is what allows beings to be. Whenever we speak or write, language gives itself in that it allows us to discuss what concerns us: "Any number of things are given voice in speaking," says Heidegger, "above all what we are speaking about: a set of facts, an occurrence, a question, a matter of concern." But when language brings things to our attention, it draws attention away from itself: "at whatever time and in whatever way we speak a language, language itself never has the floor." The act of speaking *in* language is to be rigorously distinguished from the act of speaking *about* language. However, the ability of language to withhold itself from attention while giving voice to the matter at hand is the condition of possibility of all speaking—and all writing. "Only because in everyday speaking language does *not* bring itself to language but holds back," Heidegger argues, "are we able simply to go ahead and speak a language, and so to deal with something and negotiate something by speaking" (59).

For Heidegger, language is a "prior grant" (*im voraus den Zuspruch*), and it is given to us in advance of every act of speech and writing (71). We could not pose a single question to the world unless language had already promised itself to us. Its promise is what makes every inquiry possible. To put questions to language therefore presupposes that there are languages in which our questions can be formulated. "If we are to think through the nature of language," says Heidegger, "language must first promise itself to us, or must already have done so" (76). Since the inquiry into the nature of language is constrained to follow in the path of language, that inquiry necessarily travels in a circle.

When it gives itself, however, language arrives from the future and not from the past. It is a promise already given, but it is an event that is always about to happen. It is the element we have always lived in, but it waits for us in every phrase that remains to be uttered. To inquire into language is to follow behind an inheritance whose arrival is forever anticipated yet has already arrived. "We speak and speak about language," says Heidegger: "What we speak of, language, is always ahead of us. Our speaking merely follows language constantly" (75). Whatever language gives, then, it gives in time.

We use language in our everyday utterances like a tool, an instrument. Though we follow in the path of language when we speak and write, we seldom have what Heidegger calls "an experience with language" (*mit der Sprache eine Erfahrung machen*) (75). We rely on language to give voice to our concerns but do not concern ourselves with language. We take it for granted without asking how it has granted itself to us. On those rare occasions when language does reveal itself as language—when it momentarily ceases to allow us "to deal with something and negotiate something by speaking" and instead makes "speaking" itself a "something" that demands to be "dealt with" and "negotiated"—the problem of language is "usually" discussed in relation to the body of the speaker and is thereby situated within "the metaphysically conceived confines of the sensuous" (98). The "usual notions of language," says Heidegger, derive from a preoccupation with speech and phonetics. "If we take language directly in the sense of something that is present," he notes, "we encounter it as the act of speaking, the activation of the organs of speech, mouth, lips, tongue" (96).

John Searle's theory of speech acts provides a classical example of the metaphysical reasoning that identifies language as a function of the human body. Since the many authors of the potlatch papers share Searle's theory of language, though they never stop to theorize it explicitly, I will invoke his book *Speech Acts* (1969) several times in the coming pages as an exhausted paradigm. It is necessary to remember, however, that Searle's theory does not describe how the discourse on the potlatch works—and that I do not endorse his metaphysics. I allude to Searle in order to show how the metaphysical understanding of discourse, which takes language to be a form of representation, *fails* to account for the textual effects generated by the potlatch papers.

To begin with, Searle ties language firmly to the "mouth, lips, [and] tongue" of the person who speaks. To make an utterance is to perform a physical act, though the speaking body never acts alone: "talking is performing acts according to rules," or to put it more broadly, "speaking a language is . . . a rule-governed form of behaviour" (22). Speech acts are events in which the law-giving body of language takes hold of the body that talks. Though it is individual speakers, not language, who give voice to thoughts, it is language, not speakers, that determines what *form* thoughts take when they are uttered. Searle's theory of "talking" explains the use of ordinary language in terms of a body whose utterances obey the strict code of a law.

One of Heidegger's goals in "The Nature of Language" is to break with the metaphysical tradition that understands language primarily in terms of the bodies that utter it—which means passing beyond the reasoning that distinguishes the nonsensuous, intellectual content of an utterance from its sensuous, bodily form. But since the step out of metaphysics is necessarily a step back toward what has been left behind, Heidegger argues that to circumvent the "usual notions of language" is to return to what was already there: language itself. It is true that language withdraws itself from scrutiny when it is used, but it is nevertheless possible to isolate certain instances when language "speak[s] itself as language." In such moments language makes an issue of *itself* instead of simply giving voice to issues that concern its speakers. Heidegger warns, though, that "to undergo an experience with language, is something else again than to gather information about language." While the linguistic research performed by linguists, philologists, psychologists, and analytic philosophers (this last group includes ordinary language philosophers like Searle) has its own justification and logic, it fails to make language speak itself as language (58–59).

To encounter language, we do not turn to the conclusions of researchers but to those familiar, everyday situations where we find ourselves at a loss for words. "But when does language speak itself as language?" asks Heidegger. "Curiously enough, when we cannot find the right word for something that concerns us, carries us away, oppresses or encourages us." So long as language serves our desire to give voice to our concerns, providing us with a reliable instrument of expression, it withholds itself from our attention. But when a word fails to arrive, the limits of language announce themselves and trouble our thoughts. "Then we leave unspoken what we have in mind," says Heidegger, "and, without rightly giving it thought, undergo moments in which language itself has distantly and fleetingly touched [*streifen*] us with its essential being [*Wesen*]" (59). Language grazes us precisely when we cannot grasp it. And while Heidegger says he wants to direct the inquiry into language away from the speaking body, he construes the essence of language as a physical density that, in its absence, stands so close to its speakers that it rubs against them yet remains so far away that it touches them only "distantly."

If the essence of language presents itself when words are absent, what happens when we want to articulate something we have never encountered before? Heidegger says that "when the issue is to put into language something which has never yet been spoken, then everything depends on whether language gives or withholds the appropriate word. . . . Such," he notes, "is the case of the poet" (59). To write poetry is to encounter the twofold play of a language that simultaneously gives and withholds itself. Yet the difficulty of arriving at "the appropriate word" for something previously unknown is a problem that also confronted the traveler, the ethnographer, and the Indian affairs administrator in nineteenth-century British Columbia. And if, as Heidegger maintains, finding new words for new things is a poet's job, then Sproat, Powell, and even Boas are, in their own way, poets. They write about a margin of coast where, according to Boas, everything remains to be seen by the gaze of Western science and where the European explorer is offered endless possibilities for research. When they record the activities of the coastal First Nations, they report on events and practices that according to Sproat, lie beyond the established limits of their civilization: practices that have "never yet been spoken" in the vast array of statements uttered, up until the late nineteenth century, by the disembodied voice of Western European science.

## WORDS AND THINGS

The white officials who undertook to regulate the Patlach in nineteenth-century British Columbia inherited the task of finding the appropriate word for a practice formerly unknown to the West, to Europe, and especially to Europe-in-western-Canada, and their search brought them into an encounter with language, drawing attention to the verbal matter in which every utterance is formed. It is hardly surprising, then, that their discourse is obsessed with the orthography and meaning of "Patlach" and its many surrogates. As they sought a standard spelling and a true sense for this word, they also ran up against the problem of reference: the relation between a thing and the word that names it. What their discourse gives us to think, in the end, is that the word makes a gift of the thing it names.

Lawrence Vankoughnet replaced William Spragge as

deputy superintendent general of Indian affairs in 1874. For the next twenty years Vankoughnet personally supervised every aspect of Canada's Indian administration from Ottawa, first in the Indian Branch and later in the Department of Indian Affairs. One of his aims as chief administrator was to keep his department's expenses at a minimum, and it is thought that the discontent that his policy aroused on the prairies helped to incite the Northwest Rebellion (some would say Resistance) of 1885. The Conservative government rewarded him for his frugality by forcing him to resign in 1893 (Titley 1986, 14; Leighton 1983, 105–8, 114–17).

Vankoughnet responded to Sproat's Patlach letter in December 1879 by sending a memorandum to Sproat, Powell, and James Lenihan, who had been Indian superintendent at New Westminster since 1874. The memo notes that the dominion government is troubled by "the custom existing among certain tribes and bands of Indians in British Columbia of giving 'Patlachs.'" "I am directed," Vankoughnet writes, "by the Right Honourable the Superintendent General of Indian Affairs [who at the time was the prime minister, and Vankoughnet's mentor, John A. Macdonald] to instruct you upon every favourable occasion that presents itself to discountenance the prevalence of this custom and to enjoin the Indians to discountenance the same" (NA, vol. 3669, file 10,691, 2 December 1879). Sproat's letter has brought the Patlach under the regulatory scrutiny of the Indian affairs bureaucracy. Henceforth the practice will be actively administered—"discountenanced" at first but afterwards outlawed—and not just criticized in letters and reports from British Columbia.

But what are Patlachs? Federal officials are about to launch an inquiry into the truth of "this custom," but they will not ask the people who potlatch to explain their own traditions. The inquiry will instead fold itself up between the two limits that Sproat has already mapped for it. The word "Patlach" will be made to refer, at once, to the giving of gifts and to the reciprocal exchange of property.

In his memo Vankoughnet takes up Sproat's version of the word, but is not sure what it means since the thing it names is utterly unknown to him. Drawing on what Sproat has told him, however, Vankoughnet infers that " 'Patlachs' . . . *seem* to comprise the parting with . . . personal property without any benefit being derived therefrom excepting the questionable one of obtaining a name for liberality" (emphasis added). The "Patlach" "seems" to signify a pure expenditure without return, "without any benefit." But this appearance is uncertain. The fact remains that one gives without return to receive, in return, the countergift of a name that identifies one as a giver, as one who gives with "liberality." How can the "Patlach" be construed as an absolute loss if it earns a nominal profit for the Patlacher? For Vankoughnet this benefit, this countergift of a name, is so "questionable" that it is not a return at all. "Patlachs," then, are occasions for circulating pure gifts which earn nothing, although a mark of prestige always comes back to the one who gives.

When Superintendent Powell replies to this memo, he opens a long debate about the meaning of Patlaching, but a debate that deals not so much with the thing known as the Patlach as with the word "Patlach" itself. Powell places "Patlach" between quotation marks whenever he uses it. Or is he mentioning it rather than using it? He begins by acknowledging that he has received Vankoughnet's dispatch "respecting the evil of the 'Patlach' or donation feasts, customary among the uncivilized Indians of this Province" (NA, vol. 3669, file 10,691, 19 December 1879). To cite the name correctly one ought to write " 'Patlach' " instead of "Patlach." Indeed, I have misled my readers by suggesting that Sproat and Vankoughnet discussed the Patlach in their letters of 1879, for they wrote not of the Patlach but of the "Patlach," which, again, ought to have been quoted as " 'Patlach.' "

Although he takes up Sproat's version of the word in reply to Vankoughnet, we know that Powell had already offered several versions of his own in previous reports to Ottawa. Each time he writes the word, he inscribes it with certain marks—such as capital letters, quotes, italics, and parentheses—that distinguish it from the words around it. Hence one finds " 'Patlatches' " in 1872, "('potlatches')" in 1875, "*potlaches*" in 1876, and "(potlaches)" in 1878 (*Sessional Papers,* 1873, no. 23, p. 10; 1876, no. 9, p. 45; 1877, no. 11, p. 36; 1879, no. 7, p. 71). If putting a word in quotations can mean that it is being mentioned as a problem rather than being used as a sign for something else, then the marks that haunt " 'Patlach' " and its surrogates—"*potlaches*," "(potlaches)"—in Powell's correspondence during the 1870s hint that the word, in all its forms, is clouded with unresolved difficulties. And the constant variations in its spelling confirm that it is a node of uncertainty. It is as if this word marks a point in the canon of Western European knowledge where the will to understanding is bound to stumble.

The word's reference—its relation to the thing it names—is especially uncertain. In his reply to Vankoughnet, Powell acknowledges this difficulty by trying to solidify the link between " 'Patlach' " and the practices of the coastal First Nations. He bluntly tells Vankoughnet that he has attached the word to the wrong thing. "I might state for your information," states Powell, "that the 'Patlach' does not altogether show the great liberality of the donor, as I infer from the tenor of your letter, for the Indian never gives or 'patlaches' except with the knowledge that he will receive his gifts with interest at a future feast. On the part of shrewd Indians it is really 'casting their bread upon the waters' in order that it may be returned to them 'fourfold' and, in many instances, without doubt it is." Powell's letter is another instance where, as Searle puts it, "[t]he word itself [here the noun ' "Patlach" '] is *presented* and then talked about, and that it is to be taken as presented and talked about rather than used conventionally to refer is indicated by the quotes" (1969, 75–76). But the distinction between use and mention is not absolute in this case. Powell does use " 'Patlach' " "conventionally to refer" to certain practices, yet he also mentions it in order to "talk about" the difficulty of determining exactly what practices it refers to. But what exactly does the act of "referring" entail? What is the nature of the relation binding a word to the thing it names?

Heidegger notes that it is customary to think of words as supplements, or prostheses, which come to fasten (*umgreifen*) themselves onto objects, actions, events, and processes that already exist somewhere outside language (1971, 68). When Sproat describes in *Scenes* how the Aht invent names for things, for example, he argues that things arrive in the world without names and afterwards people encounter them and decide to find words for them. If language itself was sent to earth from God, then words are artifacts fashioned by individuals skilled in their manufacture. What strikes him is the readiness with which the natives invent names for any new objects. A compound word is suggested by some individual in the tribe who is considered skilful in forming appropriate names, and who, for the sake of sound [like Searle, Sproat understands language in terms of speech and the voice], subjects the roots [the basic morphemes which, he says, are "expressive of natural sounds and generic ideas"] to great change and, often, abbreviation in the process of compounding. Yet all who hear the new word at once recognize its meaning, and it is added to their vocabulary. It is surprising to find how quickly any such new names become universal. (1987, 87–88)

For Sproat, naming is a collective speech act in which the speakers of a language agree to fasten particular words to particular objects. It makes reference possible by attaching a sign to something that already exists in a nameless state.

Searle says that speakers bind words to things through the act of pointing. Words themselves do not point. Rather, people use them to point. Names are tied to things in speech acts, and "speech acts are performed by speakers in uttering words, not by words" alone (28). Words that have been firmly bound to things are "referring expressions." As Searle points out, "Referring expressions *point* to particular [and individual] things," including processes, events, and actions, and "answer the questions 'Who?' 'What?' 'Which?' " (1969, 26–27, emphasis added). There are between three and four classes of referring expressions in English, including the class of proper names.

But the question that Powell raises in his 1879 reply to Vankoughnet is whether " 'Patlach' " is qualified to serve as a referring expression at all. Powell wants " 'Patlach' " to point to the act of exchange rather than the gift, but it serves just as well, in the dispatches of Sproat and Vankoughnet, to point toward the gift instead of exchange. Although a speaker is supposed to be able to answer the questions "What?" and "Which?" by aiming a referring expression at one thing only—as if to say "That one there"—" 'Patlach' " refuses to point in a single direction. Government officials deploy it repeatedly but are never quite sure that it is aiming the right way, toward the right "thing, process, event, action," for it simultaneously points *away* from the thing it is said to refer to. No matter what its authors intend for it, therefore, " 'Patlach' " is an unreliable pointer because it points in two opposite directions at once. It has one referent too many and thus has no referent at all.

Of course, it is not unusual for a single word to refer to several things. Searle notes for instance "that both riversides and financial houses are called 'banks,' " and he considers it "too obvious to need stating" that "one does not prove a word meaningless by pointing out that it has several meanings" (170). Is it not wrong, then, to suggest that " 'Patlach' " loses it ability to refer when it points toward two things at once? The answer depends on the "at once." It is a question of simultaneity. A word can indeed drain itself of reference if it is said to refer to one thing only but is used to refer to two different things *at the same time.* "Bank" would be rendered nonsensical if it were agreed that it points to a single object and that this object is at once a riverside and a transnational institution dealing in financial services. Yet this is precisely how Sproat, Vankoughnet, and Powell deploy " 'Patlach.' " In their texts it gestures toward one thing alone, and this thing is at once an act of giving and an exchange of payments: it is simultaneously itself and the direct opposite of itself. And it is as absurd to say that a gift is an exchange as it is to say that a riverside is a financial institution.

Because the word refuses to point in a straight line toward a single referent, the inquiry into the truth of the " 'Patlach' " follows a circular path. Sproat says in 1868 that the distributions performed by the "Aht" belong to a general system of exchange where every expense is ultimately repaid, yet in October 1879 he declares that the property circulated in these same distributions never comes back home to the giver. The effort to define the practice comes full circle when Vankoughnet repeats Sproat's second argument, which ties the " 'Patlach' " to the pure gift, only to have Powell respond that " 'Patlachs' " are reciprocal exchanges and not acts of gift giving at all.

Since the Euro-Canadian understanding of the " 'Patlach' " revolves from exchange to the gift and back to exchange again, it is only logical that the reasons for condemning the " 'Patlach' " also go round in circles. Sproat's letter of 1879 alleges that the " 'Patlach' " is a limit blocking the movement from barbarity to civilization. But the " 'Patlach' " has the authority to trace such a limit only when defined as a mode of gift giving.

In his reply to Vankoughnet, though, Powell redefines " 'Patlaching' " as a system of investment that bears no relation to the gift, and by changing the meaning of the word he strips " 'Patlach' " of its power to divide civilization from its beyond. The word occupies a zone of his text where the two sides of a limit overlap. "Were the system not so general," he writes, "*I do not know that it is different* from that prevalent among more civilized beings—nine out of ten of whom expect a commensurate return for a gift. But the Indians who make a practise of it will deprive their families and even themselves of necessaries in order to obtain 'patlach' capital" (NA, vol. 3669, file 10,691, 19 December 1879; emphasis added). When Powell makes the gift vanish, declaring that he does not know that " 'Patlach' " distributions are "different" from exchanges, he erases the mark distinguishing uncivilized peoples who spend without return from "civilized beings" who (on average: nine times out of ten) prefer a return "with interest."

Without this mark, it is impossible to "know" with certainty whether the now giftless " 'Patlach' " is an obstacle to the assimilation of the First Nations into settler society or a sign that they were civilized before the European gaze arrived to villainize them. If Powell defines civilization as that which gives no gifts and seeks a profit from every present, then all giftless cultures must be equally civilized. And if, for Powell, gift giving is the privileged sign of "barbarity," then the lack of the gift among the British Columbia First Nations collapses the distance between the "barbaric" circulation of aboriginal "capital" and the "civilized" exchanges of the Euro-Canadian economy. There is no longer any reason to condemn the " 'Patlach' " because it has been transformed into a mark of civilization, a pointer that points directly away from the act of pure expenditure that Europe-in-Canada so abhors.

Powell refuses to admit that his own logic leads to this conclusion and inserts a "but" into his reply in order to relieve aboriginal people of any qualities that might render them equal, in his gaze, to Euro-Canadian colonists. Aboriginal people may well give and take like "civilized" beings, "[b]ut," he says, they are so eager to accumulate "capital" for investment that they deprive themselves and their families of the very "necessaries" of life. It is as if each aboriginal family and indeed each individual ("the Indians who make a practise of it will deprive their families and even themselves") were composed of a capital-holding class that jealously guards its surpluses and a working class that is too poor to meet its most basic needs. Ironically, Powell's analysis of the struggle between accumulation and necessity, surplus and lack, applies as much to his own society as to aboriginal societies, yet he nevertheless insists that the will to accumulate at any cost sets aboriginal people at a firm remove from white Canadians. The effort "to obtain 'patlach' capital" is, he says, "directly opposed to the inculcation of industrious or moral habits" (NA, vol. 3669, file 10,691, 19 December 1879).

Is it necessary to recall that these observations contradict the arguments advanced by Sproat in 1879? His " 'Patlach' " letter states in its self-contradictory way that the " 'Patlach' " ought to be suppressed because it *prevents* aboriginal people from accumulating property. Banning the " 'Patlach,' " Sproat argues, would allow Canada to decrease the funds it spends providing " 'Patlachers' " with "necessaries" that they refuse to keep for themselves.

For Sproat it is the failure to store up wealth that situates aboriginal people outside the bounds of Europe-in-Canada and justifies Canada's attempt to take over the administration of their lives. But this failure *fails* to occur in Powell's letter of December 1879 because he reverses each of the terms that Sproat deployed to insert a limit between Canada and the First Nations. For Powell, the *failure of the failure* to accumulate marks a limit that was formerly marked by the *failure* to accumulate.

This overlapping of the civilized with the uncivilized occurs whenever a postal-colonial author draws a limit between Europe-in-Canada and everything that it situates outside itself. Above all the fold governs every facet of Canada's discourse on the " 'Patlach' " and undermines every attempt to justify putting the practice to death. The impossibility of vindicating the administration of Indian affairs is no reason not to proceed with it, however, for Canadian administrators do not hesitate to act on their conclusions even when the reasoning that supports them proves to be nothing but a tissue of contradictions.[11]

*giving*

# A DOUBLE INSCRIPTION

## The Bureaucratic Fetish

In 1880 the dominion government closed the Indian Branch and replaced it with the Department of Indian Affairs. Although renamed and reorganized, the Indian bureaucracy remained attached to the Department of the Interior, which was charged with overseeing the colonization of western Canada, and the minister of the interior continued to serve as superintendent general of Indian affairs. In 1881 the Indian administration in British Columbia underwent a parallel restructuring. James Lenihan was relieved of his duties, and Powell was appointed the sole Indian superintendent for the province. Also, six Indian agencies were established: the Cowichan, West Coast, and Kwawkewlth Agencies on Vancouver Island, and the Fraser River, Kamloops, and O'Kanagan Agencies on the mainland. Each of these administrative districts was placed under the supervision of an Indian agent. By 1882 two more agencies were planned: one in the Williams Lake region and the other high on the north coast of the mainland (*Sessional Papers*, 1882, no. 6, p. xii; 1883, no. 5, p. xxi; *Statutes of Canada, 1880*, chap. 28, secs. 2–8).

Prime Minister Macdonald continued to oversee the Department of the Interior, and the new Department of Indian Affairs came under his supervision. His annual report on Indian affairs for 1882 does not fail to mention what he names the " 'Potlache.' " While I call the report "his," however, it is not certain that he was its author. His signature is indeed attached to the report, but it was more likely written by Vankoughnet on Macdonald's behalf since Vankoughnet often wrote letters and reports that were to be understood as issuing from the desk of the superintendent general.[12] It does not matter who the author was, however. It is enough to underline the possibility that one of two administrators could have penned this report. The significance of this seemingly trivial detail will soon become clear.

When Macdonald (or is it?) discusses the " 'Potlache' " in 1882, he breaks with the circular logic that had governed the correspondence of Sproat, Vankoughnet, and Powell in the 1860s and 1870s and deploys a rhetoric that allows two contradictory themes to be true at the same time. Reviewing Indian affairs in British Columbia, Macdonald writes that "[i]t is satisfactory to be able to report that the old heathen feast known as the 'potlache' is gradually being abandoned on the east coast [of Vancouver Island]" (*Sessional Papers*, 1883, no. 5, p. xxiii). This statement is unremarkable in itself, since it merely echoes the 1882 report of W. H. Lomas, the agent in charge of the Cowichan Agency. Like Macdonald, Lomas insists that "[t]he 'Potlaches,' once so common [among the Salish people in the agency], are, I believe, gradually dying out" (55). But when Macdonald sets out to define this "dying" practice, his rhetoric sets out an irreducible paradox.

What is "known" as the " 'Potlache,' " what the name refers to in Macdonald's (or Vankoughnet's) report, is a distribution of goods that invokes a counterdistribution. "At these celebrations," Macdonald continues, "a large quantity of personal property is wont to be squandered in largesses from one tribe to another, the lucky (?) [*sic*] recipients being expected to return subsequently as much as if not more than they receive" (xxiii). His report points " 'Potlache' " where Powell told Vankoughnet to point it in 1879: toward a cycle of reciprocal exchanges that generate profits in the form of interest.

But Macdonald (or not) points " 'Potlache' " in a second direction too. For the very words that describe the practice as an exchange of goods simultaneously identify it as a form of gift giving. The things distributed in a " 'Potlache' " cannot be gifts because they have to be returned, and thus paid for, "subsequently," yet these same things are nevertheless "largesses" that are "squandered" the moment they leave the hands of the giver. In a " 'Potlache' " as Macdonald construes it, whatever is given away is eventually given back—yet it never arrives home. Everything is returned but nothing is repaid. Nothing is lost, but "a large quantity of personal property" is wasted. When Macdonald writes "Potlache," the word points to two different practices at once. What makes this double and contradictory reference possible? His text enacts a logic that Freud has named fetishism. As I turn to Freud to explain this notion, though, my goal is to give a name to the structure of Macdonald's (or Vankoughnet's) text, not to analyze the workings of its author's unconscious. Fetishism here names a way of organizing concepts into discourse.

In "Fetishism" ([1927] 1957) Freud discusses the case of "a young man [who] had exalted a certain sort of 'shine on the nose' into a fetishistic precondition" for erotic enjoyment. How did this attachment come about? It seems that as a boy he had firmly believed that his mother had a penis. When he discovered that she did not, says Freud, this knowledge meant "his own possession of a penis was in danger" and made him fear the possibility of being castrated. The child theorist dealt with his fear by adopting a peculiar mode of reasoning. He set up a substitute, a fetish—in this case the nose—in place of the absent penis, so that he could continue to believe it was there although he knew it was not. "He has retained that belief," notes Freud, "but he has also given it up" (152–54). Fetishism is thus a mode of doubling. The fetishist's logic holds that two contradictory propositions can both be true at once. It is this idea of a simultaneous balancing of opposites that I want to bring to bear on Canada's discourse on the "Potlache."

Macdonald's report draws attention to the "at-once": the textual structure that allows a word to refer to a single thing as if it were two opposite things at the same time. As Derrida (1986, 210) notes in another context, in the logic of fetishism, the "at-once, the in-the-same-stroke . . . of the two contraries, of the two opposite operations, prohibits cutting through to a decision within the undecidable." The weighing of two simultaneous contraries makes it impossible to decide exactly which practice—gift giving or exchange—the word " 'Potlache' " refers to. When Macdonald (or is it Vankoughnet? and is it merely a coincidence that in this instance there could be *two* authors?) maintains that the " 'Potlache' " entails both profit and loss, he overlaps two opposing referents, folding them one over the other, instead of "cutting through to a decision" about the precise relation between the word and the thing it names. The reference of " 'Potlache' " will remain undecidable so long as it is frozen between two these contradictory possibilities.

It is no coincidence, though, that Macdonald's (?) report keeps both possibilities in view. When he states that the " 'Potlache' " includes gifts *and* exchanges, he is obeying a logical imperative. His report claims to set Europe-in-Canada at a clear remove from the coastal First Nations

63

*giving*

of British Columbia, and it is impossible to trace a limit between Europe and its beyond without deploying the discursive structure of the "at-once."

Powell's 1879 reply to Vankoughnet has shown that to identify the " 'Potlache' " as a form of exchange is to cease to "know that it is different" from the exchanges practiced by Euro-Canadians. If the limit dividing Europe-in-Canada from the First Nations is to be maintained, however, the " 'Potlache' " has to continue to be identified as a mode of gift giving even after it has been declared an exchange, because in the logic of the discourse on Indian affairs it is the gift that distinguishes the First Nations from a settler society that interprets civilization as an attribute belonging only to itself. Canada wants to distance itself from the people it calls uncivilized, just as Freud's fetishist wants his body to remain different from his mother's. And just as the fetishist works, at all costs, to fend off the realization that he might someday lose his most prized possession, his penis, so Canada wants to protect itself from admitting that it too could lose its most cherished attribute: its whiteness. It is whiteness, after all, that permits Euro-Canadians to consider themselves superior to the original inhabitants of their new nation. If they were to lose their precious color, they would have no mark to reassure them of the justness of their mission to put aboriginal cultures to death.

As we have learned to expect, the people whom white administrators situate farthest from Europe—the absolute others of Western civilization—are the Kwakw<u>a</u>ka'wakw. "The Kwahkewlth Agency comprehends 25 bands and 2,264 Indians, who are the most depraved and uncivilized in the Province," writes Macdonald, and he adds that "[t]he ruinous Potlache feast is constantly held by them" (xxiii). The most uncivilized people on the coast are those who hold themselves close to the gift by maintaining the " 'Potlache' "—even though a " 'Potlache,' " it is said, gives no gifts. It is true that the Nuu'chah'nulth also continue the practice of " 'potlaching,' " but Macdonald places them a little farther from the gift and a little closer to Europe and its ways than the Kwakw<u>a</u>ka'wakw. Though he admits the Aht are "much addicted to 'potlaching' feasts, and gambling," which is what Blenkinsop had said in 1874 and 1875, "they are much more industrious and amenable to law than their neighbors the Kwahkewlths" (xxiii).[13] It seems the great crime of the Kwakwaka̱'wakw is their refusal to endorse Canadian standards of labor and legality: a refusal to become white.

## Fighting with Property

In the summer of 1885 George Dawson's work for the Geological Survey of Canada brought him to "the northern part of Vancouver Island and its vicinity." A self-styled ethnographer, Dawson found time among his other duties to write his *Notes and Observations on the Kwakiool People* . . . and present them to the Royal Society of Canada in May 1887. His paper repeats the simultaneous balancing of contrary assertions that organizes Macdonald's (or Vankoughnet's) 1882 account of the " 'Potlache' ": the potlatch is once again—and *at once*—an act of gift giving and a circular economy of expenditure and return.

Like Macdonald (or Vankoughnet), Dawson locates the people he calls the "Kwakiool" beyond the outermost limit of Europe and its civilizing influence. "The difficulties attendant on any effort toward the improvement of the condition and mode of life of the coast tribes of British Columbia, are very grave," he writes, emphasizing that "the actual results of missionary labours, such as those carried on by Mr. Hall among the Kwakiool, and other self-sacrificing persons elsewhere, are in most cases, to all appearance, small." He offers two reasons why the "Kwakiool" have not raised themselves into the hierarchy of Euro-Canadian civilization. The first—which echoes Blenkinsop's 1874 report from Barkley Sound—is that their traditions are like stones holding them down in a state of near bestiality. Weighed down by a culture that is sheer nature, they "herd" together like animals. "It is difficult to induce individuals to abandon their old customs and bad habits," he says, "and nearly impossible to prevent them from *relapsing* from time to time, owing to the fact that they still live promiscuously among and herd together with the mass of the tribe" (87, emphasis added).

Yet the main reason why the "Kwakiool" have failed to become white—and for Dawson this is the second obstacle to their progress—is whiteness itself. Like the Sproat of the 1860s, Dawson maintains that in recent years "the Kwakiool, equally with other tribes, have became [*sic*] in a word 'demoralised.' " Though they have given up their traditions—the same ones that hold them down—shedding this weight has not lifted them any higher. Instead it

65

*giving*

has stripped them of "their spirit and self-respect . . . replacing it by nothing." They find work on farms at harvest time, he says, but do little more than eat for the rest of the year. What has brought about this crisis? The process of "demoralisation" has been under way only "[s]ince the arrival of the whites" (87). The "Kwakiool" were not uncivilized until the lack of civilization arrived on their shores *from Europe,* and the greatest obstacle to their upward movement into civilization is nothing less than civilization itself. For Dawson, as for Sproat, Europe-in-Canada is at once a force that draws people to the height of human achievement and a weight pulling them down to the level of animals who can barely feed themselves—although eating is almost all they do.

Among the "old customs and bad habits" that weigh heaviest on the "Kwakiool," though not so heavy a restraint as progress itself, is the "pernicious effect of the extension and frequent recurrence of the potlatch" which, in a further proliferation of names, is also known "as *pus-a* and *ya-hooit,* these terms probably denoting special forms of the ceremony appropriate to certain occasions. In speaking of the custom," adds Dawson, "I will, however, use the commonly recognised word *potlatch* as being the most convenient." He warns that the custom is spreading: "Mr. George Blenkinsop" and "the Rev. A. J. Hall" have observed its growth firsthand. It appears, therefore, that as the "Kwakiool" approach absolute "demoralisation," they are at once abandoning their traditions and pursuing them with increased intensity, as if their long descent into death were actually enriching their cultural life (79).

The potlatch, as Dawson describes it, is "a struggle for social pre-eminence" that takes the form of a ceremonial distribution of blankets: whoever can accumulate and then give away the most blankets gains enhanced prestige within a social hierarchy. To lose is a public humiliation: "should the aspirant [to a position of eminence] be beaten," says Dawson, "[he or she] would feel mortified and ashamed." Determined to prevail at any cost, "wives even rob their husbands to assist a brother, or some other relative, in amassing blankets" and competing for social status (79–80). This is a theme that will become typical, indeed stereotypical, in the ethnography of the Kwakwa̱-ka'wakw for years to come: the potlatch is a war fought with property.

However, the distribution of blankets is more than a hostile act of expenditure. Obeying the double logic of fetishism, Dawson argues that the potlatch is at once a loss and an accumulation. It includes moments when gifts are freely given away, yet every gift has a place within a general system of investment. Anyone planning to distribute blankets begins by lending them out to people from other villages, "giving larger numbers to those who are well off, and particularly to such as are known to have the intention of giving a potlatch in return." "This loan is reckoned a debt of honour," says Dawson, "to be paid with interest at the proper time." One lends blankets and receives, in return, a payment of interest that doubles the amount loaned. "It is usual to return two blankets for every one borrowed," he adds, but "Indians *with liberal ideas* may return even more" (80, emphasis added). Hence the debtor has the option of giving back, and thereby giving away, a supplement of interest in excess of the amount owing.

The potlatch is not held until this long cycle of preliminary exchanges has finished. Then people from different communities gather in the lender's village, and, when "all is ready," says Dawson, "with the accompaniment of much bombastic speech-making and excitement [as well as 'feasting' and 'ceremony'], the mass of blankets is distributed in exact proportion to the social position of those taking part—or, *what is the same thing*, in proportion to their individual contributions" (80, emphasis added).

Dawson offers two equally possible scenarios here. Either the value of the gifts one gives in the bid to improve one's prestige matches the social position of each recipient, or—"what is the same thing" but also a thing different enough to be worth noting separately—the value of the gifts must be "in proportion" to the interest one has received from one's debtors before the potlatch. If the second hypothesis is correct—a second hypothesis that is "the same" as the first and thus the *only* hypothesis—then potlatch gifts are a repayment of the interest earned from loans. Indeed, the potlatcher returns even those extra payments of interest, those supplemental gifts, that were paid by debtors with "liberal ideas." One earns nothing from potlatching because the profit made while preparing the potlatch is repaid during the final distribution of blankets.

But there is more to a Dawson potlatch than a repay-

67

*giving*

ment of the interest accrued on loans. It is also a return of interest—*with interest*. One begins by lending out blankets. Later one receives, in return, both the blankets that were loaned and a supplement of interest. To end the cycle, one gives back the interest to those who paid it—and then gives them the blankets that they had previously had to borrow. The Dawson potlatch is therefore all gift and no profit though everything is arranged to suggest that each gift received is a profit earned. While in 1882 Macdonald's diction of gift giving described the " 'Potlache' " as an instance of exchange, in 1885 Dawson's diction of exchange construes the potlatch as an act of gift giving. In both texts, however, the "potlatch"—or " 'Potlache' "—balances these two contrary operations at once.

Dawson notes that the competition for prestige among the "Kwakiool" sometimes leads to the outright destruction of goods that might otherwise have been given away. "Should an Indian wish to humiliate another for any reason," he writes, "he may destroy a great number of blankets or much other valued property." If the adversary fails to destroy an equal amount "or if possible a greater amount of property," then "he lies under the reproach of having been worsted by his foe" (80). The destruction of property—often a destruction "with interest"—is an absolute gift, an expenditure that cannot be returned because what was spent no longer exists, except in the memory of two "foes."

## DOCTORING

Dawson says that if the "Kwakiool" communities are to give up the potlatch and become "very valuable members of the community of the west," it will be necessary "to establish industries among them" where they can be trained to work like Western Europeans (88). The notion that "industry" is capable of lifting barbarity into civilization also governs Macdonald's report for 1882, where he notes that it is the "industrious" nature of the "Aht" that brings them nearer to whiteness than the "[d]epraved and uncivilized" "Kwahkewlths." Superintendent Powell too was known to laud the civilizing power of industrial education in his correspondence, but he advocates a more violent means of putting the "Potlache" to death in his annual report for 1882.[14]

As he describes the tour he made of the Kwahkewlth Agency in June 1882, Powell suggests that the government has little choice but to force the Kwakwa̱ka'wakw to embark on the path to whiteness because they refuse to do it by themselves. "I was glad to be able to visit the Kwahkewlths in a ship of war," he says, "not from a probability of actual rebellion on the part of these otherwise wild and reckless people, but because a proper show of authority is still necessary when endeavouring to break up any of their old and demoralising customs to which they seem devotedly attached" (*Sessional Papers*, 1883, no. 5, p. 162). It is no longer enough to discountenance the "old customs." They are to become the target of a whole apparatus of outright coercion.

To support his call for "a proper show of authority" Powell sums up the experience of Alfred Hall, who retreated to Alert Bay in 1880 after spending two years trying and failing to Europeanize the "incorrigible" residents of Fort Rupert.[15] "Mr. Hall is labouring in a field," writes Powell, "where he meets the daily discouragements incident to the reforming of people who are opposed to his work. . . . He informed me, that the chief obstructions to his efforts were the liquor traffic, the potlaches and barbarous medicine feasts, which he thought should be prevented by law, now that an Agent, who might enforce such an enactment, was stationed there" (162). Citing Hall, indeed using him as a postal relay, Powell advances the idea of banning the practices that "obstruct" the uplifting influence of missionaries and government administrators, though he remarks elsewhere that if a law were passed, the dominion would have to absorb the expense of building a jail and hiring constables to make arrests (NA, vol. 3628, file 6244-1, 22 November 1882).

The statute foreseen by Powell (via Hall) would forbid not only "potlaching" and the sale of liquor to aboriginal people but a whole class of events known as "barbarous medicine feasts." Though it remains undefined, the "feast" surfaces here as a new object to be scrutinized and regulated by the Indian affairs bureaucracy. Powell says it is a mark of barbarity since, like the potlach, it traces a fragile limit between those who practice it and those who declare themselves the (Indian) agents of civilization.

The 1882 report of the agent for the new Kwahkewlth Agency—Powell's old colleague George Blenkinsop—

suggests the Indian affairs administration had already moved to suppress the practice of "feasting" in British Columbia. But Blenkinsop insists the people recently placed under his paternal supervision "are so wedded to their old customs, and even filth, that they have to be driven to make the least effort to rise above their present degraded level" (*Sessional Papers*, 1883, no. 5, p. 65). In 1882, as in 1874, Blenkinsop articulates the relation between Europe and its beyond as a hierarchical opposition between high and low, raising and sinking, elevation and degradation. Yet if in 1874 it was gambling and giving away that kept the "Aht" from lifting themselves into the ranks of Western civilization, in 1882 he says the Kwakwaka'wakw are weighed down by " 'potlatching' " and an activity named the " 'Tamanowes.' "

"The question of 'potlatching' has engaged my most serious attention," he writes, adding that

> [a] general tone of despondency prevails among the elders of the different tribes on account of their being obliged to give up this old custom.
>
> I have pointed out to them over and over again, the evils attending it, which the younger members do not fail to recognize, and even appreciate its intended abolishment.
>
> They have had due warning, and those who in future choose *to risk or lend* their property to uphold such a pernicious system will experience a difficulty in recovering it. (66, emphasis added)

70

The new agent rehearses a theme that will become a standard part of the discourse against " 'potlatching' " for years to come: young people support and even "appreciate" the abolition of this practice, while their elders refuse to give it up. Yet it is the children of these same young people who will be jailed for " 'potlatching' " fifty years later.

" 'Potlatching' " appears in quotation marks here, as if it were destined always to be a node of uncertainty in the utterances that condemn it, but Blenkinsop does not hesitate to point out its proper referent. It is—at once—a circulation of gifts and a "system" of loans, and like all forms of investment it involves an element of "risk." Indeed, in

*giving*

1882 the risks are greater than ever before. If in the pot-latch, as Dawson explains it, one distributes property knowing it will be returned, the arrival of an Indian agent means that in future creditors may be prevented from calling in their debts—a situation that would leave many people in a state of financial crisis.

Blenkinsop ends by reporting that "[t]he 'Tamanowes' was attempted to be carried out last winter in this camp, but the steps taken to prevent it caused the disgusting part of the performance to be abandoned, under threat of prosecution for assault." Like " 'potlatching,' " the word " 'Tamanowes' " envelops itself in quotation marks here, as though it were covertly calling attention to the difficulty of deciding exactly what it is. Not even an experienced observer like Blenkinsop can explain what thing, what practice, this other name refers to. He declares simply, "I have reason to hope it has seen its last days" (66). The "it" withdraws from view, and the reader is left asking what he finds so "disgusting" about its "performance." If " 'Pot-lache' " is a sign that points nowhere because it gestures toward two mutually exclusive things at once, then Blenkinsop's " 'Tamanowes' " points nowhere because it has nothing to point to in the first place.

Adhering to a by now familiar pattern, the indecision clouding the relation between this word and its referent is matched by the undecidability of its spelling. When Macdonald mentions the suppression of the practice at Fort Rupert in his report for 1882, he substitutes " 'Tamawawas' " for Blenkinsop's " 'Tamanowes.' " "The medicine dance, 'Tamawawas,' was celebrated in the camp last winter at Fort Rupert," writes Macdonald (or, again, Vankoughnet), "but threats to prosecute for assault had the desired effect of preventing the disgusting portion of the performance" (*Sessional Papers*, 1883, no. 5, p. xxiv). It seems that "medicine dance" and " 'Tamawawas' " are equivalent terms—but terms for what? The only certainty is that there is something about this object that the colonial gaze, like the eye of Freud's fetishist, refuses to see.

Dr. Powell explains in his 1882 report that the standard means of curing illness in aboriginal communities is the " 'Gamanawas.' " But the cure itself functions as a disease. "The usual amount of sickness always exists in Indian camps," he says, "and on account of the absence of professional assistance much suffering is often experienced. To this want may be attributed, in a great measure, the continuance of the 'Gamanawas,' or Indian doctoring, and its attendant evils among semi-civilized tribes" (166). Where there is " 'potlatching' " there is sickness, and where there is sickness, there is the "evil" " 'Gamanawas.' " The two practices support each other like the two sides of an arch.

Although Powell says the "Gamanawas" is a form of "doctoring" here, he had already defined it elsewhere as an act of cannibalism. In February 1881 the bishop of Victoria sent the superintendent general of Indian affairs a petition asking for the suppression of the "Tamanawas dances" in the Cowichan Agency. The petition was written by Catholic missionaries but articulates the interests of local Salish people who had adopted European practices. It describes the "Tamanawas" as a rite of initiation into a secret society. Everyone who participates is prevented from acceding to industriousness and, in particular, to whiteness.

> We see with [fear?] every winter, (the season that the initiations take place), young men who had settled themselves upon their land, worked it industriously and built themselves a little house, after the white fashion, a step towards civilization of which a white man can scarcely appreciate the importance—drawn into the society, sometimes by actual violence, and falling back into all their former Indian habits. Henceforth, they quit their land to live in the villages and spend the greatest part of the summer in roving about in their canoes, and the winter in the degrading practise of the Tamanwas dances. There is not a part of our reservation [where] one cannot behold one of the houses alluded to, deserted and falling into ruins. (NA, vol. 3737, file 27,590, 2 February 1881)

According to this "we," "Tamanwas dances" are directly opposed to "the white fashion" of being. To be white is to reside in one place and practice agriculture. It does not include "roving about" and neglecting one's property.

Vankoughnet responded by asking Powell to determine what steps might be taken to curb "the influences & practice of said society" (NA, vol. 3737, file 27,590, 30 March 1881). Called on once again to play the role of ethnographer, the Indian superintendent reported "that 'Tamana-wās' or Medicine Work is a prominent and chief feature of savage life in every part of the world and it is somewhat singular that so much similarity in the practice or mode of carrying it out exists among heathen tribes whose habits are quite dissimilar in other respects" (NA, vol. 3737, file 27,590, 25 April 1881). The " 'Tamanawas,' " like the gift, obstructs the passage from savagery to whiteness and has to be overcome "before any progress can be made in inducing Indians to entertain the *enlightening* influences of christianity and civilisation" (emphasis added). "Formerly," Powell says, "the custom was followed by every tribe on the coast," but missionaries have suppressed it in many communities. In his account of it the " 'Tamanawas' " appears to be a sort of grisly meal: "the ceremony used to begin in October lasting until March, and consisted of orgies of the most disgusting character, namely biting the arms of spectators, eating or rather tearing to pieces dogs and human bodies (exhumed for the purpose), and occasionally, killing slaves with this object in view." It is indeed ironic that Powell interprets an alleged practice of eating human and animal flesh, of assimilating others into oneself, as an obstacle to the assimilation of aboriginal people into the white body of European Canada.

Like "Potlach," the fourfold " 'Tamanowes' "-" 'Tamawawas' "-" 'Gamanawas' "-" 'Tamanawas' " points toward two opposite practices simultaneously. It is a mode of healing bodies that are sick and the act of devouring the bodies of animals and people who have died. Unlike the word "bank," though, "tamanawas" does not refer to different things in different contexts but rather claims that one thing is two things at once—as if a being could at the same time be absolutely equal and absolutely other to itself.

## CORRESPONDENCES

By the middle of the 1880s the effort to name two practices previously unknown to Western observers had drawn Canada's discourse on Indian affairs into an encounter with language itself. Government agents and administrators had initiated a debate about "potlatch" and "tamanawas" but had failed to decide what they mean, what knowledges they convey. The difficulty of fixing their proper

*giving*

meanings was compounded by the problem of determining precisely what things, what actual practices, "potlatch" and "tamanawas" refer to. Even their spelling proved undecidable. But what is meant by "meaning"? And what does "reference" entail? Before proceeding further in this interpretation of a postal literature, it is necessary to ask what is a name, a word—a sign—and how does it function? It will then be possible to decide whether "potlatch" and "tamanawas" are signs at all.

Although the authors of the potlatch papers seem to share Searle's "classical" notion of what a word is, the classical theory of the sign fails to explain either the structure or the impact of their texts. Searle defines words like "bank" as "referring expressions" that people use in speech acts "to point to particular things." Heidegger warns, however, that any theory of language that reduces signification to the act of pointing belongs to a Western metaphysics that has reached its limit and begun overturning itself from within its own borders. When language is viewed as a system of sounds articulated in the mouths of speaking subjects, it is assumed that "[written] letters are signs of sounds, the sounds are signs of mental experiences, and these are signs of things." Metaphysics defines the sign as "something that signifies and to some extent shows something else" (1971, 97). It is a pointer linking the abstract and nonsensuous contents of a mind to a sensuous world of concrete things. Yet it will soon become clear that this is exactly what "potlatch" and "tamanawas" are not.

In an essay that situates itself in the wake of "Heidegger's uncircumventable meditation" on the difference between Being and beings, Derrida ([1972] 1982, 9) says that in metaphysics the sign is "usually" thought to be a substitute, a proxy, that replaces a thing when it cannot make itself present—" 'thing' here standing equally for meaning and referent." A sign "stands in" either for a meaning that remains unuttered or for a person, object, action, or event that is absent when it is under discussion. "The sign represents the present in its absence," says Derrida. "When we cannot grasp or show the thing [whether it is a meaning or a referent], state the present, the being-present, when the present cannot be presented, we signify, we go through the detour of the sign." The sign points to things by pointing out that they are not there, presenting itself as the absence of what it signifies. What the following pages will show, however, is that the things that "potlatch" and "tamanawas" refer to were never present to begin with.

Searle (1969) makes the "classical" definition of the sign into a definition of the proper name. One reason "why we have the institution of proper names," he says, "is that we need a convenient device for making identifying references to commonly referred to objects when the objects are not always themselves present." The name, as he defines it, points toward an object that is not there when a speech act is made. Names allow us to "talk" in words about things that are not themselves words (74–75). Searle classes names within the larger category of "acts of reference" but limits his discussion of referential acts to those that are "singular" and "definite." Acts of reference are singular and definite when they answer the question Who or what in particular? rather than Who or what in general? (85–86). Proper names such as "John Searle" are the "most obvious cases," and noun phrases are another, though not every noun phrase can be said to refer. In a sentence like "My brother left me in the lurch," for example, "lurch" does not refer because it does not "serve to pick out or identify some object or entity" from the world of things (72–73). Searle deals exclusively with referring expressions—whether names, noun phrases, or pronouns—that point to people, objects, events, and activities that supposedly have a concrete existence beyond the play of signs. A speaker is said to have successfully uttered a singular, definite referring expression only if a hearer—who alone decides if speech acts are successful—understands exactly what entity the speaker intends to point out.

What class of singular definite referring expressions would "potlatch" and "tamanawas" belong to? Are they proper names? Searle includes only the names of people and places—for example "Socrates," "Russia," and "Everest"—in this group. Perhaps he would class "potlatch" and "tamanawas" among "noun phrases," which in their simplest form are composed of concrete nouns and their articles, as in "the bank."

Searle distinguishes "fully consummated" acts of reference, which identify an object for the hearer without ambiguity or doubt, from "successful" ones, which leave it unclear precisely what is being discussed. Two necessary conditions have to be satisfied if a speaker is to perform a "fully consummated" reference. First, the referent itself, and not just the expression that refers to it, must be singular and definite. There must exist only one object for the referring expression to point to, and it must be possible to demonstrate it by showing it to someone—as if to say, This one right here (82). Second, the referential speech act has to give the hearer the means to *identify* a single, definite object without doubt or ambiguity (85). Hence the fully consummated reference does not point to the object itself but to the trace of difference that divides that particular object from all others. To refer fully a phrase such as "the potlatch" must allow a hearer to tell a single kind of potlatch from all the other forms of potlatch practiced along the northwest coast. For Searle sense and reference are inseparable: reference is a speech act that describes an object by rehearsing what is known about it, pointing the hearer toward a sensuous thing (a referent) by directing his or her attention to a nonsensuous idea of that thing (a meaning).

When Searle says that "objects cannot be named independently of facts," he makes the act of reference depend on an already established relationship between objects and knowledges (93). His theory of reference is therefore grounded in a theory of truth as old as Western European philosophy. Writing in the 1770s, Immanuel Kant notes in his *Critique of Pure Reason* that "logicians" have long defined truth as "the agreement of knowledge with its object" (1929, 97).[16] According to the classical definition, truth binds ideas to things in a relation of adequation. An idea is true when it is determined to be equal to the thing it describes, and it is the word that points out the agreement between them. Words circulate between a nonsensuous knowledge and a sensuous object and tie them together in an act of judgment. Since knowledge and object need a go-between to mediate the gap that separates them, the role of the word is built into the truth relation

In the metaphysical definition of truth, then, knowledge and its object *correspond*, as if by mail. The subject who knows what is true addresses a word to the object known, just as Powell mails his yearly reports to Ottawa confident they will arrive in the Department of Indian Affairs. As it travels the path from knowledge to object and back again, the word functions as a dispatch, a letter, or perhaps a postcard. If truth is to remain true, though, the mail must not go astray. Truth is true only when knowledge is delivered to its proper object via the proper word, but it is always possible that knowledge will address itself to the wrong destination and, going astray, establish a relation of falsehood between an object and itself—just as a letter sometimes gets lost in the post and ends up at the wrong place. "If truth consists in the agreement of knowledge with its object," says Kant, "that object must thereby be distinguished from other objects; for knowledge is false, if it does not agree with the object to which it is related, even though it contains something which may be valid of other objects" (1929, 97). Knowledge goes astray when it arrives, via the word, at the wrong address. Only the word that arrives safely at the proper destination can serve as a postal relay bringing knowledge into a proper correspondence with the thing known.

Since Searle's admittedly "incomplete" theory of reference understands truth as an act of correspondence, he insists that reference and truth necessarily misfire unless they direct themselves toward a single definite object, their true object, to the exclusion of all others. Reference and truth alike are in constant danger of going astray. It is always possible for them to single out an inappropriate object without knowing they are pointing in the wrong direction. And it is always possible for them to address themselves to objects that simply do not exist.

At every instant the chances of error threaten to block the paths that truth travels as it circulates from post to post. They are about to undermine the very foundations of Canada's discourse on the "potlatch" and "tamanawas," for these two marks obey neither the classical theory of the sign nor its correlative, the correspondence theory of truth.

77

## POTLACK

When it was enacted, the statute banning the " 'Potlach' " and " 'Tamanawas' " prohibited two words rather than two practices. Within the frame of the legal text " 'Potlach' " and " 'Tamanawas' " took up position as referring expressions that failed to address themselves to two referents, two things, existing somewhere in the world. The problem was that they had no meaning or perhaps too many contradictory meanings, and referring expressions that do not communicate "the facts" about their object point to nothing at all. Here " 'Potlach' " and " 'Tamana-was' " designated hollow knowledges: they were signs sent astray, postings without destination. Or perhaps they were not signs at all. Perhaps they were, at best, mere half signs: signifiers without signifieds, verbal traces without any meaning to give them weight and bind them to things. What is certain, though, is that the law that banned them was quashed the first time it was enforced. Its failure marks the breakdown of an entire apparatus of truth conceived as a correspondence sent from a sign to an idea and from an idea to a thing signified.

By 1882 the Department of Indian Affairs had received several dispatches from white officials recommending that the potlatch and tamanawas be suppressed. Vankoughnet had officially "discountenanced" distributions of property while Powell had urged that they be banned altogether. Blenkinsop had interfered with the winter dances at Fort Rupert in 1882. Then in the first months of 1883 the department received the "Petition of the [Coast Tsimshian and Nisga'a] Chiefs at Port Simpson, Kincolith, Green-ville and other places [on the north coast], praying that the system of Potlatching as practised by many Indian Tribes on the Coast of British Columbia may be put down" (NA, vol. 3628, file 6244-1, 13 April 188[3]; in this section sources are from this file unless another file is given). The text of the petition is missing from the public archives, though Cole and Chaikin (1990, 16, 186 n. 6) surmise that it was "[t]ransparently inspired and written by Methodists Thomas Crosby [a missionary at Port Simpson] and A. E. Green [a missionary working on the Nass River], perhaps with the collaboration of Anglican Thomas Dunn at Kincolith."

It is tempting to dismiss the petition as a forgery com-posed by a group of white authors who acted without con-sulting the aboriginal community they claimed to repre-sent. According to this interpretation, the petition would have put the arguments of settler society into the mouths of the First Nations, inviting readers to hear in its pages the prayers of a people longing to be freed from their own culture in order to accede to the ranks of European civili-zation. Yet the petition can also be interpreted as the work of an aboriginal community that saw reforming the pot-latch as a legitimate way of dealing with the violence in-flicted on it when Europe-in-Canada arrived on its shores.

John Borrows (1991, 6) argues that "Native society has long been written about from a western perspective in the areas of religious life, social customs, economic practices, historical genesis, political routines, and legal customs." He adds, "These accounts of Native society have often portrayed us in a way that does not capture the active and transformative role we played in reacting to settler institutions." What he suggests is that the petition of 1883 was perhaps an effort by aboriginal people to use a white institution to serve their own interests rather than a heavy-handed attempt by white missionaries to erase aboriginal cultures from the map of a young nation. It is necessary to keep in mind that, while for years many aboriginal people opposed and successfully resisted the suppression of the potlatch, others actively worked to do away with it. Thus the struggle over the potlatch is not a simple dispute between Euro-Canadian colonizers and a number of colonized First Nations. Since aboriginal people took an active role on both sides of the conflict, it is impossible to draw a clear limit here between "Canadian" initiatives and "Indian" ones. The aboriginal people of nineteenth-century British Columbia were never passive victims of government policies, and they never stopped trying to control their own destinies. Moreover, it would be patronizing to assume that they did not hold a diversity of views and opinions—or that they did not often disagree when it came to deciding how best to manage their own lives.

Vankoughnet sent the petition to Powell in April 1883, asking him to discuss the text with Land and Works Commissioner Trutch and to submit a report of their deliberations. Powell replied on 19 May 1883. With Trutch's endorsement, he suggests that "every practicable means should be adopted by the Government to put a stop to the custom," noting that it is "often associated with Gambling, Medicine dances (Tamanaw[as]) and similar Indian vices." The civilizing efforts of missionaries and Indian agents are the best means of suppressing "vice" on the north coast, he admits, but a statute is also necessary— even though there is "really no crime in the Potlach"— because the First Nations have such respect for "the Queen's law" that they would soon give up all their "reprehensible customs" if one were enacted. Powell predicts that no single measure can kill the potlatch. To make sure it dies, he urges the department to replace traditional aboriginal governments with "Indian Municipal Councils" empowered to pass bylaws—an idea he rejected when Sproat suggested it in his " 'Patlach' " letter of 1879.

Vankoughnet sent Powell's report to Prime Minister Macdonald in June and recommended that the government pass an order in council "disapproving" of the potlatch and tamanawas. Vankoughnet says the order "would in his opinion probably have the effect of greatly reducing the number" of distributions and dances, yet he advances the idea as a provisional measure to be replaced later by legislation banning "such ceremonies" outright (11 June 1883). Eight days later Vankoughnet addressed a memorandum to the Privy Council requesting that "strenuous measures . . . be adopted to put a stop to the heathenish custom in vogue among the Indians of B.C. known as the 'Potlach' "— a custom that, he says, is "worse than useless" (19 June 1883). To support his request Vankoughnet quotes long passages from Powell's report and from Sproat's " 'Patlach' " letter. He also notes that the department plans to ask for legislation against the "Potlach" in the next session of Parliament.

The Privy Council's reply, dated 7 July 1883, touches on all the difficulties of interpretation that have haunted the discourse against the " 'Potlach' " up till now. The cabinet does not resist Vankoughnet's proposal. Indeed, it dispatches the order in council without delay. What stands out, though, is a clerical error made as the government's actions were being recorded for posterity. The report of the Privy Council approves the suppression not of the " 'Potlach' "—but of the " 'Potlack.' " To be precise, it advises that a letter be sent to the lieutenant governor of British Columbia asking him to "use his best efforts for the suppression of the 'Potlack' " and to circulate the governor general's proclamation discountenancing this "heathenish custom."

Whoever transcribed this cabinet decision added a tail to the word naming the thing to be prohibited. By substituting $k$ for $h$, strapping a tiny prosthesis onto its midsection, the anonymous copyist transforms the word into a warning that what it refers to is lacking. No doubt the mistake was made by chance, but it obeys a necessary law, for the addition of a supplementary mark to " 'Potlach' " tells the truth about its status as a referring expression: "Potlach" points, in the end, to a "Pot*lack*." It does not gesture toward an object nor to what is known about that object. Or rather what it refers to is the absence of its referent, and its meaning is that it has no meaning. The word points, in truth, to the truth about truth: it points to the truth that truth itself is not to be found in the act of pointing.

When Powell learned the order in council was in place, he responded that the "Queen's objection" was unlikely to have any influence on the " 'Potlach' " and renewed his call for legislation (15 August 1883). Early in the new year, however, Cornelius Bryant—a Methodist missionary working in the Nanaimo Salish community—urged the department to use persuasion rather than coercion to stop a practice that, he agrees, "seems to be on the increase among the Indians of this Coast" (30 January 1884). Bryant admits that steps must be taken to suppress the potlatch but says it would be better to reward people for renouncing it than to punish them for keeping it alive. He does not oppose the passing of a law. He simply believes it is unlikely to achieve its goal.

Bryant's definition of the potlatch turns it away from the concept of exchange and circles back toward the notion of absolute expenditure and the gift without return. He claims that "giving away" reduces the people to "beggary," that traveling to potlatches exposes them to misery, and that potlatches themselves are moments of "debauchery" and "intoxication" that lead to the use of "knives" and "fire-arms." Above all he notes that "the reckless and spendthrift customs which are maintained at these potlatches" bring "impoverishment" to children and the old, and squander wealth that he would rather see spent on houses, roads, fences, and the local cemetery. He also hints that the potlatch is an obstacle to missionary work because "[t]he church and school cannot flourish where the 'potlatching' holds sway."

Just days after Bryant warned the potlatch could not be legislated away, the Roman Catholic missionary at Cowichan wrote Indian agent W. H. Lomas to demand a ban on the "heathenish practices of 'Potlatching' and 'dancing' " (2 February 1884). "I respectfully request you Sir in the name of the civilized Indians," writes Father G. Donckele, "to beg the Indian Department to have a law to stop the disastrous practice of 'Potlatching' and especially dancing as it is carried on by the Indians of Vancouver

Island." He says the question of " 'Potlatching' " and
"dancing" has divided the community where he works,
bringing people who support the traditional way of life into
conflict with those who prefer to adopt the ways of settler
society. He urges the government to protect those who
have embarked on the upward climb into European civilization—which is also a climb into whiteness—from those
who remain loyal to their own aboriginal civilization. Although improvement was supposed to have happened "as
soon as the young people adopted the habits of the
whites," it is impossible, he says, for the young to rise into
whiteness when they continue to have access to nonwhite
"habits." The battle over " 'Potlatching' " continued to be
construed as a conflict between two colors—between two
qualities of light—and whiteness considers itself threatened wherever another shade is allowed to persist.

Lomas addressed his own recommendations to Powell
three days later. "I have come to the conclusion," he
writes, "that before the Indians of this coast can be perma-
nently benefited a law must be passed for the prevention
of the foolish, wasteful, and demoralising custom of 'potlatching' and for the punishment of any Indian allowing
a Tom-an-ōēs dance to be held in any house of which he
is owner or part owner" (5 February 1884). " 'Potlatching' " not only weighs down the ascent of "Indians"
into whiteness, he argues, but causes population decline,
the destitution and misery of the old, the sickness and
death of children, a general indifference to education, and
the neglect of farms and livestock in winter. Paradoxically,
while it is said to lie at the very root of social decay in
Coast Salish villages, the potlatch must end only on the
condition that it immediately begin again. Its death must
overlap its birth: "But in the event of any law being passed
it would be advisable to allow a fixed time for its coming
into force, as potlatches are in reality a lending of a certain
amount of property which has to be returned at an uncertain date with interest, or rather with an additional
amount, which at some future date has also to be returned
either by the recipient or if he lie dead by some of his
sons." The discourse against the potlatch will never cease
folding together two contradictory themes. Bryant states
on January 30 that the Coast Salish potlatch is an "im-
provident" act of gift giving, yet less than a week later Lomas maintains that it is a system of loans that have to be

repaid at enormous rates of interest. Just as in the Lomas potlatch one gives in order to add to one's wealth, so in the Euro-Canadian definition of the potlatch there is always a surplus, "an additional amount," of meaning and reference. The potlatch is never just an exchange for profit, nor is it a mere expenditure without return, gift without countergift. It always includes a certain "amount" of both—at once.

Lomas maintains that when a father dies before paying what he owes, his debts are assumed by the son. But the potlatch is itself both father and son, and though the white nation-state will soon condemn the father to die, the son is bound to assume his obligations. The moment the law kills the potlatch-father, the son will take his place, and an "additional amount" of potlatch will survive its own death. It has to replace itself with itself so that property owing from previous potlatches can be returned.

The superintendent general of Indian affairs brought legislation before the House of Commons on 12 February 1884. According to Cole and Chaikin (1990, 17–18), "Macdonald introduced debate in committee by noting that the government had received strong representations from both agents and missionaries"—including Bryant, Donckele, and Lomas. The minister of justice quoted from their letters when he delivered the bill to the Senate, where it passed "without a role call or recorded vote." The new statute came into effect on 1 January 1885 and in 1886 took up its place as section 114 in chapter 43 of the Revised Statutes of Canada. Ironically, the full title of chapter 43 is "An Act *Respecting* Indians" (emphasis added); its short title, of course, is "The Indian Act."

Section 114 promises harsh penalties to anyone who holds a potlatch or dance and to anyone who collaborates in potlatching or dancing. And it rigorously distinguishes between "Indians" and "persons." I quote it in full.

> 114. Every Indian or person who engages in or assists in celebrating the Indian festival known as the "Potlach" or the Indian dance known as the "Tamanawas," is guilty of a misdemeanor, and liable to imprisonment for a term not exceeding six months and not less than two months:
> 2. Every Indian or person who encourages,

either directly or indirectly, an Indian to get up such a festival or dance, or to celebrate the same, or who assists in the celebration of the same, is guilty of a like offence, and shall be liable to the same punishment.

By enclosing " 'Potlach' " and " 'Tamanawas' " in quotation marks, the very orthography of the law once again calls attention to all the problems that gathered around these words as they circulated through the government's mail over the years. The legal text mentions the words as nodes of uncertainty and does not just use them to refer to things known to exist in the world.

The majority of British Columbia's aboriginal people responded to the new law by actively defying it. Indeed, for most of its history, and even before it arrived in the mail, the First Nations consistently made the government aware of their opposition to the law, and the government consistently retreated before their protests and sought to appease them instead. Just days before it came into effect, W. H. Lomas wrote Powell that the people of the Cowichan Agency were "dis-concerted" to learn the government had taken steps against the "Potlach," and "they are strongly supported by Indians from the West Coast, and New Westminster Agencies" (27 December 1884). Lomas repeats that people who have debts owing from previous "Potlaches" are concerned the law will prevent them from recovering their investments. It is therefore urgent that the Cowichan people be allowed a supplement of potlatch. "I cannot help thinking," he writes, "that the enforcement of the new Act had better be delayed for a while, or, that each Band be allowed by special license to hold one returning 'Potlach' with the distinct understanding that no additional property shall be lent." The banning of the "Potlach" leads only to another "Potlach."

When he forwarded Lomas's proposal to Ottawa on 7 January 1885, Powell confided that "the holding of one or two 'Potlaches' in [Lomas's] district might pass without notice on the understanding that they would be the last." To mask the fact that he was bowing to the protest of the Cowichan people only a week after the law came into force, Powell endorsed a scheme proposed by Lomas: the government could sponsor an "Industrial Exhibition" as a forum for repaying debts. The "Potlach" would be allowed to continue under a different name. The First Nations thwarted the law even before the government tried to enforce it.

By the spring of 1885 the question of the supplemental "Potlach" came to crisis around the case of Lohah, an elder in the Cowichan village of Comeakin, which in the potlatch papers is also spelled "Comiaken." On 8 April Lohah and his supporters wrote the department for permission to hold a final distribution of property. Promising to lend no more, Lohah states that he is responsible for repaying his own debts and those of his son, who has recently died. Indeed, it was the death of his son that prevented him from making a return before the law came down. "It cannot be wrong to pay what we owe," he insists, "& this is the only way to do it—we are not yet like white people—and it is one of our laws that these payments shall be done in public."

Lohah's petition presents itself as the product of a conflict between two legal systems, and the laws of his society leave him no choice but to break the law passed by the legislature in Ottawa. His obedience to his own traditions also marks his difference from "white people" and keeps him from becoming too much "like" them. The battle over the potlatch continued to be interpreted—by whites and the First Nations alike—both as a clash of cultures and as a clash of colors. And the First Nations moved skillfully to block the schemes of government administrators intent on constructing a homogeneously "white" society.

However, it would be wrong to assume that all the Cowichan people supported the potlatch. The aboriginal community had its own internal divisions and was not everywhere equal to itself, and some people took an active role in helping the government implement its antipotlatch policy. Antoine Seseawon, for instance, declares he is in favor of putting the "Potlach" to rest and explains his opposition by rehearsing the argument that potlatching demands absolute expenditures—a giving of all—which leave the donor and the donor's family destitute. "I am always against the Potlach," he says, "I have no interest in Lohah's, I know if I join the Potlach party, I shall be poor, my children will be poor and suffer" (8 April 1885). While he opposes the "Potlach" in general, though, Seseawon affirms his sympathy and his support for Lohah: "but I feel for Lohah, he has always tried to help white men and now the law is against him, and all the old Indians are sneering at him, it will kill him and I would like to see him raised up for he is a good man." Unlike its white critics, Seseawon does not interpret the potlatch as a stone weighing down Lohah's progress into a higher Western European civilization. Indeed, the opposite is true. The "Potlach" is a "raising up" that preserves Lohah's dignity in the eyes of his peers by letting him fulfill the obligations that knit him into the social order. To the observer who stands within the potlatching culture, the Potlach has no authority to mark a limit between civilization and its beyond.

We know from Blenkinsop's 1882 report that it was not uncommon for white administrators to argue that it was exclusively men who performed distributions of property, especially "old men" who did not have the support of the young. But in Lohah's petition Cehawilawet of Comeakin notes that women have their own "Potlach" debts to pay. She and her husband owed a total of 350 blankets, and she insists that they "must pay it in public." What is more, her remarks identify the flaw that undermines the authority of the law forbidding her to pay her debts, though the problem will not surface until the legal machine breaks down four years later. She says simply, "[T]he white Chief does not understand our ways." What Cehawilawet suggests, and what the white administrators refuse to admit, is that the two words cited in the statute do not correspond to the practices that they ban. This problem of the *non*correspondence between word and thing, a problem that brought Western metaphysics to crisis out on its westernmost limit, haunted each subsequent version of the law until the final version at last dropped from the books. In the following pages I will take Cehawilawet's argument literally and explore its implications in detail—so that in the last analysis the remainder of this book is little more than an extended meditation on a cryptic remark made in opposition to a law that, in its original form, had been defeated before it was even enforced.

Charles Nowell, who was fifteen or sixteen when the law came into effect, joined Cehawilawet in deploring the ignorance of white officials determined to abolish a practice that they were not in a position to understand—and which they perhaps did not want to understand. He notes in his autobiography, really a collaborative ethnography, that their knowledge of the thing they call the "potlatch" belongs to a discourse white observers exchange back and forth exclusively among themselves, a postal literature that circulates endlessly yet always returns to sender. One of the more troubling features of the discourse against the potlatch, therefore, is that it stubbornly ignores the stories of the First Nations. It occupies an absolute fold that buries indigenous narratives under a mass of administrative documentation. And since the foreclosure of dialogue is the most basic premise of this discourse, it operates in the mode of speaking for rather than speaking with. Says Nowell: "When one of the Indian agents first came to Alert Bay, he came to visit us at Fort Rupert, and he begin to talk to us about the potlatch and say he is going to stop it, for it is no good. I ask him how he knows. He says: 'I know all about it. I know more than you do.' I says: 'You must be older than I am, because I have lived all my life amongst them, and I still don't know everything about it.' He says: 'I've been told.' And, when I ask him who tells him, it is always another white man" (1941, 106). The "potlatch" invariably posed itself as a problem of "knowing," of "understanding," but at the same time it marked an impasse in the theory of knowledge. What whites understood when they said or wrote "potlatch" does not correspond with what Nowell understood by the same word. Indeed, the white "potlatch" missed the Fort Rupert "potlatch" altogether and, because it missed it, it gave itself something else to refer to. While the Kwagiulth of Fort Rupert routinely used "potlatch" to point to an art of living, a practice that Nowell himself participated in and that exceeds any individual's effort to "know everything about it," white "agents" used "potlatch" to signify an object that is a gift of their own discourse, and they were careful to ensure that their knowledge of that object circulated only among themselves and never among the so-called potlatchers. So if the Indian agent claimed to know "more" about it than Nowell did, that is because what "the white man" knew is that supplement of potlatch that his own law had given to the world. It is a prosthetic potlatch.

The signifier "potlatch" therefore inhabits the disjunction that simultaneously joins and divides Canada and several distinct First Nations. In this gap European Canada speaks directly to aboriginal people and understands nothing they say because it is not yet possible for there to be a dialogue between them. Though the First Nations actively engage with Euro-Canadian concepts, Canada desires to remain pure of aboriginal ones, and though many "potlatches" are practiced along the coast, the white agents stubbornly insist that theirs is the only one. In this study, however, I will not continue the colonial tradition of attempting to "know all" about the potlatch. My aim is not to define it but to *read* a set of definitions deployed in a specific historical—and colonial—context of debate and contestation.

On 20 April 1885 Superintendent Powell reported that he had visited Comeakin at Lomas's request and struck an agreement to ease the local people's hostility toward the new statute. "I explained that a Potlach meant the donation of property in order to get back the original and interest," Powell reports, "and that an assemblage such as they now desired did not constitute a Potlach *as referred to in the Act*" (emphasis added). His pragmatic interpretation denies that the Potlach that Lohah wants to hold is an expenditure that invokes a return. It is instead an absolute and final gift that will leave no debts outstanding. Powell had given in to the demands of Lohah and his supporters. Cole and Chaikin (1990) explain that he had no way of enforcing a law that the Cowichan people intended to defy anyway—despite the "good grace" of their protest. "Against a background of Metis, Cree and Assiniboine discontent on the prairies and the armed conflict of the Northwest Rebellion in late March and early April, Powell quickly realized that enforcement would be both unwise and futile." Hence he "capitulated" (31). Through careful yet forceful diplomacy the people had asserted their right to that "additional amount" of "Potlach."

Powell's solution to the standoff at Comeakin hinges on the question of reference. If a Potlach continues to be called a Potlach even when it does not "constitute a Potlach as referred to in the Act," what exactly does "Potlach" refer to? How can two contrary practices—lending and "donation," profit and loss—be named "Potlaches" at the same time? "Potlach" always means more than it wants

*giving*

to mean, refers in a single instant to more objects than it wants to refer to. But there is never enough "Potlach" because something is lacking in it. The name means nothing by meaning too much, points to nothing by pointing in two contrary directions at once. The same can be said of "tamanawas."

Powell does not say how the people of Comeakin reacted to the sight of a white doctor from Victoria standing before them and defining them to themselves, telling them what is and what is not a Potlach. He reports only that his words "gave great satisfaction and delight." Then, as if to excuse himself for failing to enforce a statute that is barely three months old but already dead, he affirms that "at the same time my visit has pretty well stamped out the continuance of the Potlach system in the District visited, as I explained to them that any goods lent (ie. potlached) hereafter, would not be likely to be returned, as the law prohibited it." He will contradict this assertion a month later when he advises the superintendent general: "I think Indians should not be prevented from assembling to return property that they owe for some time to come" (22 May 1885).

There will always be a little more Potlach. In fact Powell had already distributed a circular that, in a circular fashion, cited the law banning the Potlach yet permitted Potlaches to continue for the repayment of debts. His circular also attempts to clarify another question of reference. Since the law forbids the "Tamanawas" without defining it, Powell notes that "[t]he term 'Tamanawas' refers to the Medicine Dance, customary among many of the coast tribes" (21 April 1885). His clarification leaves the question unresolved, of course, because the phrase "Medicine Dance" itself goes undefined.

In April 1886 A. E. Green complained in a letter to Ottawa that the potlatch would have "died out" if Powell's circular had not allowed "potlatching for the return of presents received" a year earlier. Powell had already defended his policy in the letter dated 20 April 1885, however, where he explains that the law must be managed with "great care" because "a large majority of Indians are opposed" to it (in a province where whites were still an anxious minority) and because the provincial government refused to enforce it for fear of losing the votes of white traders who sold many of the goods distributed in potlatches. Throughout the 1870s and early 1880s British Columbia assumed no responsibility for upholding the Indian Act, and this lack of cooperation between provincial and federal governments allowed the antipotlatch and antidance law to go unenforced for more than four years. As Cole and Chaikin (1990, 34) point out, "The provincial government, while accepting its responsibility to enforce federal criminal law, maintained that the Indian Act was solely a federal responsibility. Victoria went so far as to refuse Indian agents the use of its jails or its police to render them any assistance." Without a law-enforcement apparatus, the dominion government was powerless to put section 114 into effect (R. H. Pidcock to Powell, 19 March 1888; Powell to the Provincial Secretary, 23 March 1888).

The impasse lasted until the fall of 1888 when Thomas White, who had replaced Macdonald as superintendent general of Indian affairs, made a deal with John Robson, the provincial secretary of British Columbia. The province agreed to enforce "the criminal laws among the Indians of B.C. . . . on the condition that the moieties of the fines imposed upon parties in B.C. for violations of the liquor clauses of the Indian Act sh[oul]d be paid over to the Prov[incial] Gov[ernmen]t" (Vankoughnet to Powell, 3 October 1888). The terms of the bargain were simple: Ottawa temporarily suspended its fear of expenditure and bought British Columbia's cooperation.

## WHITE PURVEYORS

Poor health forced Powell to retire in 1889, but the debate over section 114 did not pause to mark his departure. In January Charles Todd, acting agent for the North West Coast Agency, advised the acting Indian superintendent in Victoria that the department should either have the statute repealed "or else make its enforcement dependent upon the pleasure of a majority of the Indians of any Indian settlement" (NA, vol. 3628, file 6244-1, Todd to H. Moffat, 22 January 1889). His request was ignored, and eight months later the statute was tested in court.

The first arrest was made on 1 August 1889 in Fort Rupert, among the people Europe-in-Canada had consistently located at an absolute distance from itself, the Kwakwaka'wakw. Ironically, the arrest was made without any help from provincial officials. Ha-mer-cee-luc of Ma-malilikulla was taken into custody by Indian agent Reginald H. Pidcock, with the help of two Native constables. But the people of Mamalilikulla acted quickly and effectively to win his release.

They protested in a petition to Lieutenant Governor Nelson of British Columbia that the arresting officers had seized Ha-mer-cee-luc in the middle of the night. They describe the arrest as an act of violence and note that Pidcock and his men broke down the door of the house where Ha-mer-cee-luc was sleeping in order to abduct him—though Pidcock later denied it (NA, vol. 3628, file 6244-1, 19 August 1889; Pidcock to the superintendent general of Indian affairs, 2 October 1889). Ha-mer-cee-luc's supporters tell the lieutenant governor they do not want to lose the potlatch because they have already lost so much—including rivers, trees, land, and fish—to white settlers. They also note that they do not know exactly what the law forbids: "why should we be threatened with arrest all the time," they ask, "when we don't know what is required of us[?]" Calling attention to the white community's ignorance had become the First Nations' main strategy for resisting the enforcement of the law.

Ha-mer-cee-luc was tried as soon as he was arrested, with Pidcock presiding as justice of the peace. He pleaded guilty to two counts of potlatching and was given the maximum sentence of six months in prison. But then the trial took a bizarre turn. While Ha-mer-cee-luc was being convicted and sentenced, he was simultaneously committed for trial in Victoria where he was to be arraigned for the same offense.

On 17 August Ha-mer-cee-luc's supporters applied to the Supreme Court of British Columbia for habeas corpus: that is, they asked the court to decide whether it was lawful to detain him for a second trial after he had already pleaded guilty as charged. On 21 August Chief Justice Sir Matthew Begbie ordered the defendant, who was now called He-ma-sak, to be released on the grounds that "he was not . . . held on a proper warrant of Committal" (*R. v. He-ma-sak*, in NA, vol. 3628, file 6244-1, Moffat to Vankoughnet, 30 August 1889). Yet Begbie's ruling gave the case a second unexpected turn. In determining that He-ma-sak had been illegally detained, he made a scathing evaluation of the antipotlatch statute.

Begbie's judgment confirms that the meaning and the reference of "Potlach" and "Tamanawas" are undecidable. He observes that "[i]t is not alleged that the nature of the charge was explained to the prisoner" when he pleaded guilty to "the offence of celebrating the Indian festival known as a Potlach." The charge could not have been explained, moreover, because nobody seems to have understood what the "Potlach" is. Says Begbie, "[F]rom all I know of the gathering, I think it would be very hard to explain" because "[d]ifferent people appear to have very different notions as to what the word means." The reason it is difficult to identify this particular kind of "gathering" is that the meaning of the word "Potlach" does not give its hearer sufficient information to distinguish the "Potlach" from the other kinds of gatherings that occur on the northwest coast. Hence Begbie's judgment upholds the laws of reference laid down by Searle: "Potlatch" fails to refer because it does not satisfy the second condition for a fully consummated act of singular definite reference: it does not give a hearer or reader facts that would make it possible to pick out a single, definite object *unambiguously* from the world of possible objects. The failure to refer derives from a failure to mean. Without a clearly defined sense " 'Potlach' " cannot help a hearer or reader identify the difference that distinguishes its referent from all other referents.

Begbie also affirms that " 'Potlach' " is a referring expression that refers to nothing in particular because it points to one thing as if it were several things simultaneously. It is an instance of pure ambiguity. "Under the name of a 'potlatch,' " he writes, "very different practices & objects may be intended." Since the word has many referents at once, it is impossible for anyone—including a judge or a jury—to decide what specific acts make up the crime of "potlaching." The set of the word's possible yet "very different" referents is finite, though, because they play themselves out between two strict limits: exchange and the gift. Although "Mr. Mills seem [*sic*] to think it [the 'Potla[t]ch'] is a formal and periodical repayment of obligations," a circular economy of goods and services, Begbie says it is a pure expenditure without return: "To me it has always appeared to be a meeting announced at very uncertain intervals, at which a chief or several chiefs to show his magnanimity either gives away or destroys all his accumulated wealth."

Just as Searle claims the meaning of a word encodes what is known about the referent of that word, Begbie argues that the meaning of " 'potlach' " is undecidable because the "potlach" itself remains an unknown quantity. As Cehawilawet hinted in 1885, white observers have a poor understanding of the truth of this "gathering" because it is still, for them, a new and unfamiliar object of knowledge. Begbie notes that " 'potlach' " points to a thing that has only recently come to the attention of Western European science and Euro-Canadian law, and he rules that "if it be desired to create an offence *previously unknow[n]* to the law there ought to be some definition of it in the Statute" (emphasis added). It "seems an abuse of the forms of justice," he adds, to have a defendant plead guilty to an offence "the facts constituting which we should ourselves be unable to set forth." "Potlach" does not point to a truth—as truth is classically understood in Western European metaphysics—because it does not denote a nonsensuous knowledge that can be put into correspondence with a sensuous object.

According to Begbie, "Tamanawas" is another referring expression that fails to refer. The problem here, he says, is that the word does not fulfill the first condition for a fully consummated act of reference. The thing known as the "Tamanawas" simply does not exist: "The dance 'Ta-má-nâ-wás' for instance referred to in the same Section is utterly unknown here, and it may well be that an Indian who had taken part in some quite innocent performance of dancing which the Legislature never intended to ban, might plead guilty to a charge of having danced." Since its referent cannot be found, since the thing it signifies "is utterly unknown," " 'Tamanawas' " is a pointer that points to nothing that is. "Until a defendant knows what those forbidden Acts are," asks Begbie, "how can he say whether he has committed them or not?"

While affirming that the law does not know what it bans, Begbie muses on the origins of the "potlach." He speculates that it "is not an old Indian custom," for "[i]f we may *judge by the name*," he writes, "the practice is of very modern origin" (emphasis added). "The name," he explains, "is Chinook jargon which as the language of trade and diplomacy has not been in use more than 50 years." What Begbie suggests, then, is that the "potlatch" could not be any older than the word that names it. "I have heard the origin attributed," he continues, "very often less than half in jest and more than half in earnest to the white purveyors of blankets and clothes."

What Begbie gives us to think is that the word " 'pot-latch' " has been delivered to popular usage by a group of "white purveyors." However, white purveyors are not just traders who sell manufactured goods to the First Nations. They are inventors who give *names* to things, and their numbers include anyone who coins words and puts them into general circulation, for example, Indian agents, administrators, ethnographers—even judges.

But what if the relation between words and things were reversed? What if the words for things were no longer signs fastened to objects and events that exist prior to language but were instead the purveyors of the things they name? It would then be words that bring things into existence. Things would not be until they had been named. The names Euro-Canadians give to entities situated outside the established archive of Western knowledge would themselves be *white purveyors,* and their task would be to draw ethnographic artifacts within range of a Western gaze trained to study and regulate them. But how would the words that operate as "white purveyors" distinguish themselves from all the other words that lend themselves to the discourses of ethnography and administration? White purveyors name without referring because they give things to the world and do not point them out. They include, for example, " 'Potlach' " and " 'Tamanawas.' "

94

White purveyors do not deploy themselves within the realm of truth as truth is understood by metaphysics. They are not postal relays that serve to communicate a knowledge that attempts to correspond with its object. They do not participate in the agreement between thoughts and things. Rather, they give things to thought and allow them to be put into writing. It is the mechanics of the white purveyor that enabled the Euro-Canadian bureaucracy and Western European science to give aboriginal cultures to themselves at the end of the nineteenth century. The white purveyor creates a set of doubles, an army of ghosts that haunt the cultures that were already there when the

Europeans arrived on the northwest coast: ghosts sent to hound those cultures into their graves.

## THE TEXTUAL GIFT

### Word and Event

In "The Nature of Language" (1971, 60) Heidegger investigates the problem of finding a name for something "previously unknown" by reading Stefan George's poem "The Word" (*Das Wort*), a monologue in which an unnamed speaker recalls how he once tried to carry a "[w]onder or dream" from a "distant land" back home to his "country's strand." It is tempting to compare the poem's speaker to the European traveler-ethnographer, such as Boas, who has gone abroad to study the local cultures of Asia or the Americas and returns home burdened with research data to be prepared for publication and ethnographic treasures to be deposited in the national museum. But George's speaker is an unlucky traveler or perhaps a failed ethnographer because he loses the thing he has found before he can deliver it safely to its new home. He reports that during the return journey "I could grasp it close and strong," but when he learned from a "twilit norn" that there was no name for this unknown thing, then, he says, "straight it vanished from my hand." Hence "[t]he treasure never graced my land." The poem ends with this maxim: "So I renounced and sadly see: Where word breaks off no thing may be."

Heidegger argues that the poem's final verse, "Kein Ding sei wo das Wort gebricht," records the poet's experience with language, an experience where language fails to voice human concerns and, by its failure, makes language itself into a matter of concern. "For this line," says Heidegger, "makes the word of language, makes language itself bring itself to language." "The Word" is written *in* language *about* language and in particular "says something about the relation between word and thing" (60). Moreover, their relation is not one of correspondence. The word does not point to a knowledge that in turn directs readers and hearers toward the thing that the word refers to. The word does not mediate between things and the facts about things: it is not a postal relay that puts the po-

*giving*

et's nonsensuous thoughts into communication with sensuous objects. Then what is a word?

We know that for Heidegger the word is what gives the gift of Being to the thing. It makes a present of the "is." "Only where the word for the thing has been found is the thing a thing," he says, "something *is* only where the appropriate and therefore competent word names a thing as being, and so establishes the given being as a being." The question to be posed now is: "how can a mere word accomplish this—to bring a thing into being?" (62–63).

Heidegger proposes that a word and the thing it names arrive together. The relation between them is an event of simultaneous delivery—the arrival of two *at once*. He describes this event as a gift, and his account is itself a gift of language because it derives from that idiomatic German phrase *es gibt*, which in English means simultaneously "there is" and "it gives." "If our thinking does justice to the matter," he argues (and we are very much concerned here with the doing and undoing of justice), "then we may never say of the word that it is, but rather that it gives [*Vom Wort dürften wir, sachgerecht denkend, dann nie sagen: Es ist, sondern: Es gibt*]—not in the sense that words are given by an 'it,' but that the word itself gives" (88). The path of our inquiry into the mechanics of the legal text has come full circle, returning to the *es gibt* and everything that it puts into circulation.

"We are familiar with the expression 'there is, there are' [*wir kennen die Wendung 'Es gibt'*]," continues Heidegger, "in many usages, such as 'There are strawberries on the sunny slope,' *il y a, es gibt*, there are, strawberries [*il y a, es hat dort Erdbeeren*]." These phrases assume that strawberries exist independently of the word that names them. It is customary to suppose that if you came across such things "there on the slope" for the first time, and had no word for them in your language, you could supply this lack by inventing a name for them and binding it to them in a speech act of reference. What Heidegger argues, though, is that you can only happen upon the strawberries on the hill because language has already given them to be encountered—both strawberries and hill. "In our present reflection, the expression *es gibt* is used differently; not: There is the word, rather: It, the word, gives [*In unserer Besinnung ist das 'Es gibt' anders gebraucht; nicht: Es gibt das Wort, sondern: Es, das Wort, gibt*]" (translation modified). "The word itself is the

96

*giving*

giver" that gives Being to things, yet it is not anything that *is*. It is neither the subject of a giving nor an object that is given. "Neither the 'is' nor the word attain to thinghood, to Being," says Heidegger, "nor does the relation between 'is' and the word." The word is instead an activity, a process: it is giving itself. Its "task" is "to give an 'is' in each given instance" (87–88).

Not just any word gives the gift of Being to beings, however. It is, above all, the name that gives. Heidegger's account of the relation between word and Being privileges the "power" of nouns and plays down the work done by other parts of speech—such as prepositions, articles, pronouns—in acts of utterance. Words that are not nouns seem not to be "words" at all.

Heidegger acknowledges that "current notions" about language tend to contradict the suggestion that words are not things. Common sense insists that words *are*, that they "can be like things, palpable to the senses." One has only to "open a dictionary" to prove that words exist just like other beings. His response to this objection is that the dictionary is filled with "terms," not words. It can "neither grasp nor keep the word by which the terms become words and speak as words" (87). What does it mean to say that terms "become words" only when *spoken* as words? Words are terms that have been enacted in utterances. They are not things that can be separated from each other and defined in isolation: they are instead events that take place in acts of discourse. They do not exist, yet they do occur. They *are* not, but they set themselves into action.

The distinction between word and term recalls an argument put forward by J. L. Austin in "The Meaning of a Word" (1961). Austin insists that words do not have meaning in themselves. They participate in the production of meaning only when put to work in sentences. Says Austin, "[W]hat alone has meaning is a *sentence*. . . . All the dictionary can do when we 'look up the meaning of a word,'" he adds, "is to suggest aids to the understanding of sentences in which it occurs" (24). A word is not defined by the facts it points out but by its ability to contribute to the performance of speech acts.[17]

Since "it gives" what it names instead of describing an already established fact or thing, the word as Heidegger thinks it serves as a mode of action, not a mode of cognition. The "it" of the "it gives" delivers the thing—for example, the potlatch or the tamanawas—in an irruptive event of presencing. Such an "event" can no longer be called by that name, however, because the gift-event cancels the very concept of "event." The gift of the "it gives" is an act that destroys itself even as it brings itself to completion.

In "Time and Being" (1972, 1–24) Heidegger gives the name *Ereignis* to the "It" that "gives" in the idiomatic phrase "it gives / *es gibt*." Although the dictionary tells us that *Ereignis* means "event," he insists that this term is to be glossed "as Appropriation or event of Appropriation" (19). The phrase "event of ap*propri*ation" fuses the notion of event with the notion of the proper, for embedded within *Ereignis* is "*eigen*," an adjective meaning "own," as in the phrase "your own words." Hence the event of appropriation delivers something over into its own, allowing it to be what it most properly is. As Derrida (1992b, 21) puts it, *Ereignis* realizes "the desire to accede to the proper." The task of the "It" that "gives" Being, then, is to allow Being to assume its proper nature as Being. The "It" lets Being hide and reveal itself as presence although, *properly* speaking, Being is nothing that is.

Like language, though, the event of appropriation gives only by withholding itself. The event that gives access to the proper has no proper essence of its own. It has no "own" of its own. Since the giver of the gift of "ownness" owns nothing of itself, moreover, the event of appropriation is an event of enownment that disowns its essence as event.

Heidegger warns that "[o]ne should bear in mind . . . that 'event' [*Ereignis*] is not simply an occurrence, but that which makes any occurrence possible." Since the event of appropriation is the necessary condition for every event but not an event itself, it cannot be understood in terms of what it makes possible. "What the name 'event of appropriation' names," says Heidegger, "can no longer be represented by means of the current meaning of the word": its meaning defines only those events that have already been given and fails to grasp the event of appropriation that at once releases and preserves them in their own essence (19–20). The "current" notion of event presupposes the event of appropriation and cannot be used to explain it. Because Heidegger rigorously distinguishes between the *Ereignis* that brings worldly events into their own and those events that are brought into their own through *Ereignis,* an irreducible difference divides the event of appropriation from all the everyday events that "it gives."

Although *Ereignis* gives, it is not therefore an origin. It engages but does not belong to the sequence of events that take the form of causes and their effects. What the gift gives to be thought, then, is a beginning that escapes the notion of the beginning altogether. Derrida (1986, 242):

> Before, if one could count here with time, before everything, before every determinable being [*étant*], there is, there was, there will have been the irruptive event of the gift [*don*]. An event that no more has any relation with what is currently designated under this word. Thus giving can no longer be thought starting from Being [*être*], but "the contrary" it could be said, if this logical inversion here were pertinent when the question is not yet logic but the origin of logic. In *Zeit und Sein* [Time and Being], the gift of the *es gibt* gives itself to be thought before the *Sein* in the *es gibt Sein* and displaces all that is determined under the name *Ereignis,* a word often translated by *event.*

The event of appropriation—the "It" that "gives" Being (*Sein*), and time (*Zeit*) in "Time and Being"—occurs as an irruption that fractures a continuum.

The event of appropriation is paradoxical because it stands outside eventhood and thus outside its own essence. What is more, while it arrives to cut across a cycle of events that were already going on without it, the gift-event is also, though this is impossible, what set the cycle going in the first place. The gift is the origin of a series but an origin that comes to meet that series and to intersect it from the future—as if the inaugural event, which can no longer be properly called inaugural, were constrained to arrive after everything it has put into play.

To read Heidegger is therefore to encounter an impossible thought of the gift: the gift is an originary event that irrupts within the smooth curve of a circle—but a circle is a figure that has neither origin nor end.

99

*giving*

Derrida affirms in *Given Time* (1992b, 7–8) that the motif of the circle has come to represent the structure of Western European metaphysics itself. The circle is, among other things, the privileged metaphysical figure for economy. "What is economy?" asks Derrida: transgressing Austin's law that the meanings of words reside in sentences, he looks to the dictionary to uncover the layers of sense that have gathered around "economy" since the Greeks delivered it to history.

Economy marks the "partition" that, working like a hinge, joins the law of the public sphere to the private confines of the home. "Among its irreducible predicates or semantic values," says Derrida, "economy no doubt includes the values of law (*nomos*) and of home (*oikos*, home, property, family, the hearth, the fire indoors). *Nomos* does not only signify the law in general, but also the law of distribution (*nemein*), the law of sharing or partition [*partage*], the law as partition (*moira*), the given or assigned part, participation" (6). The meaning of the word "economy" points at once to distribution in general and, in particular, to the circular exchange of goods and services that ties the home to the laws of the marketplace.

> Besides the values of law and home, of distribution and partition, economy implies the idea of exchange, of circulation, of return. The figure of the circle is obviously *at the center,* if that can still be said of a circle. It stands at the center of any problematic of *oikonomia,* as it does of any economic field: circular exchange, circulation of goods, products, monetary signs or merchandise, amortization of expenditures, revenues, substitution of use values and exchange values. This motif of circulation can lead one to think that the law of economy is the—circular—return to the point of departure, to the origin, also to the home. (6–7)

The law of economy is the law of the return home, and it dictates that whatever is spent has to circle back to its place of origin. Everything paid out must be paid back. Economy is best represented by the figure of the circle because economics requires that every exchange end where it began.

The gift, however, is precisely that which does not return to sender. It is related to the circle of economy but works to interrupt it. The gift does not, indeed cannot, come back home because it ceases to be a gift the moment it invokes a repayment, a debt, or a countergift. "It must not circulate," says Derrida, "it must not be exchanged, it must not in any case be exhausted, as a gift, by the process of exchange, by the movement of circulation of the circle in the form of return to the point of departure. If the figure of the circle is essential to economics, the gift must remain *aneconomic*" (7). The gift does not belong to any system where expenses circle home as profits: it is an event that breaks (with) the curve of circulation, distribution, reciprocity, and exchange altogether.

When a giver and recipient participate in an act of giving, they enter into an unsigned agreement—a contract—that dictates what a gift is and how it is to be distributed. Derrida reduces the law of the gift to a brief axiom: "In order for there to be gift, gift event, some 'one' has to give some 'thing' to someone other." This law generates a paradox, though, since "these conditions of possibility of the gift (that some 'one' gives some 'thing' to some 'one other') designate simultaneously the conditions of the impossibility of the gift" (11–12). What makes this impossibility possible?

If I wish to give a gift, then I must insist that nothing circle home to me as the profit of my giving. A gift, by definition, does not invoke a countergift: "there must be no reciprocity, return, exchange, countergift, or debt" (12). Yet it is not enough that I receive nothing back. In order to give I must not even know that I have given. What is more, the recipient of my gift must not know that she or he has received it because, as Derrida notes, "The simple identification of the gift seems to destroy it" (14). If I know that I have given, then, at the very least, I receive, in return, the knowledge of my own generosity and I congratulate myself for my deed. But as soon as I take satisfaction from my gift, I begin to pay myself back and my gift returns to me. Similarly, if the recipient of my gift perceives it as a gift, then at the very least that person owes me a debt of gratitude. Yet as soon as the recipient is obliged to pay something in return—even if that "payment" only means acknowledging that I have given—my gift runs "the risk of its being annulled in thanks, in the symbolic,

in exchange or economy, indeed, of its becoming a benefit" to the person who gives it (Derrida 1989a, 149).

Since every gift is destroyed the moment it is recognized, a gift remains a gift only if it occurs within an instant
of absolute forgetting. "For there to be gift, it is necessary
that the gift not even appear, that it not be perceived or
received as gift" (Derrida 1992b, 16). It must neither be
taken into consciousness nor retained in memory. Moreover, the forgetting of the gift is not a mere repression in
the psychoanalytic sense of that term, for whatever is re-
pressed from consciousness is, by definition, merely dis-
placed and immediately returns to consciousness under
another guise. The unconscious invariably gives back
whatever is given to repression. To be what it is, the gift
has to destroy itself utterly the moment it is given, leaving
no trace of itself within consciousness or within the unconscious. Otherwise it is annulled. Thus the gift can be only
on the condition that it has no being—that it *is* not.

Derrida follows Heidegger in making the gift a figure
for the impossible itself. A gift-event can happen only on
the condition that it never happen, because a gift ceases
to be a gift not only when it is returned but when it is
given. The gift-event cannot occur and remain a gift. It is
not an event at all.

### Time and the Gift

However, the gift-event does not sacrifice itself so com-
pletely that it is never given. A gift leaves nothing behind
itself, yet something of it nevertheless remains. "For there
to be gift event," says Derrida, "(we say event and not act),
something must come about or happen, in an instant, in
an instant that no doubt does not belong to the economy
of time, in a time without time, in such a way that the
forgetting forgets, that it forgets *itself,* but also in such a
way that this forgetting, without being something present,
presentable, determinable, sensible or meaningful, is not
nothing" (1992b, 17). The gift happens without happening. It is neither "present" nor "presentable" because it
does not deliver itself during a present moment, a now.

If in its self-incineration the gift exceeds every present,
that is because it interrupts the metaphysical representation of time. "One of the most powerful and ineluctable
representations, at least in the history of metaphysics," says
Derrida, "is the representation of time as a [process or

movement that takes the form of a] circle" (1992b, 8). Heidegger had already launched a critique of "this privilege of circular movement in the representation of time" in *Being and Time*.

Heidegger ([1927] 1962, 476) remarks in the final chapter of book 2, for example, that metaphysics thinks time as a series of present moments: "It is held that time presents itself proximally as an uninterrupted sequence of 'nows.'" Temporality "ensnares itself in the Present, which, in making present, says pre-eminently, 'Now! Now!'" (459). Metaphysical time consists of the now of the present present, the no-longer-now of the past present, and the not-yet-now of the future present. Moreover, the three modes of the present—the past now, the present now, and the future now—ceaselessly circle into each other. The present forever advances into the future—"Every last 'now,'" as '*now*,' is always *already* a 'forthwith'"— while the future occurs as a mode of the *past*: every "forthwith" to come is already "a 'forthwith' that is no longer [*ein Sofort-nicht-mehr*]; thus it is time in the sense of the 'no-longer-now'—in the sense of the past." The past, however, occurs as a mode of the future: "Every first 'now' is a 'just-now' [a past] that is not yet [a past that has yet to happen] . . . thus it is time in the sense of the 'not-yet-now'—in the sense of the 'future.'" The present is the ever-recurring instant in which the future revolves into the past and past into future, and time is an infinite series of nows that ceaselessly ends where it begins—only to begin again. "If in characterizing time we stick primarily and exclusively *to such a sequence*," argues Heidegger, "then in principle neither beginning nor end can be found in it" (476). It is customary to represent infinity as a circle. Hegel, for example, insists on the circularity of an infinite return home, as if time endlessly repays itself for every moment it has spent: "Infinity has rightly been represented by the image of the circle, because a straight line runs on indefinitely and denotes that merely negative and false infinity which, unlike true infinity, does not *return into itself*" ([1821] 1991, 54, emphasis added).

Derrida (1992b, 9) argues that the metaphysical representation of time necessarily excludes the gift: "wherever *time as circle* (a 'vulgar' concept, Heidegger would therefore say) is predominant, the gift is impossible." Just as it breaks with the circle of economy, the gift relates itself to time's

*giving*

circle by cutting it up. A gift is, by definition, a moment of rupture: "A gift could be possible, there could be a gift only at the instant an effraction of the circle will have taken place, at the instant all circulation will have been interrupted and *on the condition* of this instant." Paradoxically, the moment when the gift cuts *through* time is not a moment *in* time. The event of the gift escapes not only eventhood but time itself: "this instant of effraction (of the temporal circle) must no longer be part of time." The gift is an instant that is not an instant in time, an instantless instant that marks the limit between metaphysical time and its beyond. The gift-event arrives in time from beyond time's circle—in an instant that severs the metaphysical sequence of nows. "There would be a gift," says Derrida, "only at the instant when the *paradoxical* instant . . . tears time apart" (1992b, 9). To think the impossible time of the gift, this instantless instant, it is necessary to entertain the possibility, the impossible possibility, that time itself is the gift of nothing temporal.

Derrida points toward the thought of a time beyond time when he says that "the structure of this impossible *gift* is also that of Being . . . and of time" (27). There remains a correspondence between the gift, Being, and time: a disjunctive correspondence set into play by the event of appropriation and its "there is—es gibt." Time, Being, and the gift are related in that they "own" themselves in the same fashion. What is the nature of their mutual "ownness"?

For the Heidegger of "Time and Being," Being is given to be thought only when it is placed in a relation to time because Being is the presence that allows present beings to be present in the world. It gives the "is" to anything that in any way is. But the presence that Being offers to present beings is also a dimension of time. Presence persists in presence only within the present moment—the now. Heidegger concludes therefore that "Being as presencing remains determined as presence by time": Being conceived as presencing would be unthinkable if time did not offer the present to thought (1972, 3). To think Being, it is also necessary to think time.

However, time is itself determined by Being. The now constantly passes, but it also stays constant. The present is held in presence even as it recedes into the past. Right now it is the present, and as this present now passes, another now takes its place. Yet the present itself remains the same during the transition between these two different present moments, these two nows. Heidegger says that "[t]o remain means: not to disappear, thus, to presence" (3). To think time, therefore, it is necessary to think Being as the presencing of what is present.

Still, "[n]ot every presencing is necessarily the present": Heidegger maintains that absence too is a way of giving presence to something (13). For example, the present moment is present only on the condition that earlier and later moments are absent from it. The present is therefore defined not by what it is but by what it is not. It presents itself insofar as it is neither the past nor the future. True time, Heidegger concludes, is not circular but four-dimensional. It comprises the past, present, and future as well as the play of difference that holds these three in a relation to each other: "the unity of time's three dimensions consists in the interplay of each towards each." Their interplay is time's "fourth dimension" and its first dimension too. For the unity of time allows past, present, and future to extend themselves toward each other without merging into a single, undifferentiated "now" (15). It is a "nearness" that holds past, present, and future together by holding them apart. Whereas metaphysics defines past, present, and future as three versions of the same thing—as three modes of the now—Heidegger defines them in terms of the differences that set them apart from one another.

Being (conceived as presencing) and time (conceived as a negative interplay of differences) determine one another but do not give each other. Being is not a mode of time, nor is time a mode of Being. Yet they are gathered into relation in an event of appropriation that is also an event of giving. Says Heidegger, "What determines both, time and Being, in their own, in their belonging together, we shall call: *Ereignis*" (19). Since it gives time and Being, the event of appropriation stands outside the world of things that belong in time and in Being. Allowing time to persist in Being and Being to remain present in time, the event of appropriation makes it possible for there to be a world where things and events are given to be thought. Whatever *is* in the world is *in time*, but whatever *is* is possible only because, as Derrida puts it, "before everything, before every determinable being, there is, there was, there will have been the irruptive event of the gift"—the gift of Being and of time.

The enabling contradiction of Heidegger's "Time and Being" is that the gift of time arrives from beyond time. The "it" that "gives" in the phrase *es gibt Zeit* occurs in an instant beyond time because it is the instant in which time is given. The *es gibt* "is" the instantless instant itself. Derrida (1992b, 20):

> In *Zeit und Sein* (1952), Heidegger's attention bears down on the giving (*Geben*) or the gift (*Gabe*) implicated in the *es gibt*. From the beginning of the meditation, Heidegger recalls, if one can put it this way, that in itself time is nothing temporal, since it is nothing, since it is not a thing (*kein Ding*). The temporality of time is not temporal, no more than proximity is proximate or treeness is woody. He also recalls that Being is not being (being-present/present-being), since it is not something (*kein Ding*), and that therefore one cannot say either "time is" or "Being is," but "es gibt Sein" and "es gibt Zeit."

Time *is* not, just as Being is not. "There is/it gives" time (*es gibt Zeit*). There is something that is time, but time itself is not a thing in time. Furthermore the gift of time breaks time apart. Heidegger insists that this rupture, if it can be called one, is not an act of violence. The giving of time marks the movement in which time accedes to what is most properly its own, for in its *Ereignis* time lays claim to itself: it owns its essence as the interplay of past, present, and future.

However, Derrida argues that the gift occurs as a rending because it tears the fabric that receives it. The gift of the name is especially violent since it arrives as an instantless instant of irruption that can have devastating consequences for anyone it touches. "The name seems produced," he says in *Glas*, "one time only, by an act without a past." It does not attach itself to what already exists but comes instead to give existence to a thing. And not every gift is necessarily good. When what is given is a name, "such a gift appropriates itself violently [in an event of appropriation that is no longer an event], harpoons, 'arraigns' [*arraisonne*] what it seems to engender, penetrates

and paralyses with one stroke [*coup*] the recipient thus consecrated." The gift of the name owns itself within a system
of power relations: it deploys itself to control the actions
of the person or thing that is named. "To give a name is
always," says Derrida, "to sublimate a singularity and to
inform against it, to hand it over to the police" (1986, 6–
7). It is hardly surprising, then, that the law that gave the
names "potlatch" and "tamanawas" to certain "previously
unknown" practices of the British Columbia First Nations
served to "arraign" them, to accuse them, to find fault with
them and bring them to trial.

And "here one need hardly mention the fact that in
certain languages, for example in French, one may say as
readily 'to give a gift' as 'to give a blow' [*donner un coup*],
'to give life' [*donner la vie*] as 'to give death' [*donner la mort*]"
(1992, 12). One might recall too that *Gift*, in German,
means "poison."

### The Continuum of Discourse

Heidegger and Derrida have put us in their debt by giving
us this schema: a gift is an event that intervenes in an ongoing series and ruptures its continuity; it is an origin that
arrives only *after* everything it inaugurates is already in
play; and it delivers itself in an instant that is not an instant
in time. But does their schema help us to understand how
words give the things they name? The mechanics of the
textual gift—which allow "potlatch" and "tamanawas" to
make presents of what they are said to represent—remains
to be explained.

By giving what they named, "potlatch" and "tamanawas" ruptured the continuity of an already established series of utterances and events, yet the government of Canada did not invent these words when it handed them over
to the police. They were recorded in dictionaries long before they were cited in the Indian Act. Begbie's judgment
shows that by the 1880s it was understood that they came
from Chinook, a trading jargon that had circulated along
the northwest coast for perhaps hundreds of years and
continued to have a role in the region's economy until the
early twentieth century. "Potlatch" and "tamanawas" cut
across a continuum by delivering things "previously unknown" to the world, but they belonged to the very continuum that they fractured.

It is said that, before it was replaced by English, Chinook was spoken on the coast from the Columbia River to the Alaska panhandle. It was an invented and fragmentary language that occupied the spaces *between* a number of natural languages, and it allowed people from different cultures to conduct trade without having to engage in the work of translation. Harry Assu of the Lekwiltok Kwagiulth recalls in his memoirs (1989) that "[e]verybody spoke this trade language when [he] was young." He also notes that the First Nations have their own names for the potlatch though different cultures do not necessarily potlatch in the same way. "We call these big potlatches pesa in our language," he says. But that is not the only name. In a language such as Tsimshian, for example, there is a form of "potlatch" that is properly called the *yaokw*, and no doubt many analogous examples could be cited (Seguin, 1984, 110; 1985, 58–61). But while the word "potlatch" was once as foreign to potlatching cultures as it was to Canadian law, today it circulates freely across cultural boundaries: "now it's called potlatch by Indians and everybody else all up and down the coast," says Assu. "One of my father's names was pesala, meaning Potlatcher." Even today, therefore, the word "potlatch" is divided within itself: there is the "potlatch" that "Indians" perform and discuss—indeed a plurality of "potlatches" that survived the Canadian government's crude attempt to ban them— and then there is the "potlatch" that "everybody else" talks about, whether they live "up and down the coast" or on the other side of the globe. What concerns me here, though, is this second "potlatch"—the one that a regulatory discourse gave to the world and that came to overlap the "potlatches" that were already going on. As for the Lekwiltok potlatch, Assu remarks: "Important families call the people to a potlatch. Then we tell our family history and show our dances and give away names that go with the dances. We give away money and goods to everybody who's invited, and that's what the word potlatch means: 'giving away' " (10). It is a "giving away," he says, but what is given away are "names" and not merely "money and goods." It is not, according to Assu, the absolute expenditure of property that has obsessed almost "everybody else" for more than a century.

Gilbert Malcolm Sproat argues in *Scenes and Studies of Savage Life* that Chinook is all that remains of the original language of the Pacific Northwest. "The truth," he says, "is that the Chinook jargon is simply a depravation of the Chinook language—an old language, which probably is the mother of all the dialects spoken on the coast between the Columbia River and the north of Vancouver Island" (1987, 97). However, Edward Harper Thomas (1935, viii) emphasizes that the Chinook jargon is not to be confused with the Chinook language. The jargon was in use before the first Europeans arrived on the coast, he argues, but did not become known to them until the early nineteenth century. It was a mixture of aboriginal languages that also absorbed European words after the fur trade began. J. V. Powell (1988) maintains, in contrast, that Chinook did not develop until *after* the Europeans arrived on the coast. It was, he says, a pragmatic mingling of English, French, and a number of aboriginal northwest coast languages, which sprang into being to facilitate the circulation of goods and services among a diverse group of people speaking a variety of languages. "It is estimated," he observes, "that more than 100,000 people could use Chinook Jargon in 1900, and it was employed widely in court testimony, newspaper advertising, missionary activity among Indians, and everyday conversation from central BC to northern California" (417).

It is possible to look up the meaning of the word "potlatch" in any number of dictionaries that translate Chinook into English and English into Chinook. In Long's *Dictionary of the Chinook Language,* for example, the word denotes both the act of giving and the thing that is given: "Pot'-latch, *n., v.* To give; a gift" (38). Thomas says the potlatch is a struggle for prestige, too: "Pot'-latch (N): A gift and to give. (When it denotes giving, it is a verb and when it is used for the gift itself or for the celebration, it is a noun.) The potlatch was a native festival common to all the tribes of the Northwest. Its feature was the distribution of gifts. The most noted chief was he who held the largest potlatch and gave away the most valuable and largest number of presents" (92–93). For Thomas, a gift remains a gift only if it later returns to the giver. A "bad gift" is one that never comes home: " 'Cultus potlatch'— a gift without prospect of recompense—a 'bad gift' in an Indian's view" (93). Good gifts find a place for themselves on the circle of economic exchange. Charles Montgomery Tate (1889, 32) defines "cultus potlatch" simply as "gift"— as if to imply that a gift remains a gift only when nothing returns to the giver. In the dictionaries, as in everyday usage, the meaning of "potlatch" oscillates endlessly between the pole of the commodity that ceaselessly revolves in the circle of economy and the pole of the pure expenditure that breaks with circulation altogether.

George Shaw's *Chinook Jargon and How to Use It* (1909) sets "potlatch" into oscillation by insisting that it points both to the gift that never comes home and to the gift that obliges a return payment. Here "Pot'latch, or Paht-latsh, n., v." means at once "to give; allot; cede"—that is, to give without return—and to "expend; pay; impart; restore"—that is, to give in order to get something back. Shaw traces a distinct limit between the "cultus potlatch,—a present or free gift; expecting no return; a donation"—and the potlatch proper, where every gift invokes a countergift, but the moment that limit is drawn, it folds together what it has just set apart. In the potlatch every expenditure comes home to the giver, yet Shaw cites an informant who describes potlatching as a sheer dissipation of wealth.

> The *potlatch* was the greatest institution of the Indian, and is to this day [note the disjunction between the two verb tenses, "was" and "is"—throughout the white discourse on "the Indian," the First Nations always seem to be both dead and alive, as if they belonged to an absolute past that somehow survives into the present]. From far and near assembled the invited guests and tribes and with feasting, singing, chanting and dancing, the bounteous collection was distributed: a chief was made penniless. [T]he wealth of a lifetime was dissipated in an hour, but his head ever after was crowned with the glory of a satisfied ambition: he had won the honor and reverence of his people. It was a beautiful custom; beautiful in the eyes of the natives of high or low degree, confined to no particular tribe, but to be met with everywhere along the coast. (20–21)

The potlatch is a "beautiful" act of loss where in an hour one gives away the earnings of a lifetime, knowing that everything is gone forever. *At the same time,* though, it is a source of profit, a further accumulation of wealth, since by giving all one receives, in return, "glory," "honour," and "reverence." "*Potlatch* (noun)" means "[t]hat which is given, bestowed, bequeathed, given, etc.,—i.e. a gift" but a gift that is "[a]lways given with the expectation, greater or lesser, of a return." The only pure expenditure is the cultus potlatch, which Shaw defines—a second time—as "a purposeless gift, that is, outright with no expectation of return" (20–21).

The "potlatch" is at once a gift and not a gift, but what do the dictionaries say about the "tamanawas"? Long (c. 1909) says it is the name for destiny: "Ta-mah-no-mas, *n*. Magic; luck; good fortune" (39),[18] while Thomas (1935) insists it is a kind of ghost that accompanies a person through life: "Tah-mah'-na-wis (C): A guardian or familiar spirit in its personal application. Every Indian had [note, again, the past tense, signifying death] his tahmahnawis." Thomas does not say that Long's definition is incorrect but rather that it is secondary, derivative: "Tahmahnawis also means magic, ghost, spirit, or anything supernatural," he writes, "and is used as the equivalent of luck, fortune and kindred words. It was applied to anything the Indians could not readily understand" (97–98).

Although section 114 says the "tamanawas" is an "Indian dance," neither Long nor Thomas associates the thing they call the "tamahnomas/tahmahnawis" with dancing. What about Shaw? He identifies the "*Ta-mah-no-us*, n." as "[a] sort of guardian or familiar spirit; magic; luck; fortune; anything supernatural; the spirits; a ghost; goblin; idol; witch." Though "tahmahnous" does not point directly to a dance, it does gesture toward the practices of the "Tah-mah-na-wis man"—"a doctor, priest, conjurer, and fortune teller, a dealer in magic and a maker and destroyer of charms for good and evil, all in the same personage." The Tah-mah-na-wis man is an organizer of dances. Shaw mentions, for example, "The red, or *pill ta-mahn-a-wis*, [which] was an assembling together, an invocation, in short, of the spirits for a good season the following summer. It lasted three or four days and consisted of singing, dancing, the beating of tom-toms, drums and the decoration of the face and limbs and body invariably with streaks and spots of red paint" (1909, 24–25).

While "potlatch" and "tamanawas" belong to a jargon belonging to no one in particular, the dictionaries define them as practices common to all of the coastal First Nations. When the law borrows these Chinook terms to name

111

*giving*

acts that have different names and take different forms in different communities, it reduces the diversity of the coastal First Nations to an unbroken sameness. It is as if, to the Euro-Canadian gaze, aboriginal societies were all in the last analysis the same—despite the differences that separate them from each other and divide them within themselves.[19]

Heidegger insists, however, that words reveal themselves as words only when they participate in saying, not when they appear in dictionaries. Saying is the event of "letting appear" in which beings come into Being through language while language withholds itself from experience. It is during the event of saying that language gives the "is" to the thing that is. Saying shows that the nature of the word "conceals within itself that which gives being" to a given thing (1971, 88).[20] But the word gives being to a thing in an instantless instant that intersects a discourse that was already going on. It does not initiate this discourse but instead irrupts within it. The gift-event occurs, without occurring, as an effraction within the infinite circulation of speech and writing.

"Potlatch" and "tamanawas" are words in precisely this sense. Before they began to "speak as words" by giving being to the things they name, they had circulated throughout the northwest coast for decades and had for many years been the topic of a sustained debate in Canada's correspondence on Indian affairs. Hence they were already inscribed in a continuum of discourse when, sometime after 1895, they assumed their role as white purveyors.

### The Return of the Dead Letter

Two months after Begbie put section 114 of the Indian Act to death, Vankoughnet wrote the deputy minister of justice to ask whether there were grounds for an appeal. "The release of the Indian [He-ma-sak] under this ruling of Judge Begbie," he notes, "has caused much dissatisfaction among the respectable white people resident in the locality of Alert Bay, Fort Rupert and such places" (NA, vol. 3628, file 6244-1, 2 November 1889). There had been an outbreak of white anxiety in that zone where Europe-in-Canada rubbed up against its outermost limit, for despite their English names the "localities" named by Vankoughnet had been the traditional village sites of the

Kwakwaka'wakw for centuries. But the deputy minister of justice had no comfort to offer the "dissatisfied" settlers living there.

Robert Sedgewick informed Vankoughnet on 13 December that "the law makes no provision for an appeal" because "if the statements of the Chief Justice with respect to the [lack?] of certainty as to the meaning of the word 'potlach' or 'potlatch' are well founded, the Minister of Justice agrees with the view to which the judgement gives expression, that it would be difficult, and probably impossible, to sustain a conviction under the provision of the statute at all" (NA, vol. 3628, file 6244-1, 13 December 1889). The difficulty of determining what the word means continues to be marked by the difficulty of deciding how it is spelled: whether " 'potlach' or 'potlatch.' " The meaning of "tamanawas" is equally uncertain, and Sedgewick advises that, if the department wished to secure convictions under section 114, it ought to table an amendment "clearly defining what is meant by the prohibition."

As in Begbie's judgment, Sedgewick's reading of the statute follows the rules laid out by Searle's metaphysics of reference. Searle says that a speaker performs a fully consummated speech act of reference by identifying an object unambiguously for a hearer. Yet a referring expression can be used to point to a thing only if that expression has a clearly defined meaning. The meaning of an expression describes what is known about the thing referred to, and this knowledge, in turn, allows the hearer to distinguish the referent from every other thing that could possibly be pointed out. According to Sedgewick, the reason "potla(t)ch" and "tamanawas" fail to refer is that they have no meaning. Without sense there is no reference, and without reference the legal system breaks down, for a law that does not define what it bans makes it impossible for police and judges to identify the practices that are forbidden. It fails to mark out the difference between crime and lawful activity. And so long as "potla(t)ch" and "tamanawas" fail to correspond to activities known to exist somewhere in the world, aboriginal people cannot know what not to do in order to avoid being arrested.

In 1893 Reginald H. Pidcock informed Arthur Vowell—who had replaced Israel Wood Powell as Indian superintendent for British Columbia (a difference of a single consonant)—that the death of section 114 made it impossible to control the potlatch in the "Kwawkewlth" Agency. Pidcock reports that he had to stand by and watch as a thousand people gathered for a potlatch at Cape Mudge in January 1893 because "[t]he law in regard to the potlatch is practically a dead letter, as Chief Justice Begbie gave it as his opinion that he could not convict under the present law, as it did not define what a potlatch was" (NA, vol. 3628, file 6244-1, 16 March 1893). However, the "dead letter" was about to be given a second life. For if it neither refers nor means, if it points neither to actual practices nor to knowledge about actual practices, then its reference and its meaning will have to be purveyed, and whatever is lacking in the first statute will be reinvented according to the government's specifications in a revised version.

Although five years elapsed before the law hauled itself from the grave and lurched back into life, it was not repealed. It rested quietly in the statute books in a state of living death. Meanwhile, supporters and opponents of the potlatch continued to debate it, and their arguments continued to focus on the word as such. Between 1890 and 1893 "potlatch" took on a set of contradictory significations, pointing toward vastly different practices at once— as if it had come to be defined by the ease with which it could be honed to suit every context. It was an empty sign to be filled with any number of meanings for any number of purposes. How else can we account for the fact that "potlatch" defined itself over a span of three years both as a benefit society that takes care of the weak and as a "curse" that degrades Canadian society?

In the winter of 1890 Captain Napoleon Fitzstubbs, the stipendiary magistrate at Hazelton, and C. W. D. Clifford, a Hudson's Bay Company manager on the upper Skeena, wrote the attorney general of British Columbia to condemn the logic behind the suppression of the potlatch. Fitzstubbs's letter weighs the arguments of white settlers against those advanced by the First Nations of the north coast and summarizes the leading themes of the discourse for and against potlatching.

> [I]t is I believe said that to get the people as far as may be, out of the tribal state, is the first step towards reformation and advancement, and that the Potlach system being imbedded,

in that tribal condition, is a great obstacle to this hoped for progress. It is further said that various evils attend the celebration of the Potlach.

The Indians on the other hand appear invariably to regard the institution of the 'Potlach' [in single quotes here] with affection, as they charish [*sic*] it as a social, and from their point of view beneficent institution which has grown up amongst them during perhaps centuries past, and has been shaped naturally by circumstances in conformity with their social needs and ideas. They ask invariably what do the whitemen propose to substitute for this ancient and popular institution?

Aboriginal people insist, he says, that the "Potlach" is a public "fair" where goods are exchanged, marriages arranged, and questions of rank decided. It is also a "benefit society" that takes care of the old. What is more, the hostility that appears to be aroused when potlatchers compete for social prestige is just a "harmless" artifice. And whatever is given away is given back a year later because potlatch gifts in fact belong to the circle of exchange and are not really gifts at all (NA, vol. 3628, file 6244-1, 13 March 1890).

Clifford argues in his "Memo" that the government has failed to answer a fundamental question—"What is 'Potlatching'?"—so he asks: "Please define it. What overt act is contrary to the law against it?" It is as if there were a law requiring the law to alert its interpreters to the difficulty of defining what words mean and what acts they refer to. Clifford answers that the potlatch as practiced "in the [northern] Interior" of British Columbia is "a primitive system of banking" where everything that is lent out ultimately returns home to the creditor with interest. It "feeds" the aged and infirm as well, while the law against it merely consolidates the power of "Methodist missionaries" determined to set themselves up as the sole lawgivers on the Skeena. "The contention of the Methodist Missionaries that it is necessary first to put down potlatching in order to civilise the Indians is false," writes Clifford, "and it is an attempt on their part to make the Indians believe, that they are the law and that the law which the Indians now

*giving*

respect is with these missionaries and is backing them up in all their monstrous claims and assertions" (NA, vol. 3628, file 6244-1, 13 March 1890). For Clifford, the Methodists incite contempt for authority by teaching that the law of the Bible takes precedence over the laws of the state.[21]

The government of British Columbia forwarded the texts of Fitzstubbs and Clifford to the secretary of state in Ottawa even as it was preparing to withdraw from its agreement to help federal officials enforce the Indian Act (Report of the Executive Council, 15 April 1890; Lieutenant Governor Nelson to Secretary of State for Canada, 19 April 1890; these and other sources in this paragraph from NA, vol. 3628, file 6244-1). However, Vankoughnet continued to hold provincial authorities responsible for enforcing criminal law in British Columbia, and in the spring of 1889 he asked Sedgewick to clarify whether the act was a provincial or a federal jurisdiction. As Vankoughnet notes, "[T]he opinion has been expressed that as the Federal govt passed the law . . . this Dept shd prosecute any parties who violate same & that the Provincial govt shd not be called upon to do so" (7 June 1890). Sedgewick answered that under the British North America Act criminal law is a provincial responsibility and the expense of enforcing it ought to be borne by the province, not the dominion, but he adds that if the government of British Columbia refuses to support the ban against the potlatch, it is up to the Department of Indian Affairs to decide whether it "should incur any expenses in the matter or should allow the law to become a dead letter" (9 July 1890). Vankoughnet suggested that in future Indian agents and local authorities should consult with each other before "interfering" with the potlatch. But the "local authorities" had resolved to heed Fitzstubbs's warning that "where the Indians are numerous, and where they [*sic*] are few white residents the attempt to enforce the law against the "Potlach" [now in full quotes, gathering marks as his text unfolds] in too summary fashion might not produce the effect desired, but rather, might defer the good results hoped for, by causing disquiet, and a disinclination to obey the law, on other points" (13 March 1890).

The story "The Evil Potlatch," published in the Toronto *Empire* on 4 February 1893, offers a less cautious opinion about how best to deal with the potlatch. It reports that a "party of missionaries" visited the Lekwiltok reserve at Cape Mudge early in 1893, "where they found the red man engaged in a great 'potlatch' "—the same potlatch that had led Pidcock to call the law a "dead letter." The author leaves no doubt as to the meaning of " 'potlatch' ": "The word means 'to give,' " and the thing it refers to is described as a celebration of "filth," "fire water," and sexual "corruption." To evoke the reader's disgust, and pleasure, the story recalls that the visiting missionaries saw "[m]en [many of them white] and women in their drunkenness actually tearing the clothes off each other, and wallowing about in reaking filth—the picture is more like hell upon earth than anything ever heard of." It affirms that potlatchers routinely neglect their children and the elderly in order to give away blankets earned not by "industry" but by "prostitution." The final paragraph ceases slandering the Lekwiltok and calls on the federal government to enforce the antipotlatch statute. "A few years ago a law was passed prohibiting the potlatch," it notes, but "[t]his was as good as winked at by some of the officials"—an allusion to the department's failure to prevent Lohah's potlatch in 1885. "The law remains on the Dominion statutes," the story concludes, "but is practically a dead letter [popular usage repeatedly affirms that the law is a letter (that is, an article of correspondence, something sent in the mail, a postal effect) and that it is dead]; and the Indians, instead of being an upright and industrious people, are a filthy, indolent, degraded set, a disgrace and a curse to our country" (NA, vol. 3628, file 6244-1, 4 February 1893).

What is to be drawn from these readings? "Potlatch" signifies "to give" and "to loan," but that is not all because there is always a little more of it. To potlatch is also to sink, to stay low in relation to Euro-Canadian civilization. It is a failure to improve oneself, to advance out of barbarity. To potlatch is to decide on one color rather than another: it is to refuse to raise oneself into whiteness and to insist, as the *Empire* puts it, on remaining "red." To potlatch is to forgo assimilation into settler society because it signifies an unwillingness to be eaten by Europe-in-Canada—though that is not how the government will define it.

A revised version of section 114 was grafted to the Indian Act on 22 July 1895. While it tries to stabilize the meaning of "potlatch" and "tamanawas," the new statute is not an exercise in truth. It does not bring knowledge into agreement with an object. It does not identify the nature of two practices that were already in being, independent of the names tacked on to them. Instead, it gives being to the things it names, adding another potlatch and another tamanawas to those already put into circulation by Canada's Indian affairs correspondence. The gifts of the legal text irrupt within an ongoing circle of events and utterances—a circle that already includes the words "potlatch" and "tamanawas"—and forces it to leave its accustomed path and rotate around a different axis.

The revised statute can be read as an effort to obey the rules laid out by Searle for performing acts of singular definite reference. To achieve a fully consummated act of reference, Searle argues, a speaker cannot simply use a referring expression to point to a thing, but must be prepared, on demand, to replace that expression with a phrase describing what is being referred to. If a hearer is presented with the referring expression but cannot tell exactly what it is supposed to point out, then the speaker must set out a group of facts that allow the hearer to identify it—or present the hearer with the referent itself. Otherwise the act of reference goes awry. The new section 114 does not contain the words "potlatch" and "tamanawas," but they are present by their very absence. They have been replaced by brief descriptions identifying the acts that are henceforth forbidden. The substitution of a description for a word satisfies what Searle calls the "axiom of identification": "If a speaker refers to an object then he [*sic*] identifies, *or is able on demand to identify,* that object apart from all others for the hearer"—whether by demonstration, description, or both at once (1969, 91, emphasis added). Begbie and Sedgewick are the "hearers" who had "demanded" that the speaker—namely the Department of Indian Affairs—describe the practices that the expressions "potlatch" and "tamanawas" refer to, and the new statute was designed to meet their requirements.

The text begins by stating the facts about the set of acts that, in the previous statute, was named the "Potlach": "Every Indian or other person [note that the law continues to distinguish between 'Indians' and 'persons'] who engages in, or assists in celebrating or encourages either directly or indirectly another to celebrate, any Indian festi-

118

val, dance or other ceremony of which the giving away or paying or giving back of money, goods or articles of any sort forms a part, or is a feature, whether such gift of money, goods or articles takes place before, at, or after the celebration of the same." Next, the acts that were formerly gathered under the name "tamanawas" are called into the open and catalogued: "and every Indian or other person who engages or assists in any celebration or dance of which the wounding or mutilation of the dead or living body of any human being or animal forms a part or is a feature, is guilty of an indictable offense and is liable to imprisonment for a term not exceeding six months and not less than two months" (*Statutes of Canada, 1895*, chap. 35, "An Act Further to Amend the Indian Act," sec. 6). This part of the statute bans cannibalism and animal sacrifice. In effect, the law that aimed to put the First Nations of British Columbia to death by helping white Canadian society swallow them alive is a law against eating others. To facilitate its project of racial assimilation, the dominion government had to outlaw the act of assimilation itself. The irony of the ban on the "tamanawas" will be analyzed later, in "Eating."

While the second section forbids a small number of acts, the first reaches into every aspect of life in aboriginal communities. For it bans all economy. The statute is a letter sent not just to rupture the circle of economy at a few selected points, but to smash it altogether. Every conceivable exchange, every possible circulation of "money, goods or articles," is forbidden here. Henceforth there can be no forum, no market, whether public or private, no "Indian festival, dance or ceremony," where something would be allowed to pass from one person to another. "Giving away" is prohibited. So too is "giving back." "Payment" is also banned. It has become impossible for an "Indian" either to buy or to sell property, to borrow or lend capital, to give or receive presents without risking imprisonment. Taken literally, the law states that as of 22 July 1895 there can be no trade between aboriginal people anywhere in Canada.

To get at the potlatch, then, Parliament had to ban all forms of distribution. It had no choice. Suppressing the potlatch meant suppressing everything that had gathered under that name, even if that included the whole circle of economy. Since white administrators had long defined potlatching as at once an act of gift giving and a moment in the reciprocal exchange of property, both the gift and the countergift had to be outlawed. After all, if the definition of what is prohibited is not broad enough, some portion of the potlatch might be allowed to go free because there always seems to be more.

There is one exception, however. Though it forbids anything that could possibly qualify as an instance of "giving away," the law does not address itself to the "civilized" pursuit of agriculture. It therefore closes with a "but" introducing a qualifying clause: "but nothing in this section shall be construed to prevent the holding of any agricultural show or exhibition or the giving of prizes for exhibits thereat."

The revised statute does not just define the word "potlatch." It grants the world an object to be observed, regulated, handed over to the police—and arraigned. From now on the potlatch will be whatever the law says it is, although, according to the letter of the law, the potlatch could be any form of trade. Because it was an object of administrative attention long before the law delivered it to history, this mode of potlatch existed before it originated. It is necessary to remember, though, that the practice that the law gave to the world was not the same as the practices that the First Nations performed. The potlatch named in the Indian Act is not, for example, the practice called *pesa* in the Kwakwala language—even though "potlatch" is used today to refer to both practices. Furthermore, while the outlawed potlatch is a gift of the legal text, it is not a fiction. It is a real object that took up its place in the order of Western European knowledge, and it gave federal administrators a reason to send people to jail. The gift of the legal text was therefore a transfer point in a system of power relations. To think such a gift is to acknowledge that texts inflict violence on people—that words wound.

The "Brief on the Bill Further to Amend the Indian Act 1896" confirms that the revised statute was meant to replace the words "Potlach" and "Tamanawas" with descriptions of the things they named. The "Brief" states that "[i]t has been held that the mere designation of the festival or dance such as Tamanawas or Potlach is not sufficient for conviction . . . but that what is done thereat which constitutes the offence must likewise be described" (NA, vol. 3628, file 6244-1, undated). It also shows that the government planned to use the new statute to attack the dances of the First Nations of the prairies.

> As there is a similar dance to the Potlach cele-
> brated by the Indian bands in the North West
> Territories known as Omas-ko-sim-moo-wok
> or "grass dance," commonly known as "Giving
> away dance" and there are, no doubt, Indian
> celebrations of the same character elsewhere,
> all of which consist of the giving away, parting
> with, or exchange of large quantities of per-
> sonal effects sometimes all that the participants
> own it is considered better to prohibit all giving
> away festivals as they are conducive of extrava-
> gance and cause much loss of time and the as-
> semblage of large numbers of Indians, with all
> the usual attendant evils.

A single law, built up around two descriptive phrases, was to suppress a variety of very different practices in a number of regions and among a number of societies. It mattered little whether the acts that the law described existed or not, for if they were nowhere to be found, it would give itself something to ban.

### Text Machine

But how is it possible for a legal text to give what it names? "How can a mere word accomplish this, to bring a thing into being?" Paul de Man sketches the mechanics of the textual gift in "Promises" (1974, 246–77), an essay on Rousseau's *Social Contract*. De Man observes that Rous-seau's text is a meditation "on the authority of legal lan-guage," but as his reading unfolds, he claims to be circling "closer and closer to the 'definition' of *text*" in general, arguing that any text, whether it is a statute or a book of political philosophy, consists of the interplay between two functions of language: grammar and "referential mean-ing." Though there is an exchange between them, gram-mar and reference are ultimately incompatible and tend to work at cross-purposes.

Grammar is the set of rules that determine how the words of a given language are to be combined into techni-cally correct utterances. "The system of relationships that generates the text . . . is its grammar," says de Man, but grammar deploys itself in "the suspension of its referential meaning" (268–69). When a text is "generated," it does not know what it is saying because it strings words into utterances while ignoring what they signify. Thus grammar operates in a purely mechanical way. "To the extent that a text is grammatical," says de Man, "it is a logical code or a machine." His claim that grammar works independently of meaning explains why the government of Canada was able to enact a law against the "potlatch" and "tamanawas" in 1885 without knowing what these words signified or, more importantly, precisely what practices were being forbidden.

But if "the logic of grammar generates texts only in the absence of referential meaning," reference and meaning resist the machinations of grammar by giving sense to the rule-bound utterances of the text. Says de Man (1979, 246), "[E]very text generates a referent that subverts the grammatical principle to which it owed its constitution." Grammar weaves the text by linking words together according to a mechanical "logic," but once it is "generated," the text disconnects the machine that set it in play and assumes its place in the world. One consequence of the interplay between grammar and "referential meaning" is that the text acquires its "referent" only after it has been constituted (268–69).

What de Man suggests, then, is that a fundamental disjunction structures every text, and this disjunction can only be thought in relation to time. For the text never arrives in a single instant. Rather, it delivers itself to the world at least twice: once in the moment when it is constituted and its "referential meaning" is suspended, and again in the moment when it is interpreted and its "referential meaning" establishes itself. Heidegger and Derrida have taught us to expect, however, that the instant when the text is generated, when it irrupts into being, is not an instant in time. The text owns itself, becoming what it most properly is, in a moment that does not belong to the sequence of moments in which it will be read and discussed. Hence the time of the text's arrival cuts across the circle of its interpretation.

It might be objected that de Man undermines the argument made in "Promises" by failing to distinguish meaning from reference. Indeed, he deploys the two terms as if they were interchangeable, at one moment affirming that grammar works by suspending the *referential meaning* of the text, while at another instant insisting that the text overthrows the suspension of referential meaning by generating its own *referent* (269). Are "referential meaning" and "referent" equivalent concepts that may be substituted one for another without violence? Searle does not think so. He holds the two far apart by maintaining that meaning is what is known about an object, while the referent is the object itself. If "reference" is another term for "referential meaning," then perhaps what de Man is saying is that first a text establishes itself according to grammatical rules and afterwards gives itself a sense to convey to its reader. But if "referential meaning" is equivalent to "reference," then his argument is that first the machine of grammar builds a text and afterwards the text gives itself something to refer to. It would be sheer metaphysics, though, to draw a rigorous distinction between reference and meaning, for that would mean inscribing an absolute limit between a sensuous thing and the nonsensuous idea of that thing. What de Man gives us to think instead is that within the frame of the legal text the boundary between reference and meaning, the sensuous and nonsensuous, collapses altogether and they join in giving the world the uniquely textual gift of a thing previously unknown.

Begbie's judgment offers a telling example of the interplay that crosses sense with reference. He says the first version of the law is defective because it does not clearly define its terms, but this lack of sense is a problem only because it makes it impossible for the court to decide exactly what Parliament intended to ban. What matters in this case is not simply that the law fails to mean, but that its failure to mean brings on a loss of reference. As de Man might say, the statute of 1885 was, like every text, generated in the suspension of meaning. The law failed, though, because it did not overturn the suspension of meaning in which it was written and give itself a thing to refer to. No definition attached itself to "potlach" and "tamanawas" after they were cited in section 114, and without a definition they were powerless to identify the practices that were to be suppressed. In contrast, the revised statute of 1895 defines "potlatch" and "tamanawas" but does not mention them. Here meaning immediately overturns its suspension and fills in the lack of sense left over when the grammatical machine generated the text—which allows the revised statute to supply itself with reference by giving itself things to condemn.

The moment the law defines the potlatch, it is inevitable that missionaries and Indian agents will seek it out and put it on trial. If they cannot find a potlatch that conforms to their knowledge, they will warp what they do find until it bends to fit their understanding of what the law prohibits. The revised statute functions as a mechanical apparatus geared to the production of potlatches, and it manufactures them in order to control the people who are said to participate in them. Hence the legal text gives a gift that is both violent and *repeatable:* it offers its world a potlatch that can be produced and reproduced many times over. What allows the law to give this gift, moreover, is the temporal gap dividing the instant when the law is stated from the instant when it acts.

Toward the end of "Promises," de Man introduces a second set of concepts to supplement the notions of grammar, referential meaning, and reference that he has already put in play. Substituting one group of terms for another allows him to arrive at his general "definition of *text.*" "A text is defined," he says, "by the necessity of considering a statement, at the same time, as performative and constative" (270). It is the disjunction between these "two linguistic functions"—the performative and the constative—that makes it possible for the legal text to give what it prohibits.

It is customary to identify J. L. Austin as the author of the terms "performative" and "constative." Austin's theory of speech acts begins with a provisional distinction between constative utterances, which function as a mode of cognition, and performative utterances, which are a mode of action. In philosophy, constatives are traditionally called statements: they give voice to knowledge and have "the property of being true or false" (Austin 1963, 22). The utterances that Austin names performatives are those "in which to *say* something is to *do* something": in performatives, language itself acts on its world (1962, 12). The class of performatives includes such sentences as "I name this ship the *Queen Elizabeth*" or "I find the accused guilty." Performatives are strictly conventional acts because they are governed by a body of rules. Not just anyone can christen a ship or deliver a verdict before a court. The person who makes such utterances has been granted the authority to do so and has to make them in an appropriate context by following accepted procedures. When a performative utterance manages to do what it says it is doing, it is said to be "happy" or "successful" or "felicitous." If it misfires, or if the person who utters it does not obey the required conventions, then it is "unhappy" or "unsuccessful" or "infelicitous." Performatives, unlike constatives, are never true or false.

Yet Austin collapses the distinction between performatives and constatives almost as soon as he sets it up. He warns in lecture 5 of *How to Do Things with Words* (1962) that "in some ways there is a danger of our initial and tentative distinction between constative and performative breaking down"—even though he had only begun to draw that distinction in his four previous lectures (54). And it does break down. In lecture 11 he concedes that constatives and performatives are both ways of doing things with words (133) and therefore moves to situate the "doctrine of the performative / constative" in a general theory of speech acts (147). Every genuine speech act, he concludes, is at once a locutionary act, the performance of an act *of* saying something, and an illocutionary act, the performance of an act *in* saying something (98–99). It is true that every statement is a constative utterance, but to say "I state" is nevertheless to perform the act of stating, just as to say "I promise" is to state that one is promising. Every constative contains an element of performativity, and every performative includes an element of constatation.

While de Man acknowledges it is impossible to separate the performative and constative functions of language, he observes that the two "are not necessarily compatible," and their mutual incompatibility takes the form of a temporal delay. In law, for example, there is a lapse between the constative moment, when the legal text states what it prohibits, and its performative moment, when it acts on its knowledge and brings its prohibition down upon the accused. When a law is understood as a speech act, its structure proves to be similar to that of the promise. "All laws are future-oriented and prospective," says de Man, "their illocutionary mode is that of the *promise*." Like the promise, moreover, the legal text is divided in two. It announces its ban in the present—"every promise assumes a date at which the promise is made and without which it would have no validity"—but it pledges to enact that ban at some time in the future—"laws are promissory notes in which the present of the promise is always a past with regard to its realization" (1979, 273). Thus while the revised antipotlatch law came into effect on 22 July 1895, pledging to fulfill its prohibition at a later date, it was not enforced, and its promise was not realized, until February 1896 and after.

Since a law cannot be enforced until it has been written, its performative function lags behind its cognitive function in time. First the law states what it bans, and only later does it ban what it states. The moments of cognition and action cannot be so neatly separated, however, because the law does not know what it bans until the moment the ban is enforced. No one can be convicted for potlatching until a potlatch is known to have occurred, but a potlatch cannot be known to have occurred until someone is convicted of potlatching. The conviction occurs at the same time as the facts are established and the evidence verified. By an unavoidable paradox the law states what it knows *before* it is enacted but cannot know what it states *until* it is enacted. As de Man puts it, "[I]f a text does not act, it cannot state what it knows," but "as soon as a text knows what it states, it can only act deceptively, like the thieving lawmaker in the *Social Contract*" (1979, 270). The law against the potlatch learns what the potlatch is by sending potlatchers to jail, but it sends them to jail by first lying about what the potlatch is. The law "acts deceptively," setting up its own version of the potlatch, because potlatchers are sentenced not for taking part in the practice that they call the potlatch (or *pesa* or *yaokw*, and so forth) but for participating in the practice that has been named potlatch by police officers and Indian agents.

As grammar is a machine, so the law is a machine, and it produces what it forbids. It does not just enact a ban. It bans what it enacts. Between the moment it is formulated and the moment it is applied, the legal machine gives itself something to refer to. If the constative utterance states something ("A law is a promise") and the performative does something ("I promise a law"), then the gift-giving utterance does what it states, setting up its constatation as a real object in the world. To think the mechanics of the textual gift-event is therefore to dissolve the limit dividing a text from its world, meaning from reference, and to acknowledge that these seemingly opposing terms fold together and interact and do not hold themselves apart in separate spheres. It is to acknowledge that texts have the capacity to strike out at the world with all the force of a clenched fist. Moreover, the gift-bearing text does not represent the practices of "other" cultures to the West. It enables the West to give other cultures to itself. When deployed on Europe's westernmost limit such a text empowers the postal-colonial nation to appropriate itself violently, owning its own essence by seeking to rob the First Nations of theirs.[22]

## DESTROYING PROPERTY

When revised, section 114 forbids every conceivable circulation of goods and services, but when it is enforced, what it prevents are acts of pure expenditure. If as a constative utterance it states that it is a ban on exchange, as a performative it takes effect as a ban on waste. What the statute forbids, in the end, is the impossible itself. The distribution of property is a crime when what is given away does not invoke a return but, as Derrida argues, it is impossible to give a gift that brings nothing home to the giver. Such a gift cannot be given and remain a gift. For as soon as the giver or the recipient recognizes that a gift has passed between them, that gift enters the circle of exchange, and the giver receives—as a countergift—the knowledge of having given, of having acted with generosity, while the recipient owes the giver a debt of gratitude in return for what has been gained. A pure gift has to take place in an instant of absolute forgetting, an instant when the thing given conceals its status as a gift. Otherwise it earns a profit for the giver—and ceases to be a gift at all.

Section 114 says it prevents aboriginal people from participating in the circle of economy, but it acts to prohibit a gift-event that breaks with every economic circle. The law bans economy only to preserve it, forbids circulation to protect its unbroken curve from a crisis that would fracture it. Perhaps, then, Parliament outlawed the event of the gift not to "lift" the First Nations into the ranks of Euro-Canadian civilization but to protect Europe-in-Canada from itself. The law marks a refusal to tolerate the thought of a distribution that renounces every profit. It takes aim at practices that point beyond the circle of economic reasoning. Indeed, it is an attack against exteriority itself. The law works to suppress the possibility that there is an event of appropriation, an *es gibt*, that gives economy to itself but remains outside every economic circle. By banning the potlatch, Europe-in-Canada forbids itself to question its own limits.

### The Crime of Waste

Only a few weeks elapsed before the revised statute was put into force. The Anglican missionary at the Nisga'a village of Aiyansh, James B. McCullagh, had tried to prosecute "some Tamanawas dancers" in 1893, well before Parliament moved to define the crime they were accused of, but the Nisga'a had simply chased away the justice of the peace who was sent to summon the accused to trial. Though they refused to let the missionary remodel their lives according to his own design, McCullagh nevertheless remained determined to bring the potlatch to an end (Cole and Chaikin 1990, 46).

In August 1895 eight Nisga'a elders traveled from the Nass River down to Victoria, where they asked Vowell to "prevent clergymen and missionaries" from "interfering with" the "Potlach" in their communities. Their petition singles out McCullagh as the main source of complaint: "the Rev. J. A. McCullagh of Naas River has, we believe unduly interfered with Us in our holding or giving potlaches." In defending the "potlach," they underline that it is not a divisive war fought with property but a way of strengthening the social bonds that link their people together: "the holding of potlaches has been a custom prevalent among our people for many generations," they write, "and a method that we have of showing our good will toward one another, and we believe it is our right just as much as it is the right of our white brethn [*sic*] to make presents to each other" (NA, vol. 3628, file 6244-1, stamped 30 August 1895). The petitioners note too that "it is the opinion of many intelligent and good white men that the clergymens meddling in our affairs is very often uncalled for and creates a feeling against them among us." Just as the Cowichan people had blocked the enforcement of the first version of the law by rallying in support of Lohah's potlatch in 1885, the Nisga'a moved quickly now, barely a month after the revised statute had passed into law, to block McCullagh's private crusade to bring an end

*giving*

to their traditional practices. However, another group of white men sitting in the federal legislature had already relieved the Nisga'a of their "right to make presents."

Vowell referred the Nisga'a petition to Hayter Reed, who had replaced Vankoughnet as the deputy superintendent general of Indian affairs in 1893.[23] Reed instructed Vowell to remind missionaries working on the Nass "that the ability to retain the law must depend on the exercise of discretion with regard to its enforcement." The Nisga'a, like the Cowichan, had won their right to that supplement of potlatch which invariably exceeds Canada's project to put the practice to death. Indeed, the idea of "discretion" was to guide the department's management of the antipotlatch law for the next two decades. Since Reed considered it unwise to ban potlatching all at once, he advised Indian agents not to interfere in potlatches held for the repayment of debts. For his part, Vowell insisted there was no need to put the potlatch to death because it was already dying of natural causes. From 1895 until he resigned in 1910, his policy was that prosecuting potlatchers would only arouse the hostility of the First Nations while doing nothing to change their practices. The potlatch would succumb to the influence of Euro-Canadian civilization, he said, but it would die gradually and of its own accord. On those rare occasions when his agents tried to enforce the law, Vowell did little to support their efforts. It could perhaps be argued that he took steps to ensure their initiatives failed (NA, vol. 3628, file 6244-1, Vowell to deputy superintendent general of Indian affairs, 6 September 1895; Reed to Vowell, 18 September and 8 November 1895).

McCullagh pursued a more aggressive policy. Since he was both missionary and justice of the peace, he had three potlatchers arraigned before him at the Aiyansh Municipal Council in October 1895. But he did not send them to jail. He sentenced them instead to be confined to the village for two months and made their attendance at school compulsory. Early in 1896 he arrested four more people but released them after they posted $100 bonds and promised "to keep the peace for two years" (NA, vol. 3631, file 6244-G; vol. 3628, file 6244-1, McCullagh to Vowell, 1 February 1896; McCullagh's report, 1 February 1896).

In the Cowichan Agency, W. H. Lomas responded to the passing of the revised section 114 just as he had responded to the enactment of the 1885 statute. He let the

*giving*

local people hold a supplement of potlatch. While the "last gathering" of 1885 was given by Lohah, the last potlatch of 1895 was held by "Chief Jim Sil-kah-met" of Nanaimo. Lomas reports in a letter to Vowell that "the Nanaimo Indians assured me that this was the last gathering of the kind they wished to hold, [and] that the old man 'Jim' had been accumulating blankets for years, which according to custom of the natives have to be returned in public" (NA, vol. 3631, file 6244-G, 21 October 1895). Lomas notes elsewhere that most of the white people living in the Cowichan Agency are not opposed to the potlatch: "I can only say that the popular feeling in this part of the Province is that we have no moral right to interfere with these harmless Indian customs" (NA, vol. 3628, file 6244-1, 18 March 1896). Jim Sil-kah-met's potlatch was the "last" of its "kind," but it was nonetheless followed by a second "last gathering" on Kuper Island in the spring of 1896. Lomas informed Vowell later that this supplementary "last" potlatch lasted ten days and attracted fifteen hundred participants as well as a crowd of white spectators (NA, vol. 3628, file 6244-1, 30 April 1896).

Lomas's practice of allowing a supplement of potlatch to survive its own death had already attracted the criticism of Charles Montgomery Tate, a Methodist missionary laboring on southeastern Vancouver Island. On 17 October 1895 (NA, vol. 3628, file 6244-1) Tate wrote Vowell to complain that there was no justification for allowing a final potlatch for the repayment of debts, and he laid "a formal charge" against Lomas for refusing to enforce section 114. "The greatest kindness that can be shown to the Indians," he says, "is to 'Firmly & kindly' put the law into effect and say to them:—if you owe any debts, go and pay them as white men do." For Tate the potlatch is a system of loans repaid at interest, but it is inferior to the "white men's" system of credit because it leads to quarreling, drunkenness, neglect of the old and the infirm, and "immorality of the worst kind"—in a word, sex. It is also a waste. He claims the potlatch incites Native people to destroy their own property. It also depletes the resources of everyone working to "elevate" them. "It is an injustice to the Govt. and to the Missionary societies who are spending their money to make a better people of the Indians," he writes, "to have these demoralizing practices propagated, and that in the face of a law, which if enforced would speedily terminate all such proceedings." The potlatch earns a profit for people who have property owing to them but imposes a loss on everyone else—notably white missionaries and taxpayers. The potlatch is therefore a minor accumulation and an absolute expenditure, but above all it is a waste of white funds.[24]

When asked to defend himself, Lomas answered that his policy conformed to Vowell's recommendation "that great care should be taken in enforcing the [antipotlatch] provisions of the [Indian] act." Also, Lomas notes that Chief Constable Stewart of the provincial police agrees "it would be unwise to strictly enforce the law preventing these gatherings until something has been devised to take their place, as action of this kind must result in bringing about a bad feeling against the authorities, *particularly as the potlatch is dying out*, and there are only one or two to take place and the custom will be over" (NA, vol. 3631, file 6244-G, Lomas to Vowell, 21 October 1895; emphasis added). In November Reed praised Lomas and Vowell for pursuing a policy of "a gradual and discreet enforcement of the law for the suppression of the Potlach" (NA, vol. 3631, file 6244-G, Reed to Vowell, 8 November 1895). Meanwhile the opponents of the potlatch continued to urge that there would always be "one or two" more if the law went unenforced. They wanted the potlatch abolished because to them it was a source of excess—an activity that ceaselessly added itself to itself.

McCullagh joined Tate in condemning the potlatch as a celebration of loss on 1 February 1896 when he wrote Vowell to complain "very much" about "the seeming laissez faire policy of the Department." McCullagh's letter calls for the active suppression of the potlatch on the grounds that it is a useless expenditure of property and of time: "The potlatch takes up, *that is wastes*, nearly five months every year," he says (NA, vol. 3631, file 6244-G; emphasis added). He understands the circle of time as a circle of economy where every instant can be calculated either as a profit or as a loss. Measured against this circle, the potlatch proves to be a pure gift of time. "For the *old time* Indians it might be harmless enough," he admits, "but for the young men and women of *the present* generation it is the shortest and easiest way of going to the bad imaginable" (emphasis added). Time is a commodity that ought never to be wasted, yet it does not matter if the elders lose time because, for McCullagh, the "old time" that they inhabit has no value. It is necessary to protect "the present generation" from loss of time, however, because "the young men and women" belong to a temporal circle where "the present" ceaselessly resolves itself into debits and credits. The present is a currency that can purchase "the good" for the generation of the present and keep them from "the bad." If they spend the time of the present profitably, their reward will be their escape from the unprofitable "old time." But that is not all that stands to be won or lost.

According to Alfred Hall the potlatch is a waste not just of property and time but of women. Hall says in a letter to the *Victoria Daily Colonist* (11 March 1896) that he "desires" "to place before your readers a few facts with regard to the potlach [with one *t*]. . . . I emphasize the word *facts*," he continues, "and wish it to be understood that I am only referring to what I have observed on the north end of [Vancouver] Island, where I have lived seventeen years." But there is no reason to assume that Hall's "facts" correspond to the events they claim to describe.

He reports that young women from the Nimpkish village of Alert Bay have made a regular practice of traveling to Victoria to buy blankets for distribution in potlatches. "I once counted thirty-two women in one month who embarked by the steamers to bring back the coveted blankets," he says. What he suggests, without stating it openly, is that these women are making their purchases with money earned by prostitution. But if Native women are selling themselves, it is Native men who are spending the profits. Hall says it is a "fact" that many women have "sacrificed" themselves so that men can maintain their social prestige by acquiring and distributing property. "In my time about fifty women under 25 years of age have died," he alleges, "all of whom have been sacrificed to maintain the potlatch [now with two *ts*]. Girls that I have taught in school have returned only to be nursed and die." The only way to stop the sacrifice of women is to make a sacrifice of the potlatch itself: "Whenever a tribe ceased to potlatch," he argues, "the life of shame, which some of these women lead, practically cease [*sic*]." However, it was white Canada's determination to prevent the waste of property, not its concern to save time or to protect women, that led to the first prosecution under the antipotlatch law.

On the day after Christmas 1895 W. H. Barraclough, a Methodist missionary stationed at Sardis in the Fraser River valley, wrote Vowell concerning a Sto:lo man from the Tzeachten reserve who had recently performed a scandalous act of giving away. "Another of our Indians," says Barraclough, using the genitive to denote possession, "by the name of Bill Uslick, only a week or so ago Potlatched nearly everything he had away and to my knowledge he has a number of White Creditors who can now whistle for their money" (NA, vol. 3631, file 6244-G, 26 December 1895). Uslick's crime consisted of giving gifts at Christmas time, yet in describing the incident, Barraclough construes the potlatch as an absolute waste that leaves only poverty in its wake. "As long as the department permit[s] the Potlatch to continue," he warns, "we will always have indigent Indians." Ironically, Barraclough ends his letter with a complaint that white profiteers are charging the Sto:lo people inflated prices for drugs and medical care. "Many of the Indians who might not be classed as indigent," he notes, "are nevertheless unable to pay the high rates asked for medical attendance and the exorbitant charges of the drug stores" in the area around Chilliwack. Some stores are charging up to $24 for a "liniment" that costs less than $3 wholesale. But it is a Sto:lo man, not profiteering merchants, who will be sent to jail for allegedly creating poverty.

The Indian agent for the Fraser Agency shared Barraclough's understanding of the potlatch. In his report to Vowell, Frank Devlin agrees that "[t]he Indian mentioned by Mr. Barraclough, Bill Uslick is one of those Indians that is very hard to manage" because "[h]e still wishes to keep up the old habits and customs, and would like to be a leader among the Indians." Devlin identifies the "waste" of capital as the defining feature of Uslick's potlatch. "I am not aware that any human, or animal bodies, were mutilated or anything of that kind occurred," he says, but "[t]here certainly was a great waste." Uslick "practically left himself destitute," he says, "having given everything away that he had in the world." Devlin advises that putting Uslick in jail for "a couple of months" would have "a good effect" since it "would deter others from following his example" (NA, vol. 3628, file 6244-1, 18 January 1896).

Vowell instructed Devlin to proceed with the prosecution, noting that "the wanton destruction of property . . .

must be stopped in the interest of the Indians and of the Department which is labouring for their advancement" (NA, vol. 3628, file 6244-1, 22 January 1896). On 31 January Reed observed from Ottawa that if "Mr. Devlin is tolerably certain of securing a conviction it would I think be well to take proceedings against Uslick," but he qualifies his instructions by adding with his usual concern for "discretion" that Uslick need not be prosecuted if "he promises to obey the law in the future" (NA, vol. 3631, file 6244-G, Reed to Vowell, 31 January 1896). A day later Devlin arrested Uslick and arraigned him before a justice of the peace named Mellard. He was sentenced to two months in the provincial jail. Afterwards Devlin noted that the Sto:lo were visibly unimpressed by his attempt to make an example of Bill Uslick: "All the Indians in the District were at the Court, and with a very few exceptions feel that Uslick should not be interfered with for giving a Potlatch" (NA, vol. 3628, file 6244-1, Devlin to Vowell, 3 February 1896). They made a point of letting the Indian agent know that they had refused to be "deterred," and it would soon be seen that the accused was as determined as any of his supporters to continue potlatching.

The prosecution of Bill Uslick did not signal a shift in the department's policy of discreet enforcement of section 114. His conviction was an exception, not the rule. But it was not the only exception. After Alfred Hall's letter appeared in the *Victoria Daily Colonist*, Vowell wrote the agent in charge of the Kwawkewlth Agency, Reginald H. Pidcock, and suggested it was time to enforce the law. The Kwakwaka'wakw must learn, Vowell says, that "the law is not a mere shadow used to frighten them," though he repeats that "the very greatest discretion must be used to avoid raising a spirit of antagonism" among them (NA, vol. 3628, file 6244-1, 16 March 1896).

Sometime in January 1897 R. J. Walker, the Methodist missionary at Cape Mudge, arrived at school to find the Lekwiltok had taken their children to a potlatch at a village "fifty miles" away, and he asked Pidcock to arrest the "Chief" who had extended the invitation. Since Vowell had already told him to enforce the law, Pidcock issued a warrant for the arrest of Johnny Moon and "the Indian named Harry." A justice of the peace and two constables went to Salmon River to arrest the accused and to summon two witnesses to testify against them. The officers seized Johnny Moon and took him to Comox, but when they tried to arrest "Chief Harry," a group of villagers refused to let him go.

Vowell informed Reed that the incident had almost led to "serious trouble." It had also angered the provincial government. When Johnny Moon was brought to trial, the attorney general of British Columbia intervened to issue a stay of proceedings—and hinted that the accused had been unlawfully detained. Johnny Moon, it seems, had been arrested for assisting in a potlatch *before* the potlatch had actually occurred. Vowell later blamed the affair on Pidcock because he had failed to go to Salmon River to supervise the arrests, but clearly it was the Kwakwaka'-wakw who had convinced the department that they were ready, if necessary, to use force to keep the revised statute from being applied in their territory. They had also successfully pitted the province against the federal government (NA, vol. 3628, file 6244-1, Vowell to Reed, 12 and 16 January 1897; Vowell to Pidcock, 15 January 1897).

On 16 January (NA, vol. 3628, file 6244-1) Vowell distributed a circular to all the Indian agents in British Columbia, reminding them that "it is the desire of the Department in regard to the putting in force of Sec. 114 of the 'Indian Act' . . . that the greatest discretion be observed by the Indian Agents so that all possibilities of creating serious disturbance between the officers putting the law in force and the natives may be guarded against as far as can be reasonably avoided." Though the circular instructs agents to be careful when making arrests, it encourages them to "avoid" enforcing the law whenever possible: "when the Indians only meet together for a friendly and harmless interchange of kindly and social relations," says Vowell, "they should not be unduly interfered with." The sorts of "kindly and social relations" that are to be permitted include the distribution of blankets ("clothing") and the giving of feasts ("food"). Only absolute expenditures are to be stopped: "when on these occasions food and clothing is distributed amongst the aged and destitute of the people assembled, no property being destroyed or otherwise wasted, such proceedings on the part of the Indians should not be considered as coming within the purview of the Amendment to the Indian Act now under consideration." Reed approved these guidelines on 29 January 1897.

While the revised section 114 describes the potlatch as

135

*giving*

a crime of economy, Vowell's circular declares that the statute prohibits crimes of waste—especially destruction. The ban on the circulation of property has become a ban on gifts that do not return to sender. But Vowell had decided it would be better to persuade the First Nations to give up the potlatch than to enforce the law against it. There would not be another potlatch trial until 1914.

### Banking

The delivery of Vowell's circular does not mean, however, that the interpretation of the potlatch had ceased to overlap the idea of the gift with that of exchange. Just when the Indian affairs administration had finally stated that potlatching is a form of waste, not trade, Franz Boas announced his opposition to section 114 by arguing the potlatch is a form of trade rather than of waste. If Canadian law sent the potlatch toward the pole of the pure gift, the discipline of ethnography defended it by edging it toward the pole of investment.

On 6 March 1897 (xi–xii) the Victoria *Province* published an anonymous letter from an "enthusiastic natural scientist," Dr. Charles F. Newcombe (Rohner 1969, 201). Enclosed was a letter from Boas, dated 11 February 1897. Newcombe introduces Boas's text by emphasizing that Boas "is a recognised authority on the Indians of our coast and has for some years been employed by the 'British Association for the Advancement of Science' to study Indian traditions and customs." Boas is an expert on "Indians," and his text is based on fieldwork he conducted in British Columbia between 1888 and 1895—sponsored in part by the BAAS committee for the study of the First Nations of northwestern Canada.

His letter within a letter begins by alluding to the recent events at Salmon River. "With much regret," he writes, "I have seen in recent newspapers that the enforcement of the provincial law forbidding potlaches has led to serious disturbances among certain Indian tribes." He insists that the tension between the Kwakwaka'wakw and settler society has resulted from a white misunderstanding although, ironically, Boas himself mistakes section 114 of the Indian Act—passed by the federal parliament—for a "provincial law." "It might have been expected," he continues, "that the attempt to enforce such a law among tribes who still adhere to the old custom would lead to disaffection and discontent." Whites would not have aroused the First Nations' hostility, he adds, if they had interpreted the "potlach" correctly before deciding to ban it: "Unfortunately the meaning of the potlach has been much misunderstood by the whites; else, I believe, the attempt would not have been made to abolish it by law without making provision for the gradual transition of the old system to a new one." If Canadian officials would only bring their knowledge of the potlatch into correspondence with the potlatch itself— if they would only arrive, via the proper signs, at the truth about the potlatch—they would see that their policy is flawed and repeal the law.

For Boas section 114 points to a failure of reading. It is the sign of a white society's inability to comprehend the "meaning" of a social practice that, he says, is common to the First Nations of the Pacific Northwest. What he fails to consider, though, is that the antipotlatch law does not aim to reveal the facts about potlatches. It gives itself practices to correspond with and does not bring its knowledge into agreement with the acts the First Nations perform. The law is a machine that manufactures lies, for as de Man explains, "the incompatibility between the elaboration of the law"—the constative instant when it states what it knows—"and its application (or justice)"—the performative instant when it acts on its knowledge—"can only be bridged by an act of deceit." Acting deceptively, the antipotlatch law does not represent the truth but rather steals it away from its owners. "Justice is unjust," observes de Man; "no wonder that the language of justice is also the language of guilt" (1979, 269).

When Boas lends his signature to the discourse opposing the law, he tries to change government policy by denouncing the untruths that have been told about the potlatch and replacing them with the latest research, as if misunderstanding is obliged to melt away the moment it is brought into the white light of the truth. As if it is enough to "explain briefly what the potlach is" to have the law purged from the legal archive. Yet the law did not collapse when confronted with the facts, because the gift-giving utterances of the legal text escape the grasp of a metaphysics that understands truth as a correspondence traveling, via the sign, between knowledge and its object.

Boas was not alone in thinking that Indian administrators would repeal the law once they arrived at a correct

137

*giving*

understanding of the thing that "potlatch" refers to. The British Columbia Legislative Assembly passed a resolution on 14 April 1897 asking the dominion government to hold "an enquiry into the origin, nature, and meaning" of the potlatch "with a view, should it be ascertained that the grievance complained of [by 'the Indians'] is well founded, to the immediate repeal" of that part of the statute that "prohibits the said custom and will allow the Indians to enjoy such custom unmolested." The aim was to convince federal officials to take another look at the thing that has been banned in the hope they would find, as Boas predicted, that their first interpretation of the potlatch had been wrong.

By 1897 the new minister of the interior, Clifford Sifton, had removed Hayter Reed from the position of deputy superintendent general of Indian affairs and replaced him with James A. Smart, a "political ally." While Reed had personally dealt with the everyday details of departmental business, "under Smart, almost all letters went out over the signature of the departmental secretary," John D. McLean (Hall 1983, 122).[25] As far as the antipotlatch law was concerned, McLean tacitly endorsed the existing policy of placing discretion before enforcement.

When the resolution of the provincial legislature was forwarded to Ottawa, McLean asked Vowell to begin an inquiry, and he responded by confessing that he had never been a willing supporter of the law. "I have always been of the opinion," writes Vowell, "that the Indians as regards their social and friendly intercourse with each other should not be interfered with" (NA, vol. 3628, file 6244-1, 22 May 1897). In defense of his "opinion" he cites Boas's argument that the law is grounded in a misunderstanding. Says Vowell, "In the minds of many people, the term 'Potlach' conveys an idea of some vicious ceremony or performance whereas it is quite the contrary in many respects. . . . As evidence of this contention," he continues, "I inclose herewith a copy of a letter written by Dr. Boaz [*sic*], who for years has made it his business to learn as much as possible of the lives, habits and customs, etc. of the British Columbia Indians amongst whom he has travelled and lived for lengthened periods at different times." By having his letter published in the *Province* Boas had come as close as he ever would to winning a repeal of the law.

Boas returned to the coast in June 1897 to begin the

*giving*

first of two field trips he conducted for the Jesup North Pacific Expedition, sponsored by Morris K. Jesup, president of the board of trustees of the American Museum of Natural History. On 3 June he wrote home noting that the night before he had eaten dinner with Charles Newcombe "and a lawyer named Martin"—presumably Joseph Martin, then the attorney general of British Columbia. Superintendent Vowell was there too. "It was a very nice evening," Boas recalls. "Just imagine, the letter I wrote to Dr. Newcombe about the potlatches led to a bill [in fact a request] to cancel the law. I only hope that it will pass" (Rohner 1969, 201). Vowell appears to have shared that hope.

Vowell's letter to McLean (22 May 1897) suggests that Parliament delete the first clause of the statute—the one banning the giving away, paying, and giving back of property—yet retain the clause banning dances that involve the mutilation and wounding of people and animals. "As the law now stands," he writes,

> great hardship and injustice may be inflicted upon the Indians by a too strict enforcement of its provisions; and although owing to instructions guarding against such a contingency having been clearly given to the Indian Agents the latter are not likely to act so unadvisedly, yet [what follows is an allusion to the incident at Salmon River] there are unfortunately Justices of the Peace over whom the Department has no control scattered throughout the Province who are at any time either from ignorance, prejudice, or pressure brought to bear upon them by interested parties, capable by injudicious proceedings of creating serious trouble through which will spring up a feeling of antagonism in the breasts of the natives against the Indian Department and the Government.

In reply McLean asked Vowell to explain why he thought it "unnecessary to make any provisions against the giving away of articles at such festivals" when "missionaries and others" had made the distribution of property one of their "chief causes of complaint." Instead of defending his proposal Vowell withdrew it, suggesting that it might be best to "pause" before repealing the law—provided that it con-

139

*giving*

tinued to go unenforced. In January 1898, after soliciting reports on the "origin, meaning and nature" of the potlatch from Indian agents in British Columbia, the department advised the Privy Council to reject the province's request for an amendment to the Indian Act. The antipotlatch law remained in place though the department promised to continue to exercise "great care" and "discretion" in its handling of the potlatch (NA, vol. 3628, file 6244-1, McLean to Vowell, 31 May 1897; Vowell to deputy superintendent general, 1 June 1897; Clifford Sifton to governor general, 18 January 1898; Extract of a Report of the Committee of the Privy Council, 22 February 1898).

Boas's letter gave both the provincial government and the local Indian superintendent a chance to excuse themselves from their responsibility to enforce the law. But exactly what did he say in defense of the potlatch? His text affirms that the true interpretation of potlatching identifies it not as an act of waste but as a system of credit. "In all his undertakings the Indian relies on the help of his friends," Boas writes. "He *promises* to pay them for this help at a later date. If the help furnished consisted in valuables—which are measured by the Indians by blankets as we measure them by money—he *promises* to repay the amount so loaned with interest. The Indian has no system of writing, and, therefore, in order to give security to the transaction, it is performed publicly. The contracting of debts, on the one hand, and the paying of debts, on the other, is the potlach" (Boas 1897a, xi, emphasis added). The "potlach" is a substitute for writing. As Heidegger (1971, 97) notes, Western European metaphysics has always held that writing is itself a substitute for speech, while speech is a substitute for thoughts, and thoughts are substitutes for things. If writing is the act of replacing one system of signs with another, is not the substitute for writing itself a form of writing? A writing unique to cultures that have "no system of writing"?

In *Given Time* (1992b) Derrida provides his own commentary on this paragraph by Boas. The commentary unfolds while Derrida discusses Marcel Mauss's *Essai sur le don* (1990), for as it turns out, Mauss cites the whole of Boas's paragraph, as well as the one that follows it, in footnote 131 to chapter 2 of *Essai*. One might ask how Boas's letter to a weekly newspaper in late-nineteenth-century Victoria transmitted itself from there to Mauss and from

Mauss to Derrida. The answer is that Boas's letter had more than one destination from the very start. He not only sent it to Newcombe for publication in the *Province* but also grafted it to the end of his "Summary of the Work of the Committee in British Columbia," which was published in the 1898 annual report of the BAAS and brought his work for the association to a close. When Derrida quotes from this text, he is citing the citation of a citation: quoting Mauss quoting Boas quoting himself. Derrida's commentary marks the only occasion when his meditation on the gift entangles itself directly in the correspondence generated around the law against the potlatch.

What Derrida underlines in Mauss's citation of Boas is Boas's claim that the potlatch is a form of public record keeping that serves as a substitute for writing. In Derrida's analysis, the passage from Boas's letter, which is also a passage from Boas to Mauss and back, reveals "a certain relation shaping up between writing or its substitute (but what is a substitute for writing if not a writing?) and the process of the gift." Boas draws a link between the act of writing and the "process"—the event—of giving. To be precise, he suggests that it is the text in particular that gives the gift. But what sort of gift? Says Derrida, "The latter is perhaps not determined only as the content or the theme of a piece of writing—accounting, archive, memoirs, narrative, or poem [or law]—but already, in itself, as the marking of a trace." The gift is not to be found in the content or meaning that a text communicates. To think the gift is to ask what makes it possible to inscribe written traces at all: an inscription that as de Man insists, is purely mechanical and occurs in the suspension of meaning and reference. "The gift would always be the gift of a writing," Derrida continues, "a memory, a poem, or a narrative, in any case, the legacy of a text." The gift is "always" a textual gift. Hence "writing would not be the formal auxiliary, the external archive of the gift, as Boas suggests here, but 'something' that is tied to the very act of the gift, *act* in the sense both of the archive and the performative operation" (43–44).

The gift is an event that occurs in writing and contains two moments that cannot be separated one from another. First, there is the constative moment when the text records what it knows and files its knowledge away in an "archive." "The Indian Act," for example, is both a constative statement and an archival record stored among the Revised Statutes of Canada. Second, there is the "performative operation" in which the text gives itself meanings to convey and objects to refer to. For instance, the Indian Act "operates" in its performative mode when it reaches into people's lives and cultures to change them, deploying itself as an act of violence. While the constative function of language generates the legal text and donates it to the archive, the performative sets the law into play, allowing it to bring down its iron hand, clenched into a fist.

If, as Boas maintains, the potlatch is a means of inscribing events in the public memory, it is a mode of inscription patterned on the rhetorical model of the promise. Ironically, it shares this structure with the law that bans it. Boas says the potlatch is divided into two moments: the date of its enunciation and the "later date" of its fulfillment. One borrows blankets in the present and pledges to return them with interest sometime in the future, which means the distribution of property cannot be contained within a framework where time is calculated exclusively in terms of the present moment. The potlatch preserves itself only if the balance of payments remains deferred. Since the value of the debts owing far surpasses the value of the currency available to repay them, the system would collapse if all debts were to be repaid in an instant. So, once again, there must always be a supplement of potlatch to come.

> This economic system has developed to such an extent that the capital possessed by all the individuals of the tribe combined exceeds many times the actual amount of cash that exists. That is to say, the conditions are quite analogous to those prevailing in our community: if we want to call in all our outstanding debts, it is found that there is not, by any means, money enough in existence to pay them, and the result of an attempt of all the creditors to call in their loans results in a disastrous panic from which it takes the community a long time to recover. (Boas 1899, 681–82)

To defend the act of giving away, Boas folds the economy of the coastal First Nations into the vicinity of the "quite analogous" economy of "our community"—the white community—overlapping Europe-in-Canada with the very cultures it desires to keep apart from itself.

Indeed, he holds the First Nations so close to European Canada that they become a mirror where "we"—the European observer—find ourselves reflected back to ourselves, and as "we" gaze upon "our" image, moreover, "we" find that the potlatch serves two purposes "which we cannot but acknowledge as wise and worthy of praise." It allows people to pay their debts honestly, and it gives parents a means of guaranteeing the prosperity of their children. Because what is loaned has to be repaid to the lender or to the lender's family "after the lapse of several years," "the potlatch comes to be considered by the Indians as a means of insuring the well-being of their children if they should be left orphans while still young" (681–82).

In his 1897 letter, and the almost identical conclusion to the 1898 "Summary," Boas justifies potlatching by conflating it with the economic practices of what he calls "civilised communities." It was not the first time he had tried to whitewash the potlatch in order to save it. Boas had already interpreted the potlatch—in his "Second General Report on the Indians of British Columbia," published in the annual report of the BAAS for 1890—as a system of loans where people distribute presents that have to be returned later with interest. "The principle underlying the potlatch," he writes, "is that each man who has received a present becomes, to double the amount he received, the debtor of the giver" (588). But because he insists the system is "common" to all the First Nations of the northwest coast, he erases the differences between the various forms of potlatch by substituting a part for the whole, as if to describe one potlatch is somehow to describe them all.

Boas observes in the 1890 report that "[p]otlatches are celebrated at all important events," including marriages, funerals, and the taking of a name or a dance. They mark the end of a long series of preparations. "When a chief has to give a great potlatch to a neighbouring tribe," he says, "he announces his intention, and the tribe resolve in council when the festival is to be given." A messenger is sent to tell the guests that a gathering is planned, and when all is ready, another messenger invites them to come. They arrive "dress[ed] up at their nicest," and their canoes "pro-

143

giving

ceed to the [host's] village in grand procession." "The chief's son or daughter . . . attired in the dress and mask of the crest animal of the sept" meets the guests on the beach and performs a dance in their honor. Then they come ashore, making sure that the highest in rank are the first to disembark. The guests receive a few blankets as they land, and finally, "after a number of feasts have been given, the chief prepares for the potlatch, and under great ceremonies and dances [and songs], the blankets are distributed among the guests, each receiving according to his rank" (588). Boas argues that those who give away property in potlatches gain influence within their community yet know that what they have given will return to them when they are in need.

In the introduction to Boas's "Second General Report" (1891), Horatio Hale points out that Boas's research offers a compelling argument for repealing the antipotlatch law.[26] "We now perceive," writes Hale, "why the well-meant act of the local [sic] legislature, abolishing the custom of potlatch, aroused such strenuous opposition among the tribes in which this custom specially prevailed [Hale is alluding here to the first version of the law, quashed in 1889]. We may imagine the consternation which would be caused in England if the decree of a superior power should require that all benefit societies and loan companies should be suppressed, and that all deposits should remain the property of those who held them in trust." When Hale, like Boas, entangles the ethnography of the potlatch—"a custom which has been greatly misunderstood by strangers" (557)—in the battle against the law, he gives the discourse of northwest coast ethnography a decidedly polemical turn. This discourse has perhaps never sought to be purely "objective," disinterested, and free of a certain political investment.

The folding together of the First Nations' economies with the economic "conditions . . . prevailing in our community" recurs when Boas sets down his canonical (though not necessarily "correct") account of the potlatch in "The Social Organization and the Secret Societies of the Kwakiutl Indians" (1897b). Boas notes that it is based largely on material collected at Fort Rupert by himself and by his informant and coauthor George Hunt.[27] Their research focuses on the social practices of the Kwagiulth of Fort Rupert but also discusses certain practices of the

Kwakwala-speaking communities at Quatsino and Sey-mour Inlet. Following a well-established pattern, Boas uses the name of the people of Fort Rupert—the Kwagiulth or, as he puts it, the "Kwakiutl"—to refer to all Kwakwala-speaking people (Assu 1989, 16).

In "The Social Organization," as in the 1897 letter and 1898 "Summary," Boas (or should I say "Boas-Hunt" to acknowledge that the text has a corporate author?) prefaces the discussion of the potlatch by alleging that whites have so far failed to interpret it correctly. "This custom has been described often," he admits, "but it has been thoroughly misunderstood by most observers." He reaffirms that its "underlying principle is that of the interest-bearing investment of property" but no longer insists that potlatch investments are made for the sake of earning a profit (341). The distribution of property is instead "the method of acquiring rank" among the Kwakwaka'wakw and throughout the aboriginal communities of the northwest coast. He affirms at the same time, however, that rank cannot be acquired because it is inherited.

According to Boas (or Boas-Hunt), the people he calls "Kwakiutl" speak three different "subdialects" of a single language and are divided into a number of distinct "tribes." Every tribe comprises a number of "clans"—though Harry Assu (1989, 57) says the Kwakwala term for clan is *ṅamina*—and the members of every clan claim to have descended from a common ancestor, "who built his house at a certain place and whose descendants [still live] at that place." "[E]ach clan claims a certain rank and certain privileges which are based upon the descent and adventures of its ancestor" (Boas 1897b, 329–34).

But the clan is not the only unit of "Kwakiutl" society to claim inherited ranks and privileges. Clans are divided into a "limited number" of families, and the ancestors of each family have passed down names and other legacies to their descendants. "The ancestor of each of these families has a tradition of his own aside from the general clan tradition," says Boas, "and, owing to the possession of tradition . . . he has certain crests and privileges of his own" (338).

A complex system of inheritance determines how a family's inherited crests and privileges, and the names that go with them, pass from generation to generation. Boas says that when a man's daughter is married, he gives his inherited privileges to his son-in-law, who does not receive them for himself but holds them in trust for their rightful owners: his children. Boas adds that "[n]ames and all the privileges connected with them may be obtained, also, by killing the owner of the name, either in war or by murder" (335). No matter how these legacies are transmitted, though, "there is only one man at a time who personates the ancestor and who, consequently, has his rank and privileges [and names]." Anyone who acquires a rank through the permitted channels holds exclusive rights to it and can neither gain nor lose it by distributing property in potlatches. "The individuals personating the ancestors form the nobility of the tribe," he says and notes that "[t]he number of noblemen is therefore fixed" (338–39).

In Boas's narrative the potlatch is where people assume the names and privileges that they have inherited. It is a method of *claiming* rank, not acquiring it. The circulation of names and privileges begins at birth and culminates just before puberty. "The child when born is given the name of the place where it is born," he says, and once that child is "about a year old," "his father, mother, or some other relative, gives a paddle or a mat to each member of the clan and the child receives his second name." As "the boy" approaches the appropriate age for assuming his third name—about ten or twelve—"he is liberally assisted by his elders, particularly by the nobility of the tribe." They lend him blankets which he promises to give back a year or so later at 100 percent interest, and he makes the return payment the following June, "giving [blankets] proportionately to every member of the tribe, but a few more to the chief." Before a month has passed, the recipients return the returned blankets with interest to ensure that he "receives treble the amount he has given" (341–42).[28]

The youth is obliged to settle this debt in June of the next year. "Up to this time he is not allowed to take part in feasts," says Boas, though after he repays his creditors, "he may distribute property in order to obtain a potlatch name." In future potlatches he will sit in the seat formerly held by his father.

> After the boy has paid his debts, the chief calls all the older members of the tribe to a council, in which it is resolved that the boy is to receive

his father's seat. The chief sends his speaker to call the boy, and his clan go out in company with the speaker. The young man—for henceforth he will be counted among the men—dresses with a black headband and paints long vertical stripes, one on each side of his face, running down from the outer corners of the eyes. The stripes represent tears. He gives a number of blankets to his friends, who carry them into the house where the council is being held. The speaker enters first and announces the arrival. The young man follows, and after him enter his friends, carrying blankets. He remains standing in front of the fire, and the chief announces to him that he is to take his father's seat. Then the boy distributes his blankets among the other clans and sells some for food, with which a feast is prepared. His father gives up his seat and takes his place among the old men.

Once the "young man" assumes the inherited privilege of giving away property, his next task is to make his name heavy. Says Boas, "[T]he man's name acquires weight within the councils of the tribe and greater renown among the whole people, as he is able to distribute more and more property at each subsequent festival." It is especially important, he argues, for the "young man" to demonstrate his greatness by distributing more property than his peers do. "Boys of different clans are pitted against each other by their elders. . . . And as the boys strive against each other, so do the chiefs and the whole clans, and the one object of the Indian is to outdo his rival. Formerly feats of bravery counted as well as distributions of property, but nowadays, as the Indians say, 'rivals fight with property only' " (342–43).

It would be easy to conclude from "The Social Organization" that the privilege of inheriting names belongs exclusively to boys and men, since Boas tends to obscure the roles that girls and women play in the potlatch. However, George Hunt insists in his bilingual *Contributions to the Ethnology of the Kwakiutl* (Boas 1925) that women too hold potlatch names and exercise the privileges that go with them, including the office of giving away property. For example, Hunt notes that his own daughter-in-law assumed eight man's names in addition to her woman's name (65–69). It is questionable, though, whether a name can continue to be called a "man's name" when it belongs to a woman. Or does one cease to be a woman by claiming such a name?

"The Social Organization" lists a number of ways of waging war with property. The goal of every battle, however, is to break up the circle of economy. Potlatch rivals strive to give each other a pure gift that will interrupt the continuum where every present eventually returns to sender in the form of a counterpresent. The gift of rivalry is never supposed to return home. To start a battle, one rival gives the other a gift so massive that it is unlikely to be repaid with the required interest. Since the failure to repay strips weight from one's name, the rival enlists the help of his or her kin to return as much as, and preferably more than, what was received. But when one rival succeeds in shaming another by giving a gift that cannot be returned, the victor nevertheless receives a countergift of prestige, a supplement of "weight" added to his or her name, in compensation for what was spent. The war of property simultaneously breaks the circle of exchange and preserves it, because even a gift of rivalry is annulled the moment it sends something home to the giver. Boas's narrative has potlatch rivals give all by giving nothing at all and has each of them buy prestige at someone else's expense.

Boas says that one "method of rising in the social scale . . . by showing oneself superior to one's rival" is to give the rival a large number of blankets at a potlatch. A strict law dictates that the rival cannot refuse this gift and obliges him or her to return it later at 100 percent interest. One can also invite the rival and "his [or her] clan or tribe" to a festival called *dāpEntg·ala*. Here one gives the rival a pile of blankets, and the rival must not only place "an equal number of blankets on top of the pile" but return "the whole pile" later at 100 percent interest. If the rival fails to repay this amount, the challenger's name grows heavy (343).

Sometimes the challenger gives the rival a canoe, which the rival then fills with blankets amounting to half its value.

The challenger keeps these blankets, and at a later date the rival has to give another canoe in return "together with an adequate number of blankets as an 'anchor line' for the canoe." Here too the rival who fails to preserve the circle of gift and countergift suffers a loss of prestige (344).

"Still more complicated," says Boas, "is the purchase or the gift, however one chooses to term it [!], of a 'copper.' " As its name suggests, the " 'copper' " is a flat copper plate built around a T-shaped frame. Since coppers represent a large investment of blankets, Boas compares them to paper money, though unlike a banknote a copper gains value every time it changes hands.

> These coppers have the same function which bank notes of high denomination have with us. The actual value of the piece of copper is small, but it is made to represent a large number of blankets and can always be sold for blankets. The value is not arbitrarily set, but depends upon the amount of property given away in the festival at which the copper is sold. On the whole, the oftener a copper is sold the higher its value, as every new buyer tries to invest more blankets in it. Therefore the purchase of a copper also brings distinction, because it proves that the buyer is able to bring together a vast amount of property.

Coppers are always sold to rivals, often to a rival tribe, and the purchaser is under pressure to pay whatever price is asked for it. "If it is not accepted," adds Boas, "it is an acknowledgement that nobody in the tribe has money enough to buy it, and the name of the tribe or clan would consequently lose in weight. Therefore, if a man is willing to accept the offer, all the members of the tribe must assist him in this undertaking with loans of blankets" (344–45).

The sale is arranged long before the copper changes hands. Then at the appointed time the buyer gives the owner blankets worth about one-sixth of the copper's value. After the owner has loaned these blankets out and earned interest on them, he or she gives them back to the buyer along with an interest payment calculated at a rate of 100 percent. The copper is sold the next day. When the people have assembled, the buyer begins by offering "the lowest prices at which the copper was [previously] sold," while the owner's supporters demand higher prices until the buyer's bid matches the current price of the copper. The owner accepts this price but asks for boxes to put the blankets in, and after these are provided, more blankets are demanded as a "belt" "to adorn the owner of the copper." The next day, all the blankets that the owner has received for the copper are distributed "among his [or her] own tribe" (345).

Boas argues that, although the purchase of a copper is an important way of gaining prestige, "[t]he rivalry between chiefs and clans finds its strongest expression in the destruction of property." Sometimes, he claims, a "chief" burns blankets, canoes, and fish oil in public gatherings to show the people that his or her mind is "stronger" and power "greater" than that of a rival. "If the [rival] is not able to destroy an equal amount of property without much delay," he says, "his name is 'broken.' " The "vanquished" rival loses influence in the community, "while the name of the other chief gains correspondingly in renown." The destruction of property breaks the rival's name by breaking the economic circle where every present returns to the giver. To burn property, one gives a gift that never comes home: a gift of smoke. The act of incineration can only be "equaled"—if it is equaled at all—by a counterincineration. But the most effective way to break a rival's name is to break a copper: "Still more feared is the breaking of a valuable copper. A chief may break his copper and give the broken parts to his rival. If the latter wants to keep his prestige, he must break a copper of equal or higher value, and then return both his own broken copper and the fragments which he has received to his rival. The latter may then pay for the copper which he has thus received." Since to repay the gift of a broken copper by breaking a copper of one's own is to remain inside the circle of exchange, of gift and countergift, destruction and counterdestruction, Boas says the most honorable way to receive a broken copper is to destroy everything and give nothing back to the rival: "The chief to whom the fragments are given may, however, also break his copper and throw both into the sea. The Indians consider that by this act the attacked rival has shown himself superior to his aggressor, because the latter may have expected to receive the broken copper of his rival in return so that an actual loss would have been prevented." Broken coppers actually increase in value when they are riveted together and put back into circulation (353–54).

The paradox at work in "The Potlatch" chapter of "The Social Organization" is that Boas begins by insisting the "underlying principle" of the potlatch is the "interest-bearing investment of property" but ends by saying that it "finds its strongest expression" in the outright destruction of wealth. His text draws the idea of the potlatch apart from the idea of waste only to fold them together again. The Boas potlatch is at once a system of banking and a mode of absolute expenditure, for it helps the Kwakwaka'-wakw to accumulate capital while urging them to spend all they have.

Isabelle Schulte-Tenckhoff argues in *Potlatch: Conquête et invention* (1986, 120–26) that Boas's interpretation of the potlatch is not just a scientific project to understand a set of diverse and complex cultural practices but a highly political attempt to defend the British Columbia First Nations from the civilizing mission of the Christian churches and the white Canadian state. Boas described the potlatch as a system of interest-bearing investments to counter the missionaries and administrators who condemned it as a great waste, yet because anthropology has forgotten the historical context that frames his narrative, arguments deployed in a local conflict to *persuade* Canada to lift its ban on the waste of property have assumed the place of primary data in the archive of Western European knowledge. Boas's potlatch is therefore a rhetorical invention—or rather a textual gift—that has been elevated to the status of positive truth. However, his narrative of the potlatch did not succeed in liberating it from the specter of waste. Indeed, in trying to wrench the two apart, he succeeded only in tying them all the more tightly together.

## SACRIFICE

I have done nothing so far but go round in circles. The theory of the textual gift that I have elaborated to explain the machinations of the antipotlatch law is itself a residue of the debate that grew up around the potlatch in the late nineteenth century. To articulate a theory of a gift-event that breaks with every metaphysical circle—including the circles of time and of economy—is necessarily to take up a position along the circle of interpretation that has not ceased trying to decide whether the potlatch is a system of exchange or a mode of absolute waste. Marcel Mauss's *Essai sur le don* is one of the points on this circle. And it is during a commentary on Mauss's *Essai* that Derrida's meditation on the gift finds its own place along the same inevitable curve.

Mauss introduces his *Essai* (1990)—*The Gift* in English translation—as an inquiry into the "organization of contractual law" and the "system of total economic services" of "primitive" and "archaic" societies. He deploys the term "primitive society" to denote a non-Western, nonindustrialized social formation—the type of society Western European ethnography takes as the object of its fieldwork. The term "archaic society" points to Western European culture in its premodern forms—for example, ancient Rome. As for the "system of total economic services" (*le système des prestations économiques*), it includes every conceivable type of transaction, exchange, and contract that circulates between people living together in a given social organization. The system of total services is what Mauss calls a "total social fact" because it draws on the whole of a society and its institutions, such as the family, government, religion, law, morality, aesthetics, and economics (3, 78).

Mauss argues that in "primitive" and "archaic" societies people have "almost always" performed the exchange of economic services by giving each other gifts, but such exchanges occur between collectivities—"clans, tribes and families"—not between individuals. The types of "economic services" that circulate in gift-giving societies include wealth and property as well as "acts of politeness: banquets, rituals, military services, women, children, dances, festivals, and fairs." All gifts are obligatory but are given as if they were voluntary. According to Mauss the distribution of presents in so-called primitive societies proves that no social order is "devoid of economic markets," while the study of the gift reveals how markets functioned before the development of modern forms of law, contract, sale, and, especially, money. The morality and social organization underlying gift-driven markets survive in "our own societies" but are "hidden below the surface" where they constitute "one of the human foundations on which our societies are built" (3–5).

Since the study of a "total social fact" confronts the researcher with many "very complex themes" and a "multiplicity of social 'things' that are in a state of flux," Mauss limits his attention to "only one" problem raised by the inquiry into systems of total economic services. "What rule of legality and self-interest," he asks, "in societies of a backward or archaic type, compels the gift that has been received to be obligatorily reciprocated? What power resides in the object given that causes its recipient to pay it back?" (3). It is the gift itself that *obliges* the recipient to send something home to the giver.

The potlatch of the British Columbia First Nations displays the system of total services in its purest form—but also passes beyond it. While it is true the potlatch is a means of exchanging gifts, it nevertheless prefigures the modern European system of individual contracts and the circulation of money. Mauss, like Boas, and in part because of him, describes the potlatch as a system of "total services of an agonistic type." "[W]hat is noteworthy" about the "tribes" of the Pacific Northwest, he says, is that their legal and economic systems are based on "the principle of rivalry and hostility" (5–7). In *Essai* the potlatch continues to be construed as a war fought with property, resulting in acts of great destruction, though Mauss extends the meaning of "potlatch" to include exchanges practiced in many different parts of the world, particularly in Melanesia and Papua.

Mauss says that among the coastal First Nations the potlatch, like every "total social fact," encompasses juridical, religious, economic, familial, and aesthetic elements (38). What is more, the things distributed there possess an inner force that imposes "three obligations" on every participant: to give, to receive, and to reciprocate (43). Everyone in the potlatching society is obliged to give to others and to receive from them because every given thing has a soul that mingles with the soul of the giver (20). To accept a gift is to accept part of the giver's spiritual essence, and the soul of the thing requires the recipient to give something in return. The exchange of gifts dissolves the boundary between people and things: "by giving one is giving *oneself*, and if one gives *oneself*, it is because one 'owes' *one-*

*self*—one's person and one's goods—to others" (46). There is danger in failing to reciprocate, for the spirit of the thing desires to return home (12).

Mauss affirms that the existence of a system of obligatory gift exchange among non-Western peoples is evidence of an "eternal morality" common to all of humanity. The Western Europeans societies have largely forgotten it, however, because they have made people into "economic animal[s]" who value things only insofar as they serve their individual self-interest. Obsessed with themselves alone, Western Europeans neglect the interest of society as a whole, as a "total fact." Since the "brutish pursuit of individual ends is harmful to the ends and the peace of all," Mauss insists that the economic rationality based on the "calculation of individual needs" has to be balanced by public expenditures that benefit the entire social order. As in those societies Mauss deems "ancient" and "primitive," where the exchange of gifts puts an end to war, isolation, and social stagnation by forging alliances between different groups, so in modern Western European societies the renewal of gift exchange would create mutual obligations between different sectors of society and produce social harmony by initiating a return to group morality. The wealthy have an obligation to guarantee the "financial security" of the working classes whose labors produce value and profits, while the workers have to reciprocate by agreeing to work for their living instead of relying on the upper classes to support them through public assistance (66–86).

I have made this detour through *Essai* in order to circle back to Derrida, who offers this commentary on Mauss's "moral conclusions": "Mauss's discourse is oriented by an ethics and a politics that tend to valorize the generosity of the giving-being. They oppose a liberal socialism to the inhuman coldness of economism, of those two economisms that would be capitalist mercantilism *and* Marxist communism" (1992b, 44). Derrida does not take Mauss to task for his middle-of-the-road liberal socialism, however, but for his apparent failure to ask if it is even possible to speak of an *exchange* of gifts. When "Mauss is describing the potlatch," says Derrida, "[h]e speaks of it blithely as 'gifts exchanged.' But he never asks the question as to whether gifts can remain gifts once they are exchanged." We know that for Derrida the gift enacts the impossible itself: it is not a gift unless it is given to someone by someone else, but it cannot remain a gift if the two parties *perceive* that something has passed between them. The thought of the gift requires that it move from giver to recipient in an instant—which is not an instant in time—of absolute forgetting. It must burn away whatever traces it has left behind in the fields of perception and memory. Derrida insists that "Mauss does not worry enough about this incompatibility between gift and exchange or about the fact that an exchanged gift is only a tit for tat, that is, an annulment of the gift" (37).

What Derrida *forgets*, though, is that for Mauss the distinction between a gift, conceived as an event that brings nothing back to the giver, and an exchange, understood as a reciprocal circulation of goods and services between two or more parties, is a "fairly recent" development peculiar to Western European societies. In chapter 3 of *Essai* Mauss notes that "our civilizations, ever since the Semitic, Greek, and Roman civilizations, draw a strong distinction between obligations and services that are not given free, on the one hand, and gifts, on the other," but the "strong distinction" between gift and exchange—a distinction that structures the whole of Canada's discourse against the potlatch—is an accident of Western European history, not a universal logical necessity. And as if to contradict Derrida's criticism in advance, Mauss does not fail to pose a number of questions that deal directly with the problem of whether, as Derrida put it, "gifts can remain gifts once they are exchanged." "Yet are not such distinctions [such as that between gift and exchange] fairly recent in the legal systems of our great civilizations? Have these not gone through a previous phase in which they did not display such a cold, calculating mentality? Have they not in fact practised these customs of the gift that is exchanged, in which persons and things merge?" (47–48).

Derrida argues that it is precisely this merging of "persons and things," which endows the thing given with a portion of the giver's soul, that permits Mauss "to pass unnoticed over th[e] contradiction between gift and exchange [*de ne pas sentir entre le don et l'échange cette contradiction*]" (39). Yet Mauss makes it clear from the outset that his aim is to learn why in certain premodern and non-Western societies total services are exchanged not *as* gifts, but *as if* they were gifts.[29] Besides, for Mauss the mingling of persons and things belongs to a historical epoch that predates the strict and strictly Western European distinction between gift and exchange. What concerns him above all is that Western European societies have lost their former moral insight that the thing given possesses a force obliging its recipient to give something back to the giver after a lapse of time.

It is not necessary to linger on the disagreement between Mauss and Derrida. What matters is not whether Derrida's reading of Mauss is somehow true, but what their debate gives us to think. As Derrida notes, Mauss's claim that the gift is a mingling of persons and things leads him to posit the concept of the "term," a concept intimately bound up with the concept of the gift. By binding the gift to the term, moreover, Mauss suggests that the event of the gift cannot be thought outside of time and narrative, for what the term "term" denotes is precisely a delay in time, which is also a delay in writing (39). To explain how Mauss uses the term "term," Derrida cites a passage from *Essai*.

> [I]n every possible form of society it is in the nature of a gift to impose an obligatory time limit. By their very definition, a meal shared in common, a distribution of *kava*, or a talisman that one takes away, cannot be reciprocated immediately. Time is needed in order to perform any counter-service. The notion of a time limit is thus logically involved when there is question of returning visits, contracting marriages and alliances, establishing peace, attending games or regulated combats, celebrating alternative festivals, rendering ritual services of honour, or "displaying reciprocal respect." (Mauss 1990, 35–36)

The term, the difference in time that distinguishes the moment the gift is given from the deferred moment of its return, belongs to the very structure of the thing given. "Here is, it seems," says Derrida, "the most interesting idea, the great guiding thread of the *Gift:* For those who participate in the experience of gift and countergift, the requirement of restitution 'at term,' at the delayed 'due date,' the requirement of the circulatory difference *is inscribed in the thing itself* that is given or exchanged" (1992b,

40). Every gift is necessarily divided within itself. It is inscribed with the trace of a time for giving back, which is entirely other to the time for giving away. Moreover, the delay between these two times is what makes it possible to give credit: to loan out property which is to be returned at a future date.[30]

Since the thing given is an archive marked by two incompatible temporalities, it shares the principle of its structure with the legal text. A law is a text that arrives at least twice: once in the moment it is formulated and later in the moment it acts. Between these moments it gives itself something to act against. The gift given by the law therefore inhabits the term, the delay between two disjunctive instants, and since it occurs between them yet belongs to neither of them, the textual gift arrives in an instant that is not itself an instant in time.

Derrida argues that the term is what makes narrative possible, for narration occurs as a process of delay that holds together the past, present, and future of a story by keeping them apart. The term puts the space of a deferral between a narrative's temporal elements without overcoming their disjunction. "The thing as given thing, the given of the gift arrives, if it arrives," says Derrida, "only in narrative" (41). Since the gift-event happens between instants of narration, what every textual gift "demands" if it is to "give" a "thing" to the world is that it be able to "take its time," that it be able, in other words, to occupy the delay, the term between the past, present, and future of a narration. It is an act of writing that does not happen all at once. "The gift gives, demands, and takes time," observes Derrida; "[t]he thing gives, demands, or takes time. That is one of the reasons this thing of the gift will be linked to the—internal—necessity—of a certain narrative [*récit*] or of a certain poetics of narrative" (41).

When the gift occurs, it drains away the meaning of the narrative that delivers it into being because in the moment a text is generated it is stripped of its "referential meaning." Narrative gives itself to the world by suspending its ability to point either to an object or to what is known about an object, and the textual gift arrives when reference and meaning overturn their suspension by presenting themselves with knowledges to convey and objects to refer to.

Derrida traces a relation between the gift and the incineration of "referential meaning" while arguing that Mauss's theory of the gift makes his sociological narrative "go a little mad" at times. Here madness is described as a loss of sense. "The madness that insinuates itself even into Mauss's text," says Derrida, "is a certain excess of the gift": a mad excess that overflows and overwhelms both the word "gift" and the gift idea which that word tries to convey. "It goes so far perhaps as to burn up the very meaning of the gift; at the very least it threatens the presumed semantic unity that authorizes one to continue speaking of gift" (45). To write of the gift—a gift that always arrives, if it arrives, as the gift of a narration—is to reproduce the rupture in meaning that, according to de Man, governs the generation of every text. It is as if one can only write about an event that suspends the meaning of the text in a text whose meaning is itself suspended.

What I want to underline, though, is that in Derrida's commentary on Mauss, the madness that gnaws at the word "gift" can only be thought with reference to the potlatch and, in particular, to the potlatch understood as a destruction of property. Derrida says that Mauss's "language goes mad at the point where, in the potlatch, the process of the gift *gets carried away with itself* [*s'emporte lui-même*] and where, as Mauss comes to say, 'it is not even a question of giving and returning, but of destroying, so as not to want even to appear to desire repayment.' " While Mauss is usually careful to call a gift a gift (though he in fact speaks of exchanges that mimic gifts), there is a passage in *Essai*, what Derrida calls the "passage of madness," where Mauss begins to mix up the concept of the gift with the concept of sheer waste, pure expenditure— in short, the destruction of property. Says Derrida, "Whereas, in the preceding paragraphs, he has shown himself to be so scrupulous, so demanding with regard to the *name* gift and the necessity of calling a gift a gift [a necessity Mauss denies ten pages later], Mauss will begin to proliferate signs—to give signs, as one says—of a lexical uncertainty, as if his language were about to go a little mad one page after it had insisted so strenuously on keeping the meaning of gift for the gift." In the passage of madness "[t]he trembling of this [lexical] uncertainty affects the word 'gift' but also the word 'exchange' with which Mauss regularly associates it" (45–46).

There is an unfortunate tendency among Western European observers to classify the potlatch as an instance of madness. In 1879 Sproat denounced the " 'Patlach' " as a form of "mania." Similarly, Ruth Benedict argues in *Patterns of Culture* ([1934] 1961, 190–91) that the "object of all Kwakiutl enterprise was to show oneself superior to one's rivals," and she concludes that this mad collective will to "self-glorification" drove the Kwakwaka'wakw to make a virtue of megalomaniac paranoia. The missionaries and bureaucrats of nineteenth-century Canada made "potlatch" the name for a waste that surpassed the limits of Western reason, while Mauss says the struggle for prestige leads to acts of "mad extravagance" that contrast sharply with the "cold, calculating mentality" of modern Western European societies. And for Derrida, the gift destroyed in the mad act of giving is a figure for a certain nonreturn that afflicts language in general. I cite Derrida citing Mauss's long "passage of madness." The interpolations are Derrida's.

> No less important in these transactions of the Indians is the role played by honor. Nowhere is the individual prestige of a chief and that of his clan so closely linked to what is spent and to the meticulous repayment with interest of gifts that have been accepted, so as to transform those who have obligated you into the obligated ones. Consumption and destruction are here really without limits. In certain kinds of potlatch, one must expend all that one has, keeping nothing back. It is a competition to see who is the richest and also *the most madly* extravagant [le plus follement *dépensier;* emphasis added]. Everything is based upon the principles of antagonism and of rivalry. The political status of individuals in the brotherhoods and clans, and ranks of all kinds are gained in a "war of property," just as they are in real war, or through chance, inheritance, alliance, and marriage. Yet everything is conceived of as if it were a "struggle for wealth." Marriages for

159

*giving*

one's children and places in the brotherhoods are only won during the potlatch exchanged and returned. They are lost at the potlatch as they are lost in war, by gambling or in running and wrestling. In a certain number of cases, *it is not even a question of giving and returning, but of destroying, so as not to want even to appear to desire repayment* [emphasis added]. Whole boxes of olachen (candle-fish) oil or whale oil are burnt, as are houses and thousands of blankets. The most valuable copper objects are broken and thrown into the water, in order to crush and to "flatten" one's rival. In this way one not only promotes oneself, but also one's family, up the social scale. It is therefore a system of law and economics in which considerable wealth is constantly being expended and transferred. *One may, if one so desires, call these transfers by the name of exchange or even trade and sale; but* [emphasis added] such trade is noble, replete with etiquette and generosity. At least, when it is carried on in another spirit, with a view to immediate gain, it is the object of very marked scorn. (Derrida 1992b, 46–47, citing Mauss 1990, 37)

It seems the more Western European observers describe the potlatch the more extravagant their narratives become. Whereas in "The Social Organization" Boas reports that names and privileges are given "weight" through potlatching but are acquired either by inheritance or by killing their owner, Mauss assures his readers that political status and "ranks of all kinds" are "won" or "lost" in potlatches that take the form of outright battles for social position and where masses of property go up in smoke.

Derrida's commentary suggests that what burns itself up in Mauss's narrative about the burning of property is not just the word "gift" but "everything that claims to know what gift and non-gift *mean to say [veulent dire]*." A "lexical madness" is at work here, and it "manages to eat away at language itself." "There is always a moment," says Derrida, "when this madness begins to burn up the word or the meaning 'gift' itself and to disseminate without return its ashes as well as its terms or germs" (47). The "word or meaning 'gift' " incinerates itself because it draws too close to its opposites. But its opposites begin to burn at the same time. Mauss's "passage of madness" destroys the concept "gift" along with its contraries—"return," "exchange," "trade," and "sale"—by simultaneously making them say the same thing as "destruction" and, in particular, "destruction without return."

Derrida has already said that the madness that annuls the meaning of "gift" here is itself "a certain excess of the gift." It is the gift that gives the gift of madness. What is more, this gift, which for Derrida is always a gift of a narrative text, irrupts within a discourse that is already going on and reorganizes the relationship between that discourse and the things it describes. In giving a gift the text destroys its proper meaning, just as the coastal First Nations are said to destroy their own property without hope of receiving any wealth in "return." But just as—according to northwest coast ethnography—the destruction of property sends back a countergift of prestige to the person whose property is consumed, so the text that incinerates its own meaning never fails to give itself a countergift of meaning and of reference to replace what was lost in the fire.

Derrida's reading of Mauss folds the thought of the gift—"always" a gift of writing—into the vicinity of the potlatch understood as a sacrifice of wealth. But were they ever far apart? In "From Restricted to General Economy . . . ," an essay on Bataille, Derrida gives a proper name to the textual event in which a narrative incinerates its own meaning. That name is "potlatch." Here, as in *Given Time*, words raze themselves of sense when they participate in a discourse that indulges in excess, a discourse that gives too much and without limit: "the destruction of discourse is not simply an erasing neutralization," says Derrida. "It multiplies words, precipitates them one against the other, engulfs them too." Yet the event of textual "sacrifice" does not "multiply" words that have no meaning to begin with, nor does it incinerate words that have been stripped of the usual, indeed "classical" meanings that they once had: what is at stake is "[n]ot a reserve or a withdrawal, not the infinite murmur of a blank speech erasing the traces of classical discourse." Rather, the textual sacrifice makes

giving

words mean nothing by making them mean too much. It sets them on fire with a surplus of signifying energy, for it is "a kind of *potlatch of signs* that burns, consumes, and wastes words in a gay affirmation of death: *a sacrifice* and a challenge" (1978, 274, emphasis added).

## AT THE LIMIT, FIRE

I have argued that the gift makes a crease in the postal-colonial text and this crease in turn marks a limit where Europe folds back over everything that it locates at an absolute and unbreachable distance from itself. For Derrida the gift itself traces both a limit and a fold. It sets the very idea of Europe apart from its exterior while drawing them into an intimate proximity.

There is a passage in *Glas*—a text that declares that "what affords reading affords reading by citations" (1986, 168)—where the thought of the gift spans the two incommensurable sides of a limit that lies at the outermost edge of European history. Here Derrida construes the gift as a burnt offering, a "holocaust," that makes the history of Being possible without belonging to it.[31] The gift of the possibility of European history stands on the threshold of Europe, neither inside it nor outside it but both at once. Says Derrida, "[T]he process of the gift (before exchange), the process that is not a process but a holocaust [*holocauste*] a holocaust of the holocaust, *engages* the history of Being but does not belong to it" (242).

How can the self-immolating "process of the gift" touch on the history of Being without touching it? It is necessary to recall that for Heidegger (a *certain* Heidegger) the history of Europe happens as the recollection of the destining, or rather the *sending*, of Being to a humanity that is uniquely exposed to it. In "Letter on Humanism" (1977) he defines destining as an act of giving. Destining is a gift that Being gives to itself, of itself. Any thinking that inquires into Being is necessarily historical (or "historial" [*geschichtlich*]) because "[t]he happening of history occurs essentially as the destiny of the truth of Being and from it. Being comes to destiny in that It, Being, gives itself." The "historiality" of Being determines how beings deliver themselves to thought in each epoch (214–15). Being, insofar as it is historial, offers the West the very possibility of its history. But

Being gives being to historical events only by directing thought away from the event of the gift, which is why the gift generates the history of beings without participating in it. Being makes a gift of Western European history but does not "belong" to any given historical epoch.

Since Being is a postal principle that delivers beings to their history but is not a being itself—since it *is* not even though it sends the "is" to whatever is—Being *at once* gives itself and burns itself up. It initiates history but never arrives there. "The gift *is not*," says Derrida, "the holocaust *is not*; if at least *there is some such*." What Being gives occupies Europe's outermost limit, for the gift-event "engages" the circle of European history without belonging to it. The gift of Being gives onto a region—which is not a region of Being—that makes European history possible but is itself neither European nor historical. Such a gift lies simultaneously inside and outside of Europe's history, on its absolute edge.

The moment this limit offers itself to thought, however, it folds Europe together with the beyond of its own history: "But as soon as it [the gift] burns (the blaze is not a being)," says Derrida, "it must, burning itself, burn its action [*opération*] of burning and begin to be. This reflection (in both senses of the word) of the holocaust engages history, the dialectic of sense, ontology, the speculative" (1986, 242; Derrida is discussing Hegel's discussion of "God as Light" in the *Phenomenology of Spirit*). Although the gift that delivers things into Being *is not*, though it gives presence to present things only insofar as it burns up its own participation in history, nevertheless the "mad energy of a gift" leaves something of itself behind after it sacrifices itself. Otherwise there would be no gift. For a gift that gives nothing is no gift at all. And the residue of the gift must *be* even if the gift itself *is* not. Since the gift by definition leaves a legacy of itself in being, it finds a place for itself within the history that it sets going but at the same time escapes. The gift-event at once brings Europe into contact with the beyond of its history—a site that is exterior to the destining of Being but makes that destining possible—and allows the history of European Being to overlap its beyond by granting it a legacy that remains with it but *is* not. There is (*es gibt*) a constraint that makes European history overlap its ahistorical exterior, and "what this constriction pro-

163

vokes," moreover, "is perforce a counter-gift, an exchange, in the space of the debt" (1986, 242–43). Europe is indebted, indeed yoked, to its exterior because it is from there that it receives the possibility of its history.

The gift of Being is a pure gift, a gift without return, in that it gives Europe its history without giving it anything that would demand a countergift. But it is an exchange, a circulation of gift and countergift, in that it leaves a residue of itself behind in the history it gives to Europe, and a gift that leaves something of itself with its recipient— bestowing a legacy that creates a debt and obliges a countergift—annuls its status as gift and makes a place for itself on the circle of exchange. The gift of Being obliges a return as soon as Europe succeeds in interiorizing it, keeping close to a gift-event that, by definition, remains heterogeneous to the history it makes possible. The gift ceases to occupy the beyond of Europe as soon as it becomes the negative of Europe, becoming what Europe is not, its opposite, its outside, for Europe endlessly absorbs its contraries and holds them within itself, sublating them. If the gift is to remain wholly other to Europe, it must refuse to leave behind something of itself for Europe to swallow.

Derrida says that Being delivers beings into their own but burns itself up, giving the gift of ownness to things while setting fire to its own presence, a presence that would, if it did not burn away, be proper to Being itself. But the gift of Being inevitably burns up the burning that incinerates its participation in Being, and in burning this burning it begins to be. The gift is therefore both a destruction of the proper and a destruction of the destruction of the proper. It is a destruction of property. It is what Boas and Mauss, Bataille and Derrida call a "potlatch." And it haunts Derrida's meditation on the gift like a ghost.

Heidegger says that the inquiry into the truth of Being brings Western European metaphysics to an end by returning it to what it has forgotten since its beginning: the thought of Being. What Derrida suggests in *Glas,* though, is that to return to the thought of Being, a Being that makes a gift both of itself and of history, is to begin thinking the potlatch. Metaphysics reaches its outermost limit, finding its beginning in its end, on the northwest coast of North America. When it can go no farther west without giving way to the East, the West finds its truth reflected back to itself from a site that is said to be neither Western nor

Eastern. On this its westernmost rim, the West rediscovers the true meaning of its Being. The truth is that Being, which cannot be thought apart from the gift, is a fiery potlatch. In this way the British Columbia First Nations have been made to serve the ends of the West: they have given it its own paradoxical truth.

# EATING
EATING

*Then the wolves offered him the water of life and the death
bringer. He thought: "That is what I came for." WīLaqā'latit
knew his thoughts and gave them to him. Then he ordered the
wolves to devour Ya'xstaL. At once they tore him to pieces and
devoured him. They vomited the flesh, and when WīLaqā'latit
sprinkled it with the water of life, Ya'xstaL arose hale and
well. He had become exceedingly strong.*

FRANZ BOAS, "THE SOCIAL ORGANIZATION AND THE
SECRET SOCIETIES OF THE KWAKIUTL INDIANS"

## GIVING EATING

### Tamanalatch

As a constative utterance, section 114 of the Indian Act
prohibited "any Indian festival, dance or other ceremony
of which the giving away or paying or giving back of
money, goods or articles of any sort forms a part, or is a
feature," while as a performative it came into force as a
ban on the waste of property, of time, and of women. Yet
the statute also banned "any celebration or dance of which
the wounding or mutilation of the dead or living body of
any human being or animal forms a part or is a feature."
In 1885 the act had given the name " 'Tamanawas' " to
this second "celebration or dance" but left it undefined. If
the "potlatch" proved to be a crime of pure loss, what
manner of thing did " 'Tamanawas' " name? Israel Wood
Powell had described it as an orgy of cannibalism in 1881,
but by the first decade of the twentieth century white ad-

*Opposite:* "Friendly and peaceful citizens"? Israel Wood Powell re-
marked in 1874 that his task as Superintendent of Indian Affairs for
British Columbia was to assimilate the coastal First Nations into the
Canadian state by pursuing "a policy of kindness, attention, and
strict justice" (Canada, *Sessional Papers*, 1876, no. 9, p. 55).
Courtesy of The Field Museum, neg. no. 17527, Chicago.

ministrators were affirming that the " 'Tamanawas' " was in fact a kind of potlatch.

Since 1897 Indian agents and the North-West Mounted Police had used section 114 to discourage the First Nations of the prairies from performing "sun" and "thirst" dances (Titley 1986, 165–67). Secretary McLean informed Arthur Vowell at the end of January 1904 that the department was planning to amend the Indian Act to "further" curtail "the practice of dancing among Indians in Manitoba and the North West Territories," and he wanted to know whether or not "similar action" was needed in British Columbia. So he instructed Vowell to determine how the legislation had contributed to the "suppression of dancing" in British Columbia and asked the province's Indian agents to submit reports on the subject (NA, vol. 3629, file 6244-2, 27 January 1904). Most agents—including those from the Williams Lake, Kootenay, Cowichan, Kamloops-O'Kanagan, North West Coast, and Babine Agencies—answered that dancing was not a problem in their jurisdictions. Only three had anything to contribute to the department's inquiry.

R. C. McDonald had just taken charge of the Fraser Agency, and he based his report on the testimony of missionaries rather than his own observations. He advised the department to find a new, less "simple" word for tamanawas dances because, "although these gatherings now go by the simple name of dances, they are nevertheless similar in many respects to what was formerly called potlatches" (NA, vol. 3629, file 6244-2, McDonald to Vowell, 12 February, 21 March 1904).

A. W. Neill's report from the West Coast Agency also stresses the difficulty of attaching names to the objects of ethnography. He warns that "the word 'potlach' must be interpreted with caution" since its field of reference ranges "from what a white man might call an invitation to dinner up to a frenzied carouse leaving the hosts *absolutely* penniless" (NA, vol. 3629, file 6244-2, Neill to Vowell, 12 February 1904, emphasis added). According to Neill, "Potlach" points to the tamanawas dance as well as feasts and "absolute" expenditures. "The subject [of 'Indian dancing'] can not be adequately discussed," he writes, "without considering also the question of 'potlaches' with which it is almost inseparably connected." "Section 114 constitutes two offenses, the potlach—and the tamanawas dance," which are really two parts of a larger whole. Neill adds that on the west coast of Vancouver Island it is incorrect to call a tamanawas a "tamanawas" since the Nuu'chah'nulth have their own name for their winter dance: "what passes here as [the] equivalent [of the tamanawas], is called—the Clokwana or wolf dance." It always includes a potlatch, he explains, but not every potlatch is accompanied by a "wolf dance." And while he admits the dance-potlatch used to have "objectionable features"—children were kidnapped, people gnawed on disembowelled dogs, men were hung up by their skin—he insists it has been "innocent" of them since the arrival of settler society. The only remaining problem, for Neill, is that of waste—specifically the waste of time—and he advises the department to keep the antidance statute on the books because "its moral influence is considerable." But he recommends that it should not be enforced.

George Ward DeBeck had taken over the Kwawkewlth Agency in 1902. He does not mention the "tamanawas" in his report but instead notes that in Kwakwala the correct name for the outlawed dance is "Ha-mat-sa." The "only objectionable dance practised by these Indians, that I know of," he writes, "is what is known as the Ha-mat-sa or Cedar Bark dance," and "this dance, like all the others practiced by them, is not a ceremony of itself, but belongs to and is a part of the potlatch" (NA, vol. 3629, file 6244-2, 19 February 1904). To be precise, the relation of potlatch to Ha-mat-sa is like that of center to margin—"the potlatch being the center or body, and the dances, feasts, etc, are what one might call the trimmings"—though it "is impossible to separate one from the other." Among the Kwakwak̲a'wakw the practices banned in section 114 are two moments of a single process: the tamanawas is the Ha-mat-sa, and the Ha-mat-sa is the potlatch. Or rather, the Ha-mat-sa is a prosthesis strapped to the "body" of the potlatch, just as in these agents' reports words are prostheses repeatedly tied and retied to things in a search for the name that fits.

DeBeck had been preparing to suppress the potlatch, with all its trimmings, since the summer of 1903 when he consulted a Vancouver lawyer about "the exact legal procedure" for enforcing section 114 (NA, vol. 3629, file 6244-2, DeBeck to William MacLaughlin, 20 July 1903; MacLaughlin to McLean, 21 July, 5 August 1903).[1] Then on 24 December the *Victoria Daily Times* published an inflammatory article about a "Ha-Matsa Dance" being held at the Koskimo Reservation. Though the article passes itself off as "news," it is actually a summary of ethnographic data drawn from Boas's "The Social Organization and the Secret Societies of the Kwakiutl Indians"—particularly from chapter 10, which describes the initiation of a Koskimo "Ha-Matsa" in the winter of 1895. The article says the "Ha-Matsa" dance is "a cannibalistic rite" and claims that the "Ha-Matsa" dancer routinely bites members of the audience, tearing "mouthfuls of flesh" from their arms. Four days after this citation of Boas was published as news, Vowell called DeBeck's attention to the story and told him that "[s]hould it be the case that the Indian medicine man actually bit the arms, etc., of other Indians and that he also indulged in cannabalistic performances . . . the ringleaders should be punished" (NA, vol. 3629, file 6244-2, 28 December 1903). Curiously, although he ordered DeBeck to enforce the law, before long Vowell began encouraging him to disobey his instructions.[2] Whenever DeBeck took measures to suppress the potlatch over the next two years, Vowell accused him of incompetence and complained to Ottawa about his lack of discretion. He undermined DeBeck's antipotlatch campaign just as he had undermined Pidcock's efforts in the late 1890s, an effort that Vowell had also set in motion (NA, vol. 3629, file 6244-2, Vowell to DeBeck, 8 January 1904; Vowell to Deputy Superintendent Frank Pedley, 30 January 1904; Vowell to McLean, 19 March, 5 April, 30 May 1904).

DeBeck's only concerted action came in April 1904 when, with the help of a police officer and a special constable, he intervened in a gathering at Fort Rupert. Instead of making arrests under section 114 of the Indian Act, however, he fined five people under section 22, a statute restricting the movement of aboriginal people between reserves, but because he had not used the antipotlatch statute against them, the Kwagiulth rightly concluded that they had beaten the law, and they went on potlatching. When DeBeck tried to break up large potlatches again in the fall of 1904 and in the summer of 1905, he received little support from either the department or the provincial government. He resigned in April 1906, and in July of that year Parliament passed a consolidated Indian act that relocated section 114 to section 149 (NA, vol. 3629, file 6244-2, DeBeck to Vowell, 17 April 1904; Extract from De-Beck's Report for April 1904).

After 1906 the discourse against the potlatch focused with renewed intensity on the social practices of the Kwa-kwaka'wakw, the people Boas had identified in the 1880s as the absolute others of Europe. What is more, Boas's "Social Organization" had somehow become entangled in the public debate over the Ha-Matsa-potlatch, making a chance irruption within an ongoing discourse when a newspaper recited his narrative as if it were the record of a recent event. But what aspect of his narrative allowed a newspaper's unacknowledged citation of him to set off another clumsy attempt to enforce the law against giving and dancing? It is in this text, above all, that Boas deploys the full weight of his reputation as "a recognized author-ity" on northwest coast anthropology to affirm that hā'-mats'a dancers are ceremonial cannibals. Yet, obeying the movement of the fold, his text withdraws this affirmation in the very act of giving it.

### Secret Societies

In "The Social Organization" (1897b) Boas states that the hā'mats'a dance, as practiced by the Kwagiulth of Fort Rupert, cannot be understood without reference to their system of marriage. "Marriage among the Kwakiutl must be considered a purchase," he writes, "which is conducted on the same principles as the purchase of a copper"—an interpretation that Indian affairs officials would soon come to share. Boas portrays the Kwagiulth woman as a com-modity that her family sells in marriage to the man of their choice. However, the purchase money that the groom pays to his wife's family buys him not only a bride "but also the right of membership in her clan for the future children of the couple." Since clan privileges pass from their owner, through his or her son-in-law, to the son-in-law's children, marriage is the primary means of reproducing the Kwagi-ulth social organization (358–59).

When a marriage is arranged and the purchase money paid, the woman's family agrees to return this investment to their son-in-law, with interest, at a future date. "The wife is given to him as a first installment of the return pay-ment," says Boas, whereas "[t]he crest of the clan, its privi-

171

leges, and a considerable amount of other property besides, are given later on, when the couple have children, and the rate of interest is the higher the greater the number of children" (359). The bride is free to leave her husband after her family repays the "purchase money." She is also free to stay. What Boas fails to consider, though, is that since the man pays for his partner on the condition that he is to be paid back later with interest, it could be said that the woman's family buys her a husband instead of selling him a wife.

During the return of the purchase money, the father-in-law gives the son-in-law clan privileges as well as the right to belong to certain "secret societies" that are watched over by "guardian spirits" endowed with "supernatural powers," though the son-in-law acquires this right for his children and not for himself. Boas asserts that "the acquisition of a guardian spirit" is an "idea" that has "attained its strongest development in America." "Every young man endeavours to find a protector of this kind," he says, and "to gain their help, the youth must prepare himself by fasting and washing, because only the pure find favour with them, while they kill the impure." The First Nations of the northwest coast are unique in North America, says Boas, in that their young people inherit a "protector" and do not find one on their own (393).

Every clan possesses stories that recall how its ancestor first encountered a guardian spirit. In these stories the spirit gives the ancestor a special power, such as a magic harpoon for hunting sea otter, along with "a dance, a song, and cries which are peculiar to the spirit." Such stories are not fictions, though, because they describe a guardian spirit who remains "in constant contact" with the ancestor's living descendants. To dance is therefore to relive an ancestor's encounter with one's own guardian. "In these dances he personates the spirit. He wears his mask and his ornaments. Thus the dance must be considered a dramatic performance of the myth relating to the acquisition of the spirit, and shows to the people that the performer by his visit to the spirit has obtained his powers and desires. When nowadays a spirit appears to a young Indian, he gives him the same dance, and the youth also returns from the initiation filled with the powers and the desires of the spirit" (396). The spirit also gives the novice a name, and according to Boas "each name of the nobility has a separate tradition of the acquisition of supernatural powers."

Though to acquire a guardian spirit is to inherit an ancestor's name, that name is to be used "only during the time when the spirits dwell among the Indians—that is, in winter," when "all the summer names are dropped, and the members of the nobility [what might be termed the name-bearing class] take their winter names." The transition from "summer" to "winter" names transforms the whole social organization: "Instead of being grouped in clans," says Boas, "the Indians are now grouped according to the spirits which have initiated them. . . . The period when the clan system is in force is called bā'xus," he adds, "which term also designates those who have not been initiated by any spirit, and might be translated 'profane.' " The winter period "is called ts'ē'ts'aēqa, the secrets," though there are other words for it. Each winter name has a fixed place within a secret society, and each society is made up of "a limited number of names" (418).

Boas argues that the Kwagiulth have two groups of secret societies: the seals, or mē'ēmqoat, and the quē'qutsa. The seal societies consist of winter name-holders who are "possessed" by guardian spirits, while the quē'qutsa "embrace those individuals who, for the time being, are not possessed by the spirits," often because they have transferred their seal names to younger relatives. The seals are divided into two groups: the la'xsâ and the wī'xsâ. The la'xsâ are the highest in rank and have been initiated by the guardian spirit BaxbakuālanuXsī'waē: they have "gone through [his] house" and "learned all his secrets." In contrast the wī'xsâ have "leaned against [the] walls" of his house but have not gone through it (420). Though Boas says here that "every young man" seeks a guardian spirit, he notes elsewhere that at least two la'xsâ societies—the Ha'mshamtsEs and the K·î'nqalaLala—are made up almost exclusively of women (438, 463).

The hā'mats'a are the highest ranking la'xsâ at Fort Rupert. They are initiated by BaxbakuālanuXsī'waē, and during their initiation, they are "possessed of the violent desire of eating men" (437). Their desire mirrors his desire, moreover, for BaxbakuālanuXsī'waē is "a cannibal living on the mountains who is always in pursuit of man." He has several helpers. They include "his servant (or wife)" Qʼō′minōqas, "who procures food for him"; his "female slave" K·î′nqalaLala, who catches people and gathers corpses for him; his slave Qoā′xqoāxualanuXsīwaē, a raven who eats the eyes of his victims; the hō′Xhōkᵘ, a "fabulous bird . . . which lives on the brains of men"; and the cannibal grizzly bear Nā′nēs BaxbakuālanuXsī′waē, "who delights in killing people with his strong paws" (394–95).

Boas names the rite of initiation into a "secret society" the "winter ceremonial." Its goal is "to bring back the youth who is supposed to stay with the supernatural being who is the protector of his society, and then, when he has returned in a state of ecstasy, to exorcise the spirit which possesses him and to restore him from his holy madness." The ceremonial "generally" coincides with the refund of the marriage-purchase money, for it is here that the father-in-law gives his seat in one of the secret societies to one of his son-in-law's children. To become eligible for a name in the hā′matsʼa society, the child must first pass through each of the lower societies. Then the youth's father invites three leading elders to his house and announces that he wants to make his child a hā′matsʼa. The elders determine whether or not the father can afford the ceremony, which is "exceedingly expensive." If he passes this test, he calls "all the chiefs of the tribe" to a meeting to be held in four days. Here the three elders tell the "young chiefs" about the planned initiation, and the father of the novice informs his father-in-law that "he desires to have the blankets which he paid for his wife returned, and that he wants to have the box containing his father-in-law's dance" (500–1). The box contains dance regalia, such as whistles and ornaments of red cedar bark (518). Four days later the three elders call the people together and ask them to prepare for the initiation. Four days later still the novice vanishes and is heard in the woods crying "hāp, hāp, hāp"—"eating, eating, eating"—the sound of the cannibal spirit, which means

*[8 November 1886]*
*This evening I went to*
*the settlement of*
*Cowichan, which is in*
*front of my house. . . .*
*There is supposed to*
*be an old cemetery up*
*here. I shall go there*
*tomorrow and try to*
*get some skulls.*
*[Rohner 1969, 55]*

174

*eating*

BaxbakuālanuXsī'waē has taken the youth to his house for initiation into the cannibal ceremonies. In four days the people will stop using their summer names and prepare to bring the novice home (503).

When the four days have passed, the father of the novice distributes ornaments of red cedar bark among the people and gives a number of feasts. Meanwhile the father-in-law calls in his debts and amasses his property, "principally food, blankets, boxes, dishes, spoons, kettles, bracelets, coppers, and box lids" (518). Then he repays the purchase money to his son-in-law. After receiving his father-in-law's winter dance and name, the son-in-law announces that he will bring his son or daughter back from the woods in four days. As the return of the novice unfolds, he will give away everything he has just received from his father-in-law (504–20).

*[15 November 1886] Today I found something worthwhile: a very old, well-preserved skull. I discovered it in the mound I spoke of yesterday. I hope to find more tomorrow. [60]*

In Boas's narrative the return and taming of the novice takes four days. First the people bring the novice home from the woods by performing a carefully selected sequence of dances and songs. Then the novice is "tamed" by women who dance for her or him and by singers who perform songs composed especially for the occasion. The ceremony ends with the "purification" of the new hā'-mats'a (431).

Why make this second detour through "The Social Organization"? It leads us back to the question of cannibalism, which has haunted this book from the outset, and draws attention once more to the mechanics of the textual gift. It also makes it possible to ask who, in the context of Canadian postal-colonialism, are the true cannibals—the Kwagiulth or the Euro-Canadian colonizers?

To grapple with these questions, it is necessary to examine how Boas's account of the cannibal dance transforms itself each time it is repeated. For the differences that irrupt when the same scenes recur in different contexts confirm that, as Derrida has predicted, the textual gift arrives between the instants of a given narrative. In chapter 8, for example, the novice who is "possessed" by the cannibal

175

*eating*

spirit is said to have a violent craving for human flesh. After returning to the dancing house, she or he "bites pieces of flesh out of the arms and chests of the people." "In olden times," adds Boas, "when the hā′mats'a was in a state of ecstasy, slaves were killed for him, whom he devoured." One informant confides that "it is exceedingly hard to eat fresh human flesh, much more so than to eat dried corpses" (438–40). After the initiation, new hā′mats'as observe a number of rituals to cleanse their bodies, which have allegedly consumed human flesh, and they give blankets to anyone they have bitten or whose slaves they have killed (443).

*[6 June 1988]*
*Mr. Hastings, the photographer, came to show me a place where there are Indian skulls. We took a boat and went out. . . . We discovered that someone had stolen all the skulls, but we found a complete skeleton without head. [88]*

At these instants, which occur in a cluster, Boas's narrative clearly states that the hā′mats'a is an authentic cannibal. Yet the text withdraws that thesis just a few paragraphs later. "Nowadays," writes Boas, "when the ceremonies have lost much of their former cruelty, *they do not actually bite* the piece of flesh out of the arm, but merely pull the skin up with their teeth, sucking hard so as to remove as much blood as possible, and then with a small sharp knife cut off secretly a piece of skin" which is returned to its owner afterwards (440–41, emphasis added). But what if both the hā′mats'a's former and present "cruelty" is a gift that Boas's text has given to the archive of Western European ethnography?

*[6 June 1888] It is most unpleasant work to steal bones from a grave, but what is the use, someone has to do it. [88]*

When Boas describes other dances, he emphasizes that every apparent act of violence is a carefully staged piece of theater. For instance, there is a *t'ō′X'uît* dancer, "almost always" a woman, who openly "invite[s] the people to kill" her as she dances (487, 489). An attendant "will appear to drive a wedge through her head from one temple to the other" but, as the use of the phrase "will appear" suggests, this murder is pure artifice. "The wedge is first shown to the people and then *secretly exchanged* for another one, which consists of two parts attached to a wooden band that is slipped over her head and covered

*eating*

with hair." A good deal of fake gore accompanies the feigned murder: "bladders containing blood, which are attached to the band, are burst, and the blood is seen to flow down her face." The blood "is seen" to be blood from the onlooker's point of view, but for the dancer it is a stage prop. Curiously, even as the text calls attention to the illusions woven by the t'ō'X'uît dancer, it stubbornly resists admitting that she is capable of artifice. At one point, the text simultaneously affirms that she "bites her cheeks" to produce blood, and that she releases artificial blood without biting herself at all: "She also bites her cheeks *or* bursts a small bag containing blood which she holds in her mouth, so that it flows out of her mouth" (489, emphasis added). Her blood is said to be real even while it is shown to be staged.

*[1 December 1894]*
*The Hamatsa danced toward the new Q'ominō'qa, who was covered all over with blood. She was surrounded by all the other Q'ominō'qa, who danced for her. . . . Unfortunately George was not here, so I did not know what was going on— especially when the new Q'ominō'qa danced with skulls in her hand. The Hamatsa danced ahead of her, and after a while took the skulls out of her hand and put them down after he had licked them and eaten the [something like maggots?]. The people were afraid to let me see this. [188]*

Why is it that when the hā'mats'a dancers bite someone, the blood they draw is declared to be real rather than artificial? If the text can admit, albeit not without contradiction, that the t'ō'X'uît is highly trained in theatrical techniques, why does it deny the same possibility to the hā'mats'a? The answer is that "The Social Organization" is governed by a pattern of give and take and, like a cannibal, the text posits a thesis only to swallow it again. It simultaneously places scenes before the reader and withdraws them from view, folding the ideas "hā'mats'a" and "cannibal" together in the act of drawing them apart.

As soon as Boas has affirmed that "nowadays" the hā'mats'as of Fort Rupert no longer practice real acts of cruelty, his discourse turns round and states the opposite, declaring instead that cannibalism plays a role in every initiation. "When a new hā'mats'a, after being initiated, returns from the woods," he writes, "he will sometimes

177

*eating*

carry a corpse, which is eaten after his dance. . . . The hā′mats′a must use for this ceremony the corpse of one of his deceased relatives." But the hā′mats′a never eats alone. His K·î′nqalaLala comes out of the woods with him. She too is a relative, and because her task is to procure food for the hā′mats′a, she carries the corpse that is to be devoured (441–42).

*[1 December 1894]*
*Today is packing day.*
*. . . George and I went*
*out to get some skulls.*
*An Indian came our*
*way, however, so we*
*could not do much. I*
*tried again in the*
*afternoon, but this*
*time a Hamatsa came*
*and I had to give up.*
*[189]*

After saying that the novice returns with a corpse, though, Boas describes the two dances that the same novice performs in the dancing house. "The first dance *represents* him as looking for human flesh to eat." Here the hā′mats′a acts *as if* he were a cannibal but not *as* a cannibal. Says Boas, "[H]is head is lifted up, *as though* he was looking for a body that was being held high up in front of him" by the corpse-bearing K·î′nqalaLala. Yet there is no body because the hands of the K·î′nqalaLala—who "dances backward in front of him"—are empty. "She stands erect and holds her hands and forearms extended forward *as though* she was carrying a body for the hā′mats′a to eat" (443–44, emphasis added).

The give and take of Boas's text works first by hiding a set of textual markers and then by revealing them. These markers include phrases like "as though," "is seen," "secretly exchanged," and "represents." When revealed, they alert the reader that the hā′mats′a's cannibalism is a sophisticated dramatization of an inherited story. When they are withdrawn, the hā′mats′a's cannibalism is given to the reader as an actual practice, and "is seen" gives way to "is." The moment the markers return, however, the reality of cannibalism is withdrawn again, and the cannibal dance resumes its status as artifice.[3]

The link tying the hā′mats′a to cannibalism is a gift of Boas's text, and that gift is delivered in the interval between the instant when the text reveals its marks of artifice and the instant when it hides them. Suspended between the moments of an ethnographic narrative, the gift arrives in an instant that is not an instant in time. The interplay of hiding and revealing erases the limit between artifice and reality altogether and enables the text to offer the hā′-

mats'a's feigned cannibalism to the world as an actual practice. It is hardly surprising, then, that by the time Boas's account was cited in the *Victoria Daily News* it had become "real"—so real that it impelled Arthur Vowell to consider enforcing a statute that he usually ignored.

## REMEMBERING DEATH

Meanwhile the potlatch correspondence was settling into its own pattern of give and take as it began to be traversed by two opposing forces. First there was a drive toward death. It compelled administrators to repeat over and over that the potlatch was nearing extinction. But there was also a drive toward life because, even as they were consigning the potlatch to its grave, the same administrators were nevertheless compelled to admit that it had been resurrected—or that it had never died in the first place.

### The Dying Potlatch

In March 1898 a Vancouver lawyer named R. W. Harris sent the superintendent general of Indian affairs a set of identically worded petitions signed by the people of several Nisga'a, Tsimshian, and Haisla villages on the north coast. The petitioners declared that their "emancipation" from "the bondage of ignorance, superstition, and barbarism is impeded, and opposed by the custom of *giving away, and destroying property,*—a custom generally called 'potlatch,' together with its preliminary, and supplementary rites and ceremonies at which the *bodies of human beings and dogs are frequently bitten and mutilated,* such rites and ceremonies, though variously designated within the tribes, being commonly known to outsiders as 'tamanawas.'" Secretary John D. McLean replied that the department's policy was to let these "festivals" wane of their own accord (NA, vol. 3628, file 6244-1, McLean to Vowell, 15 March 1898; Harris to minister of the interior, [9] March 1898; McLean to Harris, 15 March 1898).

About a year later three Nisga'a elders hand-delivered a petition against the potlatch to British Columbia Attorney General Joseph Martin.[4] "We did not know that there could be a dead law on the Law Book," they write, "[b]ut the Potlatch law seems to be dead" (NA, vol. 3628, file 6244-1, Martin to Sifton, 29 April 1899). Superintendent Vowell answered that it was "the custom" that was "dying

179

*eating*

out gradually," not the law, though in September he received another Nisga'a petition thanking him for ignoring the potlatch's opponents (NA, vol. 3629, file 6244-2, Vowell to McLean, 25 May 1899; petition, 13 September 1899).

Vowell repeated his prophecy of death in 1904 when McLean asked him to gauge the impact of antidance legislation in British Columbia. Vowell described the winter dances as a waste of time and a cause of poor health but insisted the old ways were steadily dying out and did not need a law to kill them. He noted later that the practice of dancing had "entirely died out" in many parts of the province (NA, vol. 3629, file 6244-2, Vowell to McLean, 9 February and 22 October 1904). When John Ford of Broughton Island wrote his member of parliament in 1906 to complain about potlatching in communities where "[u]ntil recently cannibalism was held sacred," the deputy superintendent general of Indian affairs, Frank Pedley, responded that "the Department for long past has been following a well defined policy which beginning with the suppression of the more objectionable features aims at the eventual extinction of these dances and festivals" (NA, vol. 3629, file 6244-2, Ford to William Sloan, 8 June 1906; Pedley to Sloan, 21 June 1906).

Not every official thought the potlatch ought to be allowed to die in peace. In 1904 George DeBeck predicted it would kill its supporters unless it were killed first. "I am determined if possible to break up this pernicious practise indulged in by these Indians," he writes, "as it is fast decimating their numbers and will in a short time exterminate the whole lot of them" (NA, vol. 3629, file 6244-2, DeBeck to Vowell, 1 April 1904). For DeBeck, the potlatch was not just an avenue for the spread of contagious and deadly diseases. Rather, it was death itself.[5]

### The Reviving Potlatch

Ironically, toward the end of 1902, while white officials were assuring themselves that it was almost dead, Bill Uslick—so far the only man to be jailed for giving all—openly asked the department for permission to hold another potlatch (NA, vol. 3629, file 6244-2, Jukes to Vowell, 13 November 1902). The vanishing tradition had refused to die on schedule. Some officials were unable to admit their predictions had been wrong, however, so they suggested that the potlatch had indeed passed away but then returned from the dead. In May 1912 former missionary A. E. Green, now employed as an Indian school inspector, reported that "[t]he Indians are becoming demoralized by the *revival* of the old 'Potlatch' " in British Columbia (NA, vol. 3629, file 6244-2, 10 May 1912, emphasis added). A year later he warned "it is spreading" (14 May 1913). In winter 1914 T. Ferrier, the national superintendent of Methodist schools and hospitals, advised the department that "[s]omething should be done . . . in the stamping out of the *revival* of the old heathen feast of the Pot Latch" (NA, vol. 3629, file 6244-2, 26 January 1914, emphasis added). But there was no reason to conclude that the reviving potlatch had ever died. What about dancing?

When Green passed through the West Coast Agency early in 1909, he observed that "[t]he Indians in the village [of 'Clayoquot'] *resurrected* the 'Wolf' dance this winter and carried it to great extremes" (NA, vol. 3629, file 6244-2, 2 March 1909, emphasis added). Indian Agent A. W. Neill replied sardonically that "[t]he wolf dance could not be spoken of as having been revived as it never died" (14 April 1909). Nor was it to die in the immediate future. Years later, in 1920, constables from the provincial police and the Royal Canadian Mounted Police (RCMP) laid informations against forty-three people for attending a winter dance and potlatch at Clayoquot at Christmas time. The accused were fined for giving presents although, as they later argued, they "were doing no more than is customary with the white people during this season" (NA, vol. 3630, file 6244-4, pt. 1, Keatta and Atlea to DIA, 12 January 1921; RCMP report, 7 January 1921).

Also in 1920 the department received a secondhand report from a missionary complaining about the "revival" of the potlatch in Gitksan communities on the upper Skeena. He described its rebirth as a fall from whiteness. "At first it began in a small way by having small feasts of the dead and conducted in a half Christian manner," he writes, but "[y]ear after year the evil increased until today they potlatch as if they were heathen" (NA, vol. 3630, file 6244-4, pt. 1, Shearer to Scott, 9 November 1920). R. E. Loring was preparing to retire from his post as agent in charge of the Babine Agency, but he posted notices warning that the RCMP was ready to enforce the law (NA, vol. 3630, file 6244-4, pt. 1, Loring to McLean, 22 December

1920). Ironically, more than twenty years earlier he had argued that it would be better to repeal the statute than to enforce it because, he said, the winter dances had already died and the potlatch was about to follow them (NA, vol. 3629, file 6244-2, 15 July 1897).

### Impossible Mourning

Why, in their correspondence with themselves, did settlers, missionaries, and government administrators pronounce the potlatch dead even as they acknowledged it was still alive? One could argue that bureaucrats predicted its death so they could avoid enforcing the law against it. Their talk was an excuse for their inaction. One could also argue that missionaries were quick to declare the potlatch dead because by dying it would show that their proselytizing efforts had not been wasted. As J. W. Grant (1984, 136) notes, missionaries often complained that it was especially difficult to disseminate Christianity among the British Columbia First Nations. But there is another reason the potlatch correspondence folds together a drive to forecast death with a drive to affirm life. According to this other reason, these two discursive tendencies belong to a system of thought that at the time allowed European Canada to conceive of itself as a homogeneously white society.

Here whiteness gives itself to be thought in the disjunction between two forms of recollection. It is a gift that negotiates the gap between an interiorizing memory that permits the white body politic to dream of absorbing aboriginal cultures into itself and a thinking memory that situates white Canada in relation to a set of aboriginal cultures that it cannot swallow, interiorize, cannibalize. Derrida (1989a) argues that the mutual incompatibility between these two forms of recollection manifests itself in the work of mourning.

And what is mourning? Freud says ([1917] 1957, 244) that "the work which mourning performs" consists of the slow and painful loosening of the "attachments" that tie us to a loved one who has died. Since we do not surrender such attachments easily, mourning allows us to prolong them by taking the departed other inside ourselves. It is an interiorization that gives us time to undo each of the "memories and expectations" that bind us to an other who is no longer present. Indeed, for Freud the European subject is what remains of a long series of cannibalizing interiorizations that begin at infancy, as if the ever-recurring figure of the "cannibal savage"—itself a textual gift—were the source of Europe's most intimate, most proper truth.

In *Mémoires* (1989a), a text that mourns the death of Paul de Man, Derrida acknowledges that "since Freud" the "normal" work of mourning has been described as "a movement in which an interiorizing idealization takes in itself or upon itself the body and voice of the other, the other's visage and person, ideally *and* quasi-ideally devouring them" (34). An interiorizing idealization is an act of virtual cannibalism. It requires the memory of the bereaved subject to preserve the dead by swallowing them.

Derrida contrasts interiorizing memory with a memory that is oriented toward the approach, rather than the departure, of the other. This other memory is not distinct from interiorizing memory, though, because it is what makes the act of interiorization possible. Derrida notes that in Freud's account "[i]f death comes to the other, and comes to us through the other, then the [departed] friend no longer exists except *in* us, *between* us. In himself, by himself, of himself, he is no more, nothing more. He lives only in us" (28). When understood as an idealizing interiorization, mourning requires that the "self" provide an enclosure where the other's existence can be prolonged until mourning has done its work, but the self-identical and self-enclosed self that acts as a container for the interiorized other constitutes itself only by putting itself in relation to an other who is never interiorized. The condition for the possibility of mourning is therefore the condition for its impossibility. It is mourning that establishes the enclosure where the other resides during the work of mourning, but that means mourning has to occur in advance of itself if it is to happen at all. And that is impossible.

The only way mourning can precede itself is by grieving for an other who has yet to die. It has to begin "even before the death of the other *actually* happens," because it is the *anticipation* of mourning that "constitutes in advance all 'being-in-us,' 'in me,' between us, or between ourselves" (28–29). The self sets up its self-enclosure in relation to an *un*departed other who is mourned but cannot be interiorized because she or he is not dead yet. "The *possibility* of death 'happens,' " says Derrida, "before" there is a "me," an "us" or a "between us" "and makes them possible." By a paradoxical turn, the interiorizing memory that prolongs

183

*eating*

the life of the other remains open to its exterior because it is built upon the memory of an other whom it can never reduce to itself. Derrida: "The 'me' or the 'us' of which we speak then arise and are delimited in the way that they are only through this experience of the other, and of the other as other who can die, leaving in me or in us this memory of the other. This terrible solitude which is mine or ours at the death of the other is what constitutes this relationship to self which we call 'me,' 'us,' 'between us,' 'subjectivity,' 'intersubjectivity,' 'memory' " (33). Although the self sets up its enclosure around the thought of an other who can die—though "[t]he 'within me' and the 'within us' acquire their sense and their bearing only by carrying within themselves the death and the memory of the other"—the memory of the other recalls a death that has yet to happen, a death that remains outstanding like an unpaid debt (33).

Perhaps the word "experience" is not adequate to name the encounter with an "other as other who can die." Since it is the experience of an event that has not occurred, this encounter does not offer itself to perception, and it cannot be recorded within an interiorizing memory that swallows the traces of past events and stores them within its self-enclosure. Rather, the encounter with "the other as other who can die" is an experience that *is* only insofar as it is *on the way*, as if it were forever in the mail, like the fulfillment of a promise. Indeed, since the "experience" of the other who can die occurs *before* the other dies, it is not an experience at all but rather a thought of death: a thought that offers itself to a memory turned toward an endlessly deferred future, toward a time that exceeds the enclosure of the interiorizing self altogether (38).[6]

## WHITE CANNIBALS

### Act of Assimilation

The disjunction between a memory that aims to interiorize an other who has died, and a memory that thinks an other who is always about to die, underlies the history of Canada's Indian policy. As John L. Tobias (1983) argues, Canadian law has "always" tried to push the people it defines as "Indians" toward two contradictory goals at once, seeking both to protect and to assimilate them. The British government's colonial policy in the middle of the eighteenth century was to help the First Nations defend themselves against the "European encroachment" on their lands and cultures. By 1830, however, the British declared that it would be better to "civilize" aboriginal people instead and encouraged them to settle on reserves where they would be taught to farm and live like Europeans but would generally be kept at a remove from European settlements. When the civilizing mission failed, the Province of Canada elected to absorb aboriginal people directly into the body of settler society and, with that end in view, granted them special legal status in the Gradual Civilization Act of 1857 (Tobias 1983, 40–42). The act distinguished "Indians," who were made disenfranchised wards of the state, from people (that is, white men), who had the rights of full citizens—including the right to vote (Titley 1986, 11).

Yet the act set the two groups apart only to fold them together again. Canada sought to distance the First Nations from itself in order to win time to instill them with European values and prepare them to live in Euro-Canadian communities. Once "civilized" they were to be given the franchise and all the other rights of white (male) citizens. By granting them special status, though, Canada ensured aboriginal people would never be assimilated into white society. Tobias (1983, 42) observes that this double bind is the "paradox that was to become and remain a characteristic of Canada's Indian policy": "the legislation to remove all legal distinctions between Indians and Euro-Canadians actually established [those distinctions]."

The self-contradictory policy of the colonial period survived intact after confederation, for the Indian Act of 1876, which set "the foundation for all [of] Canada's future Indian legislation," included "all the protective features of the earlier legislation" and introduced new ones. By preserving the colonial policy of "protection," moreover, the Indian Act continued to check the absorption of the First Nations into settler society even though it was designed, and later amended, to encourage assimilation through enfranchisement. The same principles of protection, civilization, and assimilation underlie the Indian Act of 1951 (Tobias 1983, 43–45).[7]

Since its inception, then, Canada's Indian policy has folded itself up between two incommensurable poles. It has served the interests of a devouring national memory that

*eating*

seeks to absorb the aboriginal other into itself, yet the moment when that other is to be eaten belongs to a future that will never arrive. Canada has aimed both to draw the First Nations into itself and to hold them beyond its outermost limit. They are to be swallowed immediately but remain always-about-to-be-incorporated. Though the nation wants to put them in their coffins, it is determined to bury them alive. The law against the potlatch has to be understood within the larger framework of Canada's plan to make the First Nations white by taking them into itself (Tobias 1983, 47–48).[8]

### Suspended Sentences

For almost three decades federal administrators were content to vilify the potlatch while doing little to keep it from happening. The policy of nonenforcement did not end until the fall of 1913 when the Department of Indian Affairs began its only sustained attempt to put the potlatch to death. The new strategy was to last for the next ten years.

The attack was led by William Halliday, who had taken charge of the Kwawkewlth Agency in 1906. In *Prosecution or Persecution* (1979) Daisy Sewid-Smith calls Halliday a "fanatic" and holds him responsible for the violence done to her community by the antipotlatch crusade. "He and others like him," she says, "thought it would be easy to stamp out a culture that had been in existence since the great flood" (1). But Halliday had not always been a foe of the potlatch. Not long after he took charge of the Kwawkewlth Agency, the Victoria *News Advertiser* published an inflammatory article about two potlatches held at Alert Bay, where he was stationed. Halliday responded by reminding Superintendent Vowell that "the potlatch is a comparatively harmless institution." Its only faults, he says, are that it involves "a great waste of time" and encourages "the sale of girls" among men. He also enclosed two photographs he had taken during the Alert Bay potlatches. The new agent appears to have been more interested in observing the potlatch than in preventing it (NA, vol. 3629, file 6244-2, 9 July 1907).

However, Halliday made it clear that he strongly opposed the marriage practices of the Kwakwa̱ka'wakw, which were inseparable from what he called the potlatch. Months before the *News Advertiser* printed its story, he had sent his own inflammatory report on "the sale of girls" to Superintendent General of Indian Affairs Frank Oliver, claiming that men in Kwakwala-speaking communities sometimes buy and sell the same woman several times to earn money for potlatches. "It has always been the custom among these people," he alleges, "to marry their girls as soon as she [*sic*] has her first menstrual flow or rather I should say before she has her second flow. In none of these cases is the girl consulted but is simply sold to the highest bidder. She is not openly put up and sold by public auction as was done in slavery times, but private offers are made to the father or nearest male relative and he almost invariably accepts the highest offer" (NA, vol. 3629, file 6244-3, 1 February 1907). It is once again a case of a white man intent on saving brown women from brown men. Ironically, one of the premises of Halliday's letter is that his own society stands as an example of the just treatment of women—an example that the Kwakwaka'wakw ought to emulate.

Sewid-Smith emphasizes that, although Halliday "made statements about our marriage custom that were pure 'rubbish,' [h]is remarks left such a guilty feeling among our old people, especially pertaining to the age they got married." It took her years, for example, to find out how old her grandmother was when she married (7). But while Halliday charged that her people made marriages for profit, he did not yet mobilize his criticisms into an attack on the potlatches where the profits of marriage were allegedly spent. Instead he advised the department to do more to educate the Kwakwaka'wakw in European ways and suggested that the Indian Act might be revised to impose the marital practices of Euro-Canadian society upon all aboriginal people.

Halliday did not turn against the potlatch until the winter of 1913 when John Antle, an Anglican missionary in charge of the Columbia Coast Mission, made a formal complaint about the department's management of the Kwawkewlth Agency. By this time Arthur Vowell was no longer in a position to deflect criticism of the department's potlatch policy. He had resigned in 1910, and the department had closed its British Columbia superintendency and divided the province into three regional inspectorates. William E. Ditchburn, a former printer, was appointed to the southern inspectorate, which included the Kwawkewlth

Agency. After investigating Antle's complaint, Ditchburn reported that, although Halliday was "inclined to be too self-opinionated and always seem[ed] to rub people the wrong way," the agency's main problem was the "deplorable custom" of the potlatch. A few months later Ditchburn observed that "the time is opportune" for the anti-potlatch statute "to be put into force" (NA, vol. 3629, file 6244-2, Ditchburn to McLean, 27 March and 28 August 1913).

Accordingly, in November Halliday had John Bagwany and Ned Harris committed for trial in Vancouver for participating in some "small potlatches" at Alert Bay. A jury found them guilty in May 1914, and the presiding judge gave them suspended sentences. Halliday recalls in his report on the trial that the jury had some difficulty deciding whether or not the acts defined in the law corresponded with the acts that the accused had performed. While "the fact of the potlatching having taken place was proved satisfactorily," the jury was not sure that this event was the type of "Indian festival, dance, or other ceremony" prohibited by section 149 of the Indian Act. Hence "in summing up" the judge "read from the unabridged dictionary from the Law Library the meaning of the words festival and ceremony." "According to that dictionary," adds Halliday, "a festival was a religious gathering and a ceremony was described as an affair that was conducted by fixed rules and regulations." But it proved impossible to match the potlatch to either of these words: "The jury disagreed as to the fact that a potlatch was either a festival or ceremony." As Searle would say, the statute did not refer successfully because it did not give its readers enough information to select its intended referent out of the field of possible referents. When a second trial was held the next day, the jury concluded that the accused had taken part in a "dance"—which the law also banned. In the end, then, the potlatch that the legal text had given to the world substituted itself for the potlatch that the accused men had attended—and they were convicted (NA, vol. 3629, file 6244-2, Halliday to McLean, 8 November 1913 and 12 May 1914).

Halliday's report shows the law once again wavering between its constative function, in which it states what it bans, and its performative function, in which it bans what it states. As a constative, the legal text has no referent to correspond with: in de Man's terms, its "referential meaning" is suspended. But since it is also a performative, it must act, and to act it overcomes its failure to refer by giving itself something to point to. The arrival of the textual gift temporarily bridges the disjunction between the two incompatible moments of the legal text. Its constative function helps the jury establish that Harris and Bagwany participated in a potlatch-dance, and its performative function allows the law to set into action as a ban on dancing.

The subtleties of the jury's deliberations were probably lost on Harris and Bagwany, though, because they did not speak English fluently and apparently the court proceedings were not translated into Kwakwala. In June 1914, after "the Salmon River, Kweakiah [Kweeka] and Cape Mudge tribes" gathered at Campbell River to discuss the trial, Jim Quatel noted in a letter to Ottawa that "[i]f Bagwany and Harris speaks english they would explain how and why. but both dont fully understand the evidence given by mr Halliday Indian Agent." Quatel's letter also includes a statement by Billy Assu, Harry Assu's father, who interprets the conflict over the potlatch as a clash between opposing systems of government: "I have give many potlatches myself and never get sorry. but I feel good, for the good work I have done. I never give away all what I have and other goods I wish to use for myself. my houses is always stays. I never lose it. I have canoes and boats and so on. The potlatch is our goverment" (NA, vol. 3629, file 6244-2, 12 June 1914). A Nuu'chah'nulth petition written at Alberni on 4 December argues that the "pot latch" is a force that "binds" one "tribe" to another and each "tribe" to itself: "we maintain that the right enforcement of the law against pot latches would have a harmful effect in breaking up the unity of the tribe. The life of the indians has for many generations been bound up with the giving of feasts and pot latches. This more than anything else . . . has brought tribe to tribe, and has established friendly relations among the members of each tribe and among the tribe themselves." These texts are two of the many petitions that aboriginal communities from all over Vancouver Island sent to the Department of Indian Affairs in 1914 to ask it to reverse its decision to enforce the antipotlatch law. However, a group of petitioners from the "Quami-chan" Reserve—writing "to strongly protest against the

*eating*

action which the Government has taken lately"—correctly observed that the government was unlikely to listen to such protests: "We are oppressed from all sides we never have any satisfaction given to our many petitions sent in—We notice that all times the white people are listened to, but we seem to be forgotten" (NA, vol. 3629, file 6244-3, 22 December 1914).

In 1914 Halliday had also laid potlatching charges against Cessaholis from Kingcome Inlet, but withdrew them after learning that the sentences of Harris and Bagwany had been suspended. A year later he laid new charges against Cessaholis as well as Kiskwagila. Cessaholis pleaded guilty to giving a potlatch at Gwyasdums and received a suspended sentence. His testimony before the court once again reduced the struggle over the potlatch to a debate over the meaning of the word "potlatch": " 'I did not give a potlatch,' he stated, 'I gave a feast for poor Indians, just like white people in Vancouver give feasts for the poor people' " (Cole and Chaikin 1990, 99). When Kiskwagila went to trial, however, the jury saw no offense in what he had done and threw his case out of court. It was becoming clear to government officials that juries in British Columbia were unlikely to send people to jail for preserving a cultural practice that had many supporters among the province's white population (NA, vol. 3629, file 6244-2, Halliday to McLean, 20 February 1915; vol. 3629, file 6244-3, Halliday to McLean, 9 February 1915, and Halliday's report for May 1915).

### Recollections

Why did Halliday and his overseers lay siege to the potlatch when they knew the public did not consider it a crime? They were, above all, driven by the necessity to think their own whiteness. They were also obsessed with tracing the borders of their "young" nation there where the First Nations had once been—and of course still are. By endlessly anticipating the death of the potlatch they made it possible for Canada to remember itself by bearing within itself the trace of an aboriginal other who was always about to die.

Halliday describes whiteness as a phantasmatic relation to the other in the first sentence of his memoirs, *Potlatch and Totem and the Recollections of an Indian Agent* (1935), where, in order to "recollect" himself and his life, he draws a rigid and impermeable boundary between "whites" and "Indians." "In very many things," he begins, "the customs of the Indians on the Pacific Coast are *directly opposite* to those of whites" (3, emphasis added). The coastal First Nations are for Halliday the absolute others, the "direct opposites," of Western European civilization and are located beyond its outermost limit.

It is the gift, moreover, that marks the boundary between whiteness and aboriginality. "The white man of the present age," he says, "considers too much the acquisition of property as being the essential sign of success," while "[t]he Indian in his native state [which, as the shift to the past tense implies, is assumed to have vanished] considered that the more he gave away, and impoverished himself, the better off he was" (3). We have seen this pattern before: to be "white" is to renounce the gift in favor of accumulation and to be "Indian" is to embrace poverty by making total expenditures. Halliday cannot remember his life— can neither think himself nor consider what is most proper to him as a "white man"—without first calculating the distance that divides him from "the Indian."

Later, when he remembers his war on gift giving, he recalls that for years the potlatch refused to die. Though "[i]t was thought that education and missionary training amongst the Indians would so open their minds to the folly of the custom that the custom itself would die a natural death without any legal proceedings having to be taken to compel it to die," he and other administrators eventually saw that, instead of dying, the potlatch was actually growing: "assuming greater and greater proportions." By surviving its own death, the potlatch continued to mark the limit between whiteness and aboriginality. But the potlatch was not supposed to survive. It was to be absorbed into the nation's memory and mourned, and the antipotlatch statute was put into force to make the work of mourning possible. As "things gradually got worse and worse," remembers Halliday, the Department of Indian Affairs had no choice but to "see that this custom was done away with entirely" (188). As the potlatch died, the border that it traced between whiteness and aboriginality was supposed to fade as well, for if it was gift giving that divided "whites" from "Indians," then the death of the gift was supposed to integrate them both into a larger totality, a single nation-state.

*eating*

Alert Bay. Photograph by William Halliday, Indian Agent for the Kwawkewlth Agency, c. 1900. Published in Halliday 1935, 85, over the caption "A Potlatch of Flour." Courtesy of Vancouver Public Library, photograph no. 8664.

Alert Bay. Photograph by William Halliday, Indian Agent for the Kwawkewlth Agency, c. 1910. Published in Halliday 1935, 35, over the caption "Redemption Property Arranged to Be Given Away." Courtesy of Vancouver Public Library, photograph no. 9896.

Alert Bay. Photograph by William Halliday, Indian Agent for the Kwawkewlth Agency, c. 1907. Published in Halliday 1935, 35, over the caption "The Redemption." Halliday sent a copy of this photograph to Arthur Vowell on 9 July 1907 (NA, vol. 3629, file 6244-2). Courtesy of British Columbia Archives and Records Service, photograph no. H-03975.

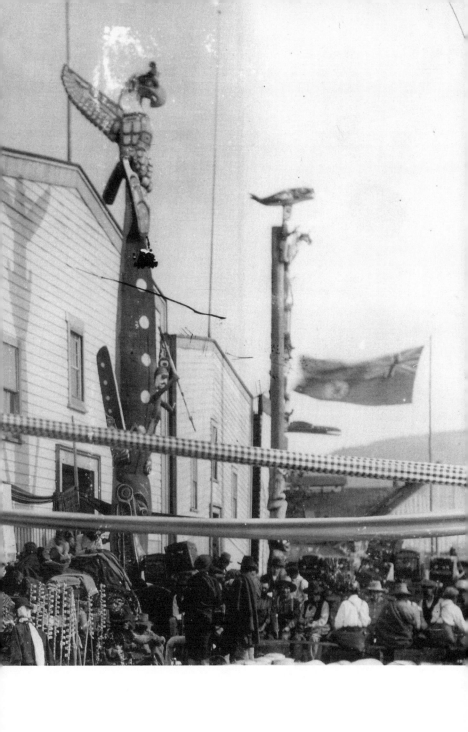

Alert Bay. Photograph by William Halliday, Indian Agent for the Kwawkewlth Agency, c. 1907. Published in Halliday 1935, 80, over the caption "A Potlatch of Flour." Courtesy of British Columbia Archives and Records Service, photograph no. H-03980.

To think himself as a white citizen of a homogeneously white country, Halliday has to perform two contradictory operations at once: he has to set his whiteness at an absolute distance from the aboriginal other, but he also has to take the other into himself so that he can "recollect" his whiteness to himself and to his reader. Thus while he begins his memoirs by setting the terms "white" and "Indian" apart, he ends by underlining the necessity of folding them together again, as if it were inevitable that whiteness will devour its aboriginal other at an unspecified future date. Indeed, his chapter "Medical Progression" suggests that white Canada has been eating away at the First Nations for several decades. "The white man," he affirms, "is largely responsible for the near extermination of the Indian" because it was white society that introduced the North American First Nations to the disastrous influence of liquor and to diseases that overcame "their powers of resistance." Yet they refused to die. Though he says "the Indian population was almost exterminated" in the nineteenth century, Halliday admits that it "has been gradually increasing for several years past," and he attributes their "better physical life" to a process that he calls "the infusion of white blood." "A very large percentage of the Indians to-day are not of pure Indian blood," he confides, "but have a large admixture of white blood, and, as one can imagine, it is not the better class of white men who have thus degraded themselves by intermingling with the Indian women [!], so that the result morally is not so great as the result physically. However, it will hasten the time when the Indians as such will be no more, but will be absorbed into the white race, and will help to carry the burden that so far has been borne by the white man for his benefit" (226–27). Halliday's vision of racial assimilation, where whiteness inexorably swallows its aboriginal other, overlaps interiorizing memory with its own other—thinking memory. Whiteness is here a life force that takes aboriginal people into itself by attacking them from the inside, not from without. Like a disease it infiltrates the aboriginal body and quietly masters its inner workings. Halliday predicts that when the process of incorporation-from-within is complete, there will be only one "race" left in Canada, the white race—a master race whose "blood," he says, is destined to overpower the "blood" of all its others. And it will do so for their own good, indeed for their own "physical betterment."⁹ Need I recall that *Potlatch and Totem* was published in 1935?

Yet Halliday's "recollection" of the moment when whiteness will have assumed its eugenic mastery over aboriginality—"the time when the Indians as such will be no more"—remains forever deferred, for the absorption of one "race" by another is not an event that has passed but one that has yet to happen. It anticipates the death of an other who can die but is never quite dead yet. What is more, an other who is always-about-to-die cannot be absorbed into an interiorizing memory and mourned. The inassimilable other can only be *thought* by a memory that recollects the arrival of future events.

In his last pages Halliday construes assimilation as a promise that Canada has made to the First Nations and enshrined in the Indian Act, a legal text and archive: "by the terms of Confederation, the Dominion Government took on themselves the oversight of the Indians with *a promise* that they should be treated fairly and squarely. *This promise* has been kept in all fidelity and honesty, and the day will come, and it is not far distant, when the Indians who are in the province of British Columbia will receive their enfranchisement; will cease to become minors in the eyes of the law, and will be honest, law-abiding, respected citizens of Canada" (239, emphasis added). Canada has signed a contract with the First Nations, pledging to make them "honest," "law-abiding," "respected"—and white. However, Paul de Man (1979, 273) points out that when "the speech act of the contractual text" is "[c]onsidered performatively"—as an utterance that acts and not just as one that states—it "never refers to a situation that exists in the present, but signals toward a hypothetical future." Every promise is suspended between the past moment when it was uttered and the future moment when it is to be fulfilled. It is the memory of an event that has not happened.

Throughout Halliday's memoirs whiteness gives itself to be thought in the disjunction between two incompatible forms of memory that are in turn governed by two equally incompatible temporalities. Whiteness recalls itself to itself as a self-enclosed political body that has absorbed the aboriginal other after the tragic moment of the other's death. But the other is not dead. Moreover, a memory geared to

201

*eating*

eating the departed other is possible precisely because the moment of death never comes. Though the memory that gives the gift of whiteness aims to devour the past, it is built upon the memory of a meal that is always about to be served. Whiteness remembers itself by thinking a past that never comes to pass because it arrives at itself from the future.

## POET OF MEMORY

### Policy Memoir

While Halliday was being pressured to kill the potlatch in 1913, the chief accountant of the Department of Indian Affairs took a moment to write a brief note to Deputy Superintendent General Frank Pedley. "It seems a great pity," he confided, "that we cannot do something to break up this abominable and wasteful aboriginal custom." Pedley coolly replied that Indian administrators in British Columbia "should be able to suggest means to deal with this state of affairs." But he would not be there to help them. By October he had been forced to resign his post after he was caught speculating on the sale of First Nations lands, and the position of deputy superintendent general went to the former chief accountant, Duncan Campbell Scott (NA, vol. 3629, file 6244-2, 14 April 1913).

In December 1879, when Scott was seventeen, his father had secured him a clerical position in the department, but by the end of the 1880s he had become the department's bookkeeper and had published his first poems in *Scribner's* magazine. He was clerk in charge of the accountant's branch by 1891 and became chief clerk and accountant in July 1893, which meant he was responsible for restricting departmental expenditures. In 1893 he also published his first book, *The Magic House and Other Poems*. Though he remained chief accountant until 1913, in 1905 he was appointed to the commission in charge of negotiating Treaty Nine in northern Ontario and was made superintendent of education in 1909.

Scott was not just a career bureaucrat in a minor government department. By the end of the nineteenth century he had established himself as one of Canada's leading literary intellectuals. He was admitted to the Royal Society of

Canada in 1899 and served as its president in 1921–22. In 1922 he was the first person to be named honorary doctor of letters by the University of Toronto. He wrote poems, stories, and essays as well as a play and an unpublished novel. In 1892 and 1893 he contributed to "At the Mermaid Inn," a weekly column in the Toronto *Globe*. His poetry is obsessed with the themes of death, mourning, and memory. It also concerns itself with light and the play of color—especially at sunrise and sunset (Titley 1986, 22–28).

Scott served as deputy superintendent general of Indian affairs until he retired on 31 March 1932. In "The Administration of Indian Affairs in Canada," a paper he presented at a conference in China in 1931, he provides an overview of the policies he pursued as Canada's most powerful Indian affairs administrator. "The Administration" records the memoirs of Scott the civil servant, if not of Scott the writer. Moreover, Scott's policy memoir, like Halliday's *Recollections*, is governed by the disjunction between an interiorizing memory that seeks to absorb the other into itself and a thinking memory that holds the other at an irreducible remove.

For example, the disjunction between these two memories structures Scott's explanation of Canada's policy of setting aside reserve lands for the First Nations. The reserve system, he recalls, "is intended to ensure the continuation of the tribal life and that of the individual as an Indian." Its aim is to help aboriginal people "protect" their distinct cultures and identities as Euro-Canadians invade their homelands. Yet it also has the opposite goal since it is intended "as well to render possible a continuous and consistent administrative policy directed towards civilization." The reserve system is supposed to help Canada devour the First Nations while holding them at an absolute distance from itself (26).

However, Canada cannot eat the First Nations if it continues to hold them apart from whiteness. Reserves contribute to the civilizing mission, says Scott, but also inhibit it by drawing a limit between Euro-Canadians and aboriginal people. "In the older provinces," he notes, "where Indians have mixed and intermarried with whites for more than two centuries, the efficiency of the reserve system tends to weaken. . . . In southern Ontario and Quebec," he adds, "there are communities of Indians who for the most part show little trace of their ancestry, either in physiognomy, colour or habits of life." Those indigenous people who, to Scott's gaze, bear no marks of race to distinguish them from the white population are ready to be absorbed into the body of Canada and should no longer live in segregation. "There is no apparent reason why these groups should not take their place in the community and assume the responsibility of citizenship." He singles out the right to vote as the privileged mark of whiteness. It is to be given only to those people who have renounced every trace of their aboriginality and given up the special legal status that is theirs under the Indian Act (26).

Scott's discourse unites the civilizing mission of the nineteenth century, a mission to Europeanize others through education and evangelism, with the eugenic project of the early twentieth century, which dreamed of solving social problems by manipulating human biology. In his lexicon assimilation means not just the absorption of one culture, one collective mode of being, by another, but the biological absorption of one "race," one "heredity," by another.[10] Yet for Scott, as for Halliday, the moment when white Canada will have swallowed the aboriginal other is deferred to a future that never arrives. "It is the opinion of the writer," he concludes, "that by policies and activities such as have been outlined, the Government *will in time reach the end* of its responsibility as the Indians progress into civilization and finally disappear as a separate and distinct people, not by race extinction [an option soon to be deployed in Europe] but by gradual assimilation with their fellow citizens" (27, emphasis added). Though Canada plans to eat its others, the nation's totem meal is scheduled for a time that lies beyond time, a deferred time that will not come to pass until time as it is currently understood has "reached" its "end." The memory that seeks to devour and then to mourn a departed other is tied to, and opposed by, a future-oriented memory that thinks the other as absolutely other, irreducible to whiteness.

In Scott's discourse there is no white self, no white subject or subjectivity, before and outside the possibility of an impossible mourning that inevitably falls short of its aim to interiorize an aboriginal other. The thought of a homogeneously white Canadian society, a pure white "us," is grounded in the bereaved memory of an other whose death is always-about-to-have-happened, but the other's death is nonetheless a possibility promised, in a past that is past, for a future that cannot come to pass or else the seamless white "us" that it institutes would be shattered. "Our" other must remain living outside "us" so that their death can be promised and by that promise give "us" our being. The promise of the other's death happens *before* the instant of death to make the thought of whiteness possible. Taking nothing in return, the other sends "us" a gift of whiteness in death, a gift of white death. "Our" whiteness is therefore impossible, for it requires "us" to eat what "we" cannot and will not swallow. Unable to absorb the other into itself, this "we" is irreconcilably divided from itself: as Derrida (1989a, 28) puts it, "*we* are never *ourselves*, and between us, identical to us, a 'self' is never in itself or identical to itself." Such a "we" is never self-identical because it establishes itself in relation to an other whom it can never assimilate to itself.

### A National Feeling

Perhaps the story of the antipotlatch law is the story of a nation trying to get a "feeling" for itself—a feeling that Scott calls "national consciousness"—by giving itself others to eat. Scott muses in "Poetry and Progress" (1947, 129) that the "feeling of nationality" is "a strong aid and incitement to a poet, no matter how much we may talk nowadays about the danger of national feeling." But how does a poet, let alone a people, come into contact with a "national feeling" that is distinctively its own, proper to one nation only? Scott remarks in "The Tercentenary of Quebec" (1947, 154) that to touch itself in the present, a nation has to devour its own past: "Our lives should be blown through and through by historical memories and national ideals, otherwise we live in a fen country without vistas, or in stifling air, like old people in a workhouse." A nation is "civilized" only insofar as it remembers itself, but its memories are of a past that "projects" itself into the future: "In a highly civilized state, accompanying the actions of each day and year, there is the shadowy, intangible, but ever-present drama of the past, existing not only in manners, forms, and precedent, but in definite characters that *project* their force into life, and feed the imagination with instances of resource and fortitude" (emphasis added). By "projecting" its past into the future, the nation recollects itself as the "country" it *will* have been, in the future perfect tense. It carries its dead within itself in order to remember a national destiny that is still to come. "Especially for such a young people as ours," says Scott, writing as an English-Canadian about Quebec, "it is wise to perpetuate old deeds and to treasure what is, after all, our chief possession—the actions of those who were all unconsciously framing our destiny." The departed arrive from the future to give the nation to itself, for "[a] state might boast of impeccable laws and enjoy the smoothest, most improved methods in the art of living," he says, "but it would be a poor, dead thing without the memory of great men and great actions" (1947, 154). The nation would itself be dead if it did not preserve its dead within a bereaved, interiorizing memory. The national self-consciousness is fashioned in an act of mourning.

If a "young" nation is to "project" its past forward onto its destiny, however, it has to distinguish between the others it wants to store within its national memory and those it wants to exclude from itself. It must make a judgment about what to remember. Freud ([1925] 1957, 236), whose discourse repeatedly circles back to the figure of the cannibal, says that the "function of judgement" makes "two sorts of decisions." It determines whether a thing has a particular attribute, and it decides whether the things represented in the mind have an existence "in reality." Freud's two functions of judgment correspond to two of the functions of language outlined by Searle: meaning and reference. The meaning of a referring expression defines the attributes of a thing, while the speech act of reference establishes whether that thing exists.

Freud argues that the two functions of judgment begin forming in the oral-*cannibalistic* phase of a child's development. When an attributive judgment is expressed "in the language of the oldest—the oral—instinctual impulses, the judgement is: 'I should like to eat this,' or 'I should like to spit it out'; and, put more generally, 'I should like to take this into myself and to keep that out.' That is to say: 'It shall be inside me' or 'it shall be outside me.' " Judgments of existence develop out of the child's efforts to rediscover what is judged to be good and to avoid what is known to be bad (237–38).

If for Freud "[j]udging is a continuation along lines of expediency of the original process by which the ego took things into itself or expelled them from itself, according to the pleasure principle" (239), for Scott the formation of a national consciousness is a process of incorporating the memories of certain others who are judged to be good and rejecting the memories of others judged to be bad. He notes in "The Tercentenary" (1947, 154) that the child-nation of Canada—"a young people such as ours"—has already absorbed a "rich" supply of French-speaking others, whom he rather patronizingly portrays as good others, into the national memory: "Peculiarly rich is our heritage in the memories of the early navigators and explorers"— he cites Cartier, Champlain, and Frontenac—"who groped their way along our coasts and founded our cities unerringly on the points of natural vantage." In the poem "Indian Place Names" (1926, 22), though, he suggests that Canada has at once eaten and expelled the First Nations. The white collectivity has absorbed them into itself, making them a part of itself, yet they remain exterior to it and haunt it from its periphery like living "ghosts": "The race has waned and left but tales of ghosts, / That hover in the world like fading smoke / About the lodges: gone are the dusky folk / That once were cunning with the throng and snare." "But," as they disappeared from the land, these "dusky folk" bequeathed their "wild names" to the white child-nation: "But all the land is murmurous with the call / Of their wild names that haunt the lovely glens / Where water lonely falls, or where the street / Sounds all day with the tramp of myriad feet." Couched in iambic pentameter, "Toronto triumphs; Winnipeg flows free / ... And Restigouche takes the whelmed sound of sea." Scott's discourse situates the "dusky" dead—dusky because related to the dusk, the waning of daylight—both inside and outside the borders of the white body politic. The "Indian" names of its cities are at once distinctively Canadian, fully assimilated into the national consciousness, and noticeably foreign, "wild," other.

By anticipating the death of the First Nations, Canada gains the power to name itself not only in aboriginal languages but in English too, the language of the colonizer.

Let me recall Scott's "Lines in Memory of Edmund Morris" (1926), where the act of naming once again coincides with a thought of death. Toward the end of this long elegy, the poet addresses an apostrophe to the departed friend and painter who accompanied him on the 1906 journey that set up Treaty Nine in northern Ontario and whose life has been prolonged in a bereaved interiorizing memory. Curiously, the apostrophe requires the departed other to "think" the death of yet another other.

> Here, Morris, on the plains that we have loved,
> Think of the death of Akoose, fleet of foot
>
> .   .   .   .   .   .   .   .   .   .   .   .   .
>
> Akoose, in his old age, blind from the smoke
> Of tepees and the sharp snow light.
>
> .   .   .   .   .   .   .   .   .   .
>
>                  Once when sharp autumn
> Made membranes of thin ice upon the sloughs,
> He caught a pony on a quick return
> Of prowess and, all his instincts cleared and quickened,
> He mounted, sensed the north and bore away.
>
> .   .   .   .   .   .   .   .   .   .   .   .   .
>
> And for these hours in all the varied pomp
> Of pagan fancy and free dreams of foray
> And crude adventure, he ranged on entranced,
> Until the sun blazed level with the prairie,
> Then paused, faltered and slid from off his pony.
> In a little bluff of poplars, hid in the bracken,
> He lay down. . . .

What the bereaved poet says to the departed, in memory of the departed, is that it is impossible to name either the land or the citizens of the young country called Canada without at the same time remembering the death of the aboriginal other. The bracken hides Akoose within itself, preserving him after his death: "There Akoose lay, silent amid the bracken, / Gathered at last with the Algonquin Chieftains" (148–49). But it is the recollection of the other's death that allows "bracken" to be uttered here at all— whether as a common noun or as a proper name—for it was not the departed "Algonquin Chieftains" who grafted this word to their resting place. The privilege of renaming the land of the colonized falls to the colonizer.

# SUMMARY OFFENSES

It was only after Scott took charge of the Department of Indian Affairs in 1913 that William Halliday began his attack on the potlatch. The majority of potlatch prosecutions occurred between 1919 and 1922, in the middle of Scott's term as deputy superintendent. It was Scott, moreover, who took the steps required to make it easier for Indian agents to send potlatchers to jail.

Until 1918 potlatching was an indictable offence, which meant that anyone charged under the statute had the right to trial by jury, and the department allowed its agents to lay charges and conduct preliminary hearings in potlatch cases. Halliday advised John D. McLean in June 1913 that potlatching ought to be made a summary offense so that trials could be heard before a magistrate—and without a jury. After the Vancouver county court freed Cessaholis on a suspended sentence in 1915, Halliday renewed his call for changes to the statute, and in 1918 Parliament amended section 149 to Scott's specifications, removing the word "indictable" and introducing the phrase "on summary conviction." This change took potlatch trials out of the courts and handed them over to justices of the peace, and under the Indian Act, Indian agents had possessed all the powers of justices of the peace since 1881. Scott's fine-tuning of the law gave them the power to act as prosecutor, judge and jury in potlatch trials (NA, vol. 3629, file 6244-2, Halliday to McLean, 20 February 1915; *Statutes of Canada, 1918*, chap. 26 [8–9 George V], sec. 9).

On October 21 Scott sent a circular to the agents in British Columbia, instructing them that, since the war in Europe had created an "urgent need for conservation" in Canada, no "wasteful practice or mode of life can be countenanced." He reminds them that they are now permitted to make summary convictions for acts of "giving away" and advises them "to exercise these powers to the full in the matter of the potlatch." "One of the objectionable features of this ceremony," he adds, "is the congregating together of numbers of individuals and the wasteful distribution of food either as presents or in feasting" (NA, vol. 3629, file 6244-3). In Scott's discourse, gifts are a form of waste, and waste has to be restricted, held in, con-

*eating*

tained—especially in time of war, which is a time of ultimate waste.

Ironically, the circular disobeys the advice that the
wood spring gives the poet in one of Scott's lyrics, "The
Wood-Spring to the Poet" (1926, 127), where the poet is
told: "Give, Poet, give! / Thus only shalt thou live. / Give!
for 'tis thy joyous doom / To charm, to comfort, to il-
lume." The wood spring instructs the poet, in particular,
to give food to those who are in mourning—"Give manna
for the mourner's mouth / Sovereign as air"—and song
to the living dead—"Give to dead souls that mock at life /
Aweary of their cankered hearts / . . . Helve them a song
of life." There is a fold at work in Scott's discourse on the
gift: giving is a virtue when directed from white poets to
the living dead but a crime when done by First Nations
who are always about to die.

Halliday responded to the 1918 circular by noting that
he had already warned the Kwakwaka'wakw "that the authorities could not look unmoved at them wasting their
time and substance at potlatches during such times as
these" (NA, vol. 3629, file 6244-3, 2 November 1918).
There is no time for the waste of time in wartime, which
is a time of absolute waste, for every instant is a precious
commodity and must be wisely spent. War is an absolute
expenditure that, according to Halliday's logic, obeys a
temporality opposed to the temporality of pure expenditure and the instantless instant of the gift. But Halliday did
not begin enforcing the law until after the war was over.
It was not until January 1919 that he sentenced Likiosa,
whose English name was Johnny Seaweed (or Sewid), and
Kwosteetsas, also known as Japanese Charlie, to two
months in prison, after Likiosa married Kwosteetsas's sister, Kaakstatos, in the traditional manner: with a distribution of property (NA, vol. 3629, file 6244-3, 29 January
1919). The brothers-in-law were freed on bail after their
lawyer, Frank Lyons, filed an appeal.

That March four more potlatchers—Harry Mountain,
Isaac the son of Abraham, John McDougall, and Chief
August—were arraigned before justice of the peace Halliday. But they were not convicted. Instead they and
seventy-three of their supporters signed an agreement to
obey the law in future, and the Crown withdrew its
charges. Likiosa and Kwosteetsas were included in the
agreement, and though the county court did not overturn

their convictions, it ruled that they would not have to return to jail (NA, vol. 3630, file 6244-4, pt. 1, Halliday to McLean, 29 March 1919; Proceedings on Hearing of Appeal, 27 March 1919).

When Harry Mountain testified before the court, he insisted that the potlatch had nothing to do with wasting time. "I work all the time," said Mountain, "*and only rest five months of the year.*" William E. Ditchburn later drew Scott's attention to this remark, noting that "[t]he statement is somewhat contradictory, though very significant" (NA, vol. 3630, file 6244-4, pt. 1, 22 May 1919). Indeed: Mountain suggests there is a time for work—a time that belongs to the circle of economy—and a time beyond economic time, a remainder of time that cannot be calculated in terms of profit and loss. The potlatch, he hints, belongs to this "rest" of time beyond time: to the other time of the gift.

The department gained an ally in its postwar battle against waste in November 1919, when Parliament merged the Royal North-West Mounted Police with the dominion police to form a national police force: the RCMP. Its mandate was to enforce federal law in the provinces, including the provisions of the Indian Act. By December two RCMP officers had arrived in Alert Bay, the center of the Indian affairs administration in the Kwawkewlth Agency, and the potlatch was one of their first targets (Cole and Chaikin 1990, 116).

In January 1920 Sergeant Donald Angermann (he seems well named) laid informations against nine potlatchers. Eight were charged and pleaded guilty. Seven were sentenced to two months in jail, while one, an elderly man, received a suspended sentence. They were the first people to be jailed for potlatching since the conviction of Bill Uslick in 1897, and Halliday interpreted their case as a sure sign the potlatch was about to die. "I think I may safely say," he wrote to Scott, "that the recent convictions of eight Indians at Alert Bay for potlatching has [*sic*] done a lot towards its extermination" (NA, vol. 3630, file 6244-4, pt. 1, 15 February 1920). But it was too soon to mourn. In January 1921 Angermann charged Mrs. MacDougall and an older man named Munday for participating in "what is commonly known as a potlatch" (31 January 1921). Their crime consisted of arranging for Munday to marry MacDougall's daughter Jennie, but their case was

*eating*

dismissed after witnesses refused to testify against them. Two of those witnesses, Bob Harris and Amos Dawson, were convicted of perjury in 1922 (NA, vol. 3630, file 6244-4, pt. 1, Angermann to Halliday, 28 January 1921; Halliday to Secretary [McLean], 19 May 1922; Angermann's Crime Reports, 15 and 22 April, 22 and 27 May 1922).

The assault on the potlatch spread into the Cowichan Agency in February 1921, after three officers from the Nanaimo RCMP attended a gathering on the Hallalt Reserve. Sergeant N. D. McLaren laid charges against Edward Hulbertson, James Gabriel, Jack Semo, Jimmy Albert, and Modest Dick, who were convicted, given suspended sentences, and set free (NA, vol. 3630, file 6244-4, pt. 1, McLaren, Crime Reports, 17 and 22 February 1921; Ditchburn to Scott, 24 March 1921). In March Angermann arrested Charles Nowell for celebrating his brother's funeral at Alert Bay (his son had died a month earlier). "I was sentenced for three months," Nowell recalls in his memoirs (1941, 224), "but after I had been there for six weeks Dr. Newcombe came to see me and got me a parole from the Governor of Victoria, and they let me out." Though his trial was intended to kill the potlatch, it served instead to bring it to life. "From then on I have been giving potlatches," Nowell remembers. "I have put my grandsons in their places ready when I die. My eldest grandson I put in my place as head chief, and the others in my other positions. I have told all the people about it, so that there will be no argument about it after I die. That's the way the Indians do before they die. Each of them has his own paraphernalia to use, so that they won't try to take away each other's. They have their own names" (218). As always the law had the effect of generating a supplement of potlatch. Indeed, the new policy of enforcement never had the impact that departmental officials claimed for it— though no doubt they had a stake in exaggerating their success. As Jim Quatel noted in 1914, "Mr Halliday says if he don't do what the government told him to do: he might lose his job." But why does he understand his "job" to be the "extermination" of the potlatch (NA, vol. 3629, file 6244-2, 12 June 1914)?

In December 1921 Angermann laid informations against Johnny Scow, George Scow, Chief Dick, Lagius, and Kasu for taking part in the sale of a copper. After Halliday sentenced each of them to two months in jail, their lawyer—Edwin DeBeck, the son of former Indian agent George DeBeck—lodged an appeal, but the British Columbia Supreme Court upheld the convictions. The five were sent to Oakalla prison on 22 January 1922. Two days later Halliday informed McLean that the potlatch was on the verge of death. "The general consensus of opinion is that if the next case is successful," he writes, "the potlatch will be absolutely dead." In the same month Peter Wilson, Edward Saxsmith, John Morrison, and Robert Wilson from the Gitksan community of Kispiox were charged with taking part in a "giving away celebration." They were tried at Hazelton and given suspended sentences of six months each (NA, vol. 3631, file 6244-5, Crime Report, 28 December 1921; vol. 3630, file 6244-4, pt. 2, Halliday to Secretary John D. McLean, 24 January 1922; Corporal Hall, Crime Reports, 6 and 8 January 1922).

By February 1922 white officials were preparing to deliver what they considered a death blow against the potlatch in the Kwawkewlth Agency. Using evidence gathered by police informants, Angermann laid informations against thirty-four people who had attended the Cranmer potlatch on Village Island at Christmas. Emma Cranmer's family had returned the property that her husband Dan had given them at the time of her marriage. Then Dan Cranmer distributed the repayment, and a large amount of other property, to the assembled guests (Sewid-Smith 1979, 55–57). Thirty-two of the accused were brought before Halliday on 16 February. Fearing he would be accused of bias if he heard the case by himself, Halliday shared the bench with a second justice of the peace, A. M. Wastell. When the trial resumed on 27 February, the lawyer for the defense offered to make a deal with the Crown: if the accused would plead guilty and agree in writing to renounce the potlatch forever, the Crown would give them suspended sentences and set them free. At Angermann's insistence, the agreement required the accused to surrender their masks, costumes, headdresses, coppers, and all the other regalia used in their hereditary dances. The court gave them a month to sign. "I firmly believe in my own mind," Halliday wrote Scott, "that the

*eating*

potlatch has been killed as they are all afraid to go on any further with it realizing that they are fighting a losing game" (NA, vol. 3630, file 6244-4, pt. 2, 1 March 1922). As always Halliday was compelled to repeat the news of a death that never arrived, for the potlatchers resisted the law with determination and consummate skill.

By the end of March many but not all of the people from three Kwakwala-speaking communities—the Lek-wiltok of Cape Mudge, the Mamililikulla of Village Island, and the Nimpkish of Alert Bay—had agreed to surrender their possessions to stay out of jail. The Kwagiulth of Fort Rupert refused. To coerce more people into signing, Angermann laid further charges stemming from the Cranmer potlatch and from some smaller potlatches held on Harbledown Island in February 1922. On 10 April twenty-two people who had not signed were sentenced and taken to Oakalla. Halliday informed Scott that "the potlatch is killed" (NA, vol. 3630, file 6244-4, pt. 2, Halliday to Scott, 10 April 1922; Angermann, Crime Reports, 19 April 1922).

Herbert (Me-Cha) Martin was one of the people who served time in prison for attending the Cranmer potlatch. Daisy Sewid-Smith records his version of events in *Prosecution or Persecution* (1979), an oral history of Halliday's anti-potlatch crusade. Martin's recollections suggest that Halliday's claim to have "killed" the potlatch was an extreme simplification. As Sewid-Smith puts it, "The Government was so sure that threat of imprisonment was going to make the people submit to their wishes but this was not to be" (59). Why then did Halliday repeatedly deploy the metaphor of putting to death? He was obeying a well-established discursive pattern. Martin's trial conformed to another, equally familiar model, for he recalls that his testimony before the court hinged on a debate over the word "Potlatch": "I spoke in English in spite of the fact that I did not really understand that language. I spoke. 'The Potlatch.' They did not understand what Potlatch meant. 'Potlatch is in the Chinook language. Give! to give! that is what Potlatch is *in Chinook*. You have told us to stop so you must think that it is bad. Potlatch is bad? To give! Take a look at the one who is putting us on trial. The Judge. This is Potlatch.' (He gives something to the judge). Is that the way it is? he said. He now knew. It was a Chinook word" (61, emphasis added). What is the difference between Martin's "Potlatch" and the judge's "Potlatch"? Martin recalls that after serving "just about two months" in jail, he and his fellow prisoners returned home—and resumed potlatching: "They did not stop our ways. We came home. It was good. There were no more arrests (for a while). After that La-geek (Peter Knox) had a potlatch in Fort Rupert. The Chieftains were afraid but we all went. They started the Red Cedar Bark Ceremony. Dan Cranmer gave as a dowry to him a Ah-klah-gey-ma. . . . James Knox was the Hamatsa. They started the Red Cedar Bark ceremony. They were going to dance that night. To our shock, Angermann and Halliday were sitting by the door." Martin danced anyway: "I was dancing the Hum-sumlth (the large Hamatsa mask) I was good at it at one time." The police officer—"that brute Angermann" —asked only if the mask was heavy (63).

Most of the articles confiscated in the aftermath of the Cranmer potlatch were sent either to the Victoria Memorial Museum in Ottawa or to the Royal Ontario Museum—which requested "one or two large totem poles"—in Toronto. They were not returned until 1979. In September 1922, however, Halliday sold a number of articles to George Heye, founder of the Museum of the American Indian in New York. By the time McLean reprimanded him for making this unauthorized sale, the property had been moved to the United States. It has never returned. The Canadian government paid a total of $1,456 for the goods it seized—including the coppers, which, to their owners, represented vast accumulations of wealth (NA, vol. 3630, file 6244-4, pt. 2, Currelly to Scott, 3 October 1922; Halliday to Secretary John D. McLean, 6 September 1922; Sapir to Scott, 1 March 1923).

The potlatch had died. But it was declared alive again by 1923. On 31 March Halliday sentenced ten people to jail for attending Quimolas's potlatch at Blunden Harbor. They appealed, and on 12 April the county court overturned their convictions on the grounds that Halliday had made errors in the warrants of committal. "The regrettable part of the whole thing," a frustrated Halliday complained to McLean, "is that all the work that has been done with regard to the potlatch will be more or less nullified and will have to be done all over again." The practice

*eating*

he had worked so hard to kill had returned from the grave. The department refused to appeal (NA, vol. 3630, file 6244-4, pt. 2, Halliday to McLean, 14 April 1923; Angermann, Crime Reports, 6 and 7 April 1923; McLean to Halliday, 4 May 1923).

In March 1927, precisely five years after heralding its death, Halliday informed McLean that the people of Kingcome Inlet had given "a real old time potlatch." Ten people were charged and pleaded guilty, but they negotiated an agreement that kept them from going to jail: "they said that if they were given another opportunity it would be the last time they would ever break the law in this respect and they pledged themselves that not only would they give up potlatching but that no potlatching would be allowed on the Kingcome Inlet Reserves" (NA, vol. 3631, file 6244-5, Halliday to McLean, 23 March 1927). Halliday gave them suspended sentences. Perhaps the Kingcome people knew that what mattered was not that the potlatch be killed but that its death be promised ("pledged") for a future that belonged to a rest of time beyond time—as if the unstated goal of the potlatch trials had not been to murder the potlatch, but to make it possible to *say* it was dead, over and over again.

Years later, in a letter to Scott dated 26 February 1931, Halliday resumed his discourse about a potlatch that is always-about-to-die. "You will remember," he begins, "that this Agency has been the cradle and nursing ground of that system known as the 'Potlatch,' for very many years, and although the prosecutions which took place some time ago killed it for the time being, I am sorry to say that I have reason to believe that it has broken out again" (NA, vol. 3631, file 6244-5). Since the nineteenth century the potlatch has died only to be reborn in a postal literature that tirelessly folds and unfolds the themes of life and death to generate an intricate system of creases. We can speculate about what drove Halliday to repeat the news of an instant that never arrived. His first three words sketch a likely answer: "You will remember." His compulsion to repeat belongs to that thought of whiteness that irrupts in the disjunction between a memory that aims to swallow the departed other and a memory that thinks an other who is always about to die but never does. While interiorizing memory seeks to preserve the present instant—"the time being"—within itself, thinking memory

*eating*

ensures that the moment of death is projected onto the horizon of an endlessly deferred future.

## EXACT INFORMATION

In June 1930 Halliday sent Scott, the poet-administrator, a manuscript copy of *Potlatch and Totem* and asked if he would agree to write a brief foreword. Halliday points out that the second section contains his recollections, while the first is, as he later confesses, a fictional account of a "typical" potlatch that "never took place" (1935, 11). The very structure of his memoirs suggests that he cannot remember himself without referring to a potlatch that is inching toward death. "The book has cost me a great deal of time," he recalls, "and I m[ay] say, considerable expense in getting all the exact information, as I have taken pains, particularly in the part relating to the Potlatch, to have every item of it meticulously correct" (NA, vol. 3631, file 6244-5, 12 June 1930). Halliday has spent his time, for him a precious currency, gathering the "exact information" about a practice that he had long identified as a waste of time, but narrative is impossible without delay, without that instantless instant of deferral that holds each of its moments apart from every other. The gift of the text irrupts in just such an instantless instant. And, as the First Nations never ceased to recall, it was the arrival of a textual gift that ensured that Halliday and his fellow administrators never sent themselves a "meticulously correct" account of the potlatch.

By 1930 the British Columbia First Nations had spent years telling Canada that the thing it had banned did not correspond to the gatherings held in their communities. After the trial of Ned Harris and John Bagwany in 1914, Jim Quatel had protested in his first letter to the department that "[i]t may be the potlatch is bad to those who know nothing about it," and he classed Halliday in particular among the ranks of the ignorant: "Mr. Halliday is not Indian, he is white-man and standing on the other"— indeed standing on others in order to kill their traditions and swallow them into the white body politic. "The potlatch is not a new and nothing unusual," he concludes. "When one give a potlatch (present) to us, we are only glad when we receive a gift and hear our chiefs tells us about the pass historys as well as to his own history (which

217

*eating*

would be about as thick as the white peoples own history books it if was printed)." A month later Charlie Smith affirmed in Quatel's second letter that "[t]hat Indian Agent Halliday is only spoils everythings because he telling you what is not correct. . . . We all like our own ways" (NA, vol. 3629, file 6244-2, 14 May, 12 June 1914).

In 1897 Boas had argued that the potlatch served as a means of record keeping in societies that had no system of writing. According to this argument, the potlatch was a poor substitute for pen, paper, and the graphic alphabet. But if the potlatch was an inferior writing, surely it would have disappeared when the people of potlatching cultures adopted the Western European system of inscription. Surely, after years of contact with Europeans and Euro-Canadians, when the First Nations needed to record their transactions, they would have chosen the information technology of Western European "civilization" over the writing performed by the potlatch. However, the potlatch did not die when confronted with another technology. Instead, people like Jim Quatel deployed writing in their defense of writing's substitute.

On 7 September 1914 the Kwakwaka'wakw joined with a number of Salish-speaking communities to protest to the white government that its hostility toward the potlatch was based on ignorance. "Indians don't understand white man's fashions," they wrote, "and white man don't understand our fashion, and they can't live as Indians does." "We earnestly pray to the Government of Canada," they conclude, "to take consideration of our plan and petition, as the Government knows this is our own and it is our fashions. We did not imitate it from no nation but our own. . . . There are people reporting saying some severe words against us, and what we've done harm to them we dont see." On 28 January 1915 representatives of the Kwagiulth and the Nimpkish wrote H. S. Clements, a conservative member of Parliament, asking him to intercede with the department on their behalf. Clements, who admitted he "had considerable sympathy in some of their grievances," sent their letter on to D. C. Scott (NA, vol. 3629, file 6244-3, 3 February 1915). In reply, Scott wrote the Department of Mines and asked the anthropological division to prepare a report on the potlatch. Edward Sapir sent Scott a copy of Boas's 1898 "Summary" and advised him to read Boas's "Secret Societies," which according to

Sapir contained "[p]robably the best account yet published of the potlatch system of the Kwakiutl Indians" (11 February 1915). "It seems to me high time," Sapir added, "that white men realized that they are not doing the Indians much of a favour by converting them into inferior replicas of themselves." But that was already the impossible goal of Scott's administration.

Sapir also mentioned that he was writing the leading scholars of northwest coast anthropology to ask "for their opinion on the potlatch." On 1 March he sent Scott letters from James Teit, Harlan Smith, Charles F. Newcombe, Charles Hill-Tout, John Swanton, and Franz Boas. They all advised against enforcing the law. "Those who have caused all the trouble of thus persecuting these Indians," wrote Harlan Smith, "dragging them many miles before the courts and imprisoning them, so far as I have ever been able to find out, knew little or nothing about Indians." He doubted that "any one person understands all about this institution" (NA, vol. 3629, file 6244-2, 16 February 1915).

Meanwhile the Kwagiulth band sent John D. McLean a petition via Halliday in order "to ask one or two Commissioners from Ottawa to come to this agency . . . and look into the potlatch themselves, so that we may explain to them what they call a potlatch . . . for we are in great trouble . . . for we are sure that these judges and lawyers do not unde[rstand] what the potlatch is but they have to go by the law." The petitioners appear to have arrived at a collective decision that the most effective way to protest against the law was to prove that it was based on misinformation, for they begin by noting that they have held "several meetings at Fort Rupert to look into the matter of the potlatch to see what is the reason the Indian Department wants to stop the potlatch and could not see any fault in it." They also observe that Halliday himself "told us he finds no fault in the potlatch" (NA, vol. 3629, file 6244-2, 2 March 1915). In 1919 Charles Nowell, Moses Alfred, and William Roberts traveled all the way to Ottawa to present their arguments directly to Scott. In the words of Cole and Chaikin (1990, 111), "The reception they received was as cool as the Rideau River in February."

However, they eventually managed to force Scott to listen to their appeals. When Harry Mountain, Isaac, John McDougall, Chief August, and their seventy-three supporters signed the agreement to give up potlatching in

219

eating

March 1919 (whether they obeyed it or not is another question), they were careful to reserve the right to petition the government to amend the law. What followed was a skillful manipulation of the white legal system. Several months later the presiding judge, H. S. Cayley, wrote Minister of the Interior Arthur Meighen and reminded him that the government had agreed to conduct an inquiry into the potlatch. When confronted with the agreement, Scott wrote his minister that "[t]he facts are already available in this Department and in the anthropological division of the Geological Survey and lately a complete survey of all our papers on the subject was made by Mr. [Marius] Barbeau of that division. . . . As a matter of fact," he continues, "we probably know more about the aboriginal custom of the potlatch than do the Indians themselves." Though he claimed to know all, Scott nevertheless agreed to ask the anthropological division to make a report and "to allow the Indians to make their representations to this Department in writing." "The Indians" had outmaneuvered him. So he kept only the first part of his promise (NA, vol. 3630, file 6244-4, pt. 1, Cayley to Meighen, 26 September 1919; Scott to Stewart, 12 January 1920).

No matter what Scott argued, though, the Kwakwaka'-wakw had never stopped insisting that, "as a matter of fact," the government knew none of the "facts" about the potlatch. On the day after Christmas 1918 a group of people from seven Kwakwaka'wakw communities signed the following petition:

> We feel that the Government has not been fully
> and correctly informed about the potlatch and
> we would respectull [*sic*] ask you to send a good
> straight man to come and see all the Indians
> so that you may know exactly what the potlatch
> is. We think the law is not right and that you
> have been mistaken in stopping the Indians
> from giving away money to our friends. We see
> our white friends giving presents to one an-
> other and why can we not do the same? Our
> white friends give feasts why can we not do the
> same? (NA, vol. 3629, file 6244-3, 26 Decem-
> ber 1918)

A petition written at Alert Bay on 28 January 1915, addressed to H. S. Clements, states: "We told you that our

Indian agent Mr. Halliday is trying to stop us from giving away money + blankets + etc to other Indians, which we all know is good for every Indians + which we know is called a potlatch by a chinook word to give." The petitioners defend the potlatch as a way of redistributing wealth from rich to poor in a time of high unemployment.

Almost five years later the Nimpkish deployed the same arguments in a petition to Duncan Campbell Scott. What the government fails to understand, they say, is that the practice known as "the potlatch" is a redistribution of wealth.

> [W]e think that if you understood our customs from the beginning that you would amend the law to allow us to go on in our old way. In order to let you know how it was carried on and why it was done we are sending you this letter.
>
> We all know that things are changing. In the old days the only things that counted were such things as food, dried fish, roots, berries and things of that nature. A chief in those days would get possession of all these things and would pass them on to those who had not got any and in many instances would call another tribe and help them out too. We wish to continue this custom. (NA, vol. 3630, file 6244-4, pt. 1, 6 April 1920)

The previous January Spruce Martin and Frank Walker had sent a letter to H. S. Clements in protest against the law. Their strategy here is to defend "the potlatch" by arguing that it is "just the same" as a number of Euro-Canadian customs. Hence their text overlaps "tribal" values with "white" ones.

> The Potlatch to us is *just the same* to us as Christmas or any other feast is to the whites. It has been carried on before us as far back as we can trace. Suppose two of our tribe get married we have a potlatch that is we give them presents *just the same as the white man dose.* Suppose some of our people are hard up we potlatch them flour or anything they want just the same as the white man dose if any of his friends are

hard up. In other words it is the religion of the Indians to help one another. And we think when the Government stops us from pot-latching they are taking away from us one of our oldest and best customs. (14 January 1920, emphasis added)

Two years later Chief Joseph of the Nuu'chah'nulth community of Clayoquot declared that "we can't possibly put away the ways of Indian dancing" (NA, vol. 3630, file 6244-4, pt. 2, 13 March 1922).

In March 1921 Edwin DeBeck began a campaign to have Scott's administration release the promised report detailing the "facts" about the potlatch—but without success (NA, vol. 3630, file 6244-4, pt. 1, 4 March, 18 May, 19 July 1921). Then, on 3 May 1922, while over twenty people were in jail for attending the Cranmer potlatch, Leon Ladner, the conservative member of Parliament for south Vancouver, inquired in the House of Commons about the report that was supposed to have been prepared by the anthropological division. Above all he asked Superintendent General of Indian Affairs Charles Stewart whether or not the report was "favourable to the Potlatch Institution" (*Parliamentary Debates*, 1922, 1377). On 11 May Ladner wrote directly to Stewart, urging him to amend the antipotlatch statute and to release the people imprisoned for the Cranmer potlatch. He reminded him that public opinion was opposed to the law. On 26 May he again asked Stewart for a copy of the report, which, as it turns out, had been ready for over a year. With pressure building Scott prepared a memo for Stewart on 6 June, advising him that "the report is neither favourable nor unfavourable" to the potlatch. "It is merely a recapitulation of all the facts with reference to the potlatch," though the question, again, is *which* "potlatch" do these "facts" refer to. "There would be no great objection to letting Mr. Ladner have a copy of this report," Scott writes, "but I think it would be inadvisable."

Ladner rose in the House on 19 June and asked, "Has the matter not been investigated, at the instance of the department, by the Anthropological Society which has made a report favourable to the lessening of these [antipotlatch] restrictions and giving back to the Indians some of their rights?" Stewart replied that "[i]f a report is in the department, it has not been brought to my attention." But he had known about it since at least 6 June. He also promised to release the report if it was available. It had been available since May 1921 (*Parliamentary Debates,* 1922, 3191–92).

Because Scott said he was "absolutely and unalterably opposed" to amending the law, it is not hard to understand why he advised Stewart not to release the report. What remains of it suggests that it is unequivocally "favourable" to "the potlatch Institution." From the outset the author of the report, D. G. Campbell, proposes "to set forth reasons why the [KWAKI]UTL Indians should not be disturbed . . . in carrying out the principle of the Potlatch." He argues that the purpose of the law—to lift the Kwakwaka'-wakw into European civilization by stripping them of traditions that white observers, especially missionaries, considered barbaric—was wrong from the start: "The Kwakiutl Indian from the nature of his peculiar characteristics and mode of life can never be assimilated with the white race." Like Boas's ethnography, the report interprets the Kwakwaka'wakw as the absolute others of European Canada. They belong outside the westernmost limit of the West and cannot be cannibalized by a white society that desires to remember itself by eating others. Since "[t]he Indian will thrive only in an atmosphere and under condition[s] and customs handed down from one generation to another," the report advises the government to give in to the petitions of the First Nations and to repeal the ban on the potlatch "as soon as possible" (NA, vol. 3631, file 6244-X).[11]

If a crime was committed during the era of the potlatch trials, it was not the distribution of property on Village Island. Rather it was Scott's suppression of the report on the antipotlatch law. Since 1915 Scott had known that the leading researchers in his own culture were opposed to the law. By the first week of May 1921 he knew that the government's research demanded a change in policy. According to the protocols of scholarship laid out by his nation's institutions, Scott was obliged to publish the findings of the acknowledged experts even if that meant having the law amended. That he refused to publish the latest data is especially striking if one recalls that throughout this episode Scott was president of the Royal Society of Canada.

He gave his presidential address, "Poetry and Progress," on 17 May 1922, while twenty-three people were serving time in Oakalla prison for potlatching. He begins by praising the "ideals of the Society." There is "something unique," he says, "in the constitution of a society that comprises Literature and Science, that makes room for the Mathematician and the Chemist, the Historian and the Biologist, the Poet and the Astronomer" (1947, 123). This "unique" society also includes the anthropologist and provides for the publication and conservation of anthropological data. "It should be remarked," Scott remarks, "that one of the objects set forth by our charter was to assist in the collection of archives and to aid in the formation of a National Museum of Ethnology, Archaeology and Natural History. Let us not weaken for a moment," he exhorts, "in the discharge of this obligation" (127). By suppressing the government's research, though, Scott broke this selfimposed "obligation" to establish "archives" where ethnographic research would be open to public scrutiny.

Perhaps his betrayal of his own principles was a consequence of his conviction that the poet's foremost ethical responsibility is to contribute to the building of a nation. In his address Scott describes literature as the producer, rather than the product, of social and political relations. He concedes that "[l]iterature in its purest form is vowed to the service of the imagination" and that "its ethical powers" are therefore "secondary," yet he affirms that, since the task of poetry is to advance the cause of "human progress," poets are burdened with a heavy ethical "obligation" (125–26). It is their duty to help raise people from barbarity and lead them toward nationhood, which he understands to be the crowning achievement of human civilization, its ultimate, rational "social state." "The poet is the voice of the imagination," he says, and the "imagination has always been concerned with endeavours to harmonize life and to set up nobler conditions of living; to picture perfect social states and to commend them to the reason" (146). Perhaps this is the reason he suppressed the report. Scott's "perfect social state" has no place for non-European cultures. The poet's duty to contribute to the building of a homogeneously white Euro-Canadian society outweighed the researcher's recommendation that Canada give up its project to absorb the First Nations into itself. Aboriginal cultures have a place in Scott's nation only if they consent to die and leave their remains—such as their names or confiscated potlatch regalia—in national archives and museums to be remembered by future generations of homogeneously white citizens.

# EPILOGUE

*But let life go, naught can be altered after*
*The heart is vacant and all shed the tears;*
*Let it be told amid ironic laughter*
*"He had given all—through all the years."*

Duncan Campbell Scott, "A Mood"

## THE IMAGE AND THE GIFT

When Andrew Paull of the Allied Tribes of British Columbia wrote the minister of the interior to demand "a relax-
ation of the Potlatch law" in 1923, he argued that the government's knowledge of the potlatch did not correspond
with its intended object. While he admitted that "[m]uch
has been said against the Potlatch," he took care to note
that "what has been said in favor of the Potlatch has been
done so by the people who are in a position to know but
the prayer of the Indians has not heretofore been given
due consideration." His argument assumes true knowledge
is a correct representation, an authentic image, of a thing
existing independently of the words that describe it. If administrators would "position" their utterances to bring what
they said about the potlatch into agreement with potlatch
itself, they would have to acknowledge that the law was an
expression of ignorance, and they would repeal it (NA, vol.
3630, file 6244-4, pt. 2, Paull to Stewart, 30 August 1923).

Paull could not have foreseen that the potlatch that the
law had banned did not belong to a metaphysics that takes
truth to be a correspondence shuttling via the postal technology of the sign between knowledge and its object. The
legal text gave administrators a potlatch to regulate, and
this thing, this ghost potlatch, could never have been a
"meticulously correct" representation of the First Nations'
traditions. It was a substitute for the potlatch, not an image

*Opposite:* Representatives of the law pose at the intersection of
three colonial technologies: the gunboat, the camera, and the postcard. Courtesy of The Field Museum, neg. no. 17527, Chicago.

of it. When Indian agents and police officers enforced the antipotlatch statute, they condemned what it had given them to condemn, not the practices that aboriginal people were performing. And no amount of education could make white administrators lift their prohibition. For if they understood nothing about the potlatch, they knew what it was that they called "the potlatch." Since it had arrived into being out of the gap between two functions of the legal text—the past moment when it defined what it banned and the future moment when it banned what it had defined—the only way to revise the government's potlatch policy was to get rid of the law that had given a thing to the world. Yet the law did not drop from the statute books until Parliament passed a new (but not too new) Indian Act in 1951 after two years of hearings by a joint committee of the Senate and House of Commons.

There is no doubt that the law sometimes changed the way the First Nations pursued their traditions. Since the statute—which was relocated to section 140 of the Indian Act in 1927—banned "any Indian festival, dance, or other ceremony" involving the "giving away or paying or giving back" of property, in the early 1930s the Kwakwaka'wakw decided they could escape prosecution by letting six months elapse between dances and distributions of property (NA, vol. 3631, file 6244-5, Ditchburn to Scott, 2 April 1931). In February 1931 Halliday made the following complaint after a large number of sacks of flour were distributed on Village Island: "There is no difficulty whatever in getting proof that the flour was given, but the difficulty arises in making any connection between the giving away of the flour and any Indian festival, dance, or other ceremony, as prescribed in Section 140 of the Indian Act" (NA, vol. 3631, file 6244-5, 26 February 1931). However, it is not certain that every potlatch divided itself in two. Two months earlier Boas had written his sister from Fort Rupert that "[t]here were all sorts of feasts here during the past weeks, especially the wedding of a couple that had been living together for several years." These "feasts" included both dancing and the distribution of property. On Christmas Eve, Boas held a feast of his own: "The Indians used this opportunity to celebrate Christmas," he writes, but not without contradiction: "that is, they had entertainment in their old style" (Rohner 1969, 294, 298).

After the Cranmer potlatch in 1922, white officials lost their desire to enforce the law. There were prosecutions in the northeast of the province, but no one was sent to jail. Silas Johnson of Kispiox received a lecture after holding a potlatch in 1927, and a potlatcher from the Nantley Reserve was given a one year suspended sentence, which was illegal under section 140. In 1928 Chief Isadore and Thomas and Margaret Kettlo pleaded guilty to potlatching, but their convictions were overturned on appeal when it was found that, as in 1889, the crown was "unable to quote an authoritative definition of this word"—" 'Potlach'." In January 1931 Moses Stevens received a one-month suspended sentence for raising a totem pole (NA, vol. 3631, file 6244-5, T. E. E. Greenfield, Crime Report, 28 February 1927; K. H. Turnbull, Crime Report, 23 July 1927; A. H. Brien, Report, 26 June 1928; M. T. Berger, Crime Report, 9 February 1931).

After Halliday retired from the Kwawkewlth Agency, his immediate successor, E. G. Newnham, tried to enforce the law but encountered resistance from the local people and from the new pastor of the Anglican church at Alert Bay, C. K. K. Prosser. In another ironic turn a church that had previously demanded that the statute be enforced—through such missionaries as John Antle and Bishop Schofield—now called for its repeal. When Murray Todd took over the Kwawkewlth Agency in 1934, he suggested amending the Indian Act to make it illegal to attend potlatches and to own regalia associated with potlatching, such as masks and coppers. He also recommended that agents be empowered to seize the property distributed in potlatches. T. A. Crerar, the new superintendent general, brought the proposed amendment before Parliament in February 1936 but in another ironic turn ran into opposition from a former Indian agent—the independent member for Comox-Alberni, A. W. Neill—along with J. S. Woodsworth and others. In 1904 Neill had advised that the antipotlatch statute be retained but not enforced. In 1936, obeying the instructions of the First Nations which had written him in protest, he helped to ensure that it became a "dead letter" once and for all (Cole and Chaikin 1990, 144–50).

## ANOTHER FOLD

Heidegger repeats in "The Way to Language" (1972) that the "essential being" of language consists of "saying." To say is to show things, and showing makes it possible to signify them: "in everything that gives itself to us in speaking, or waits for us unspoken, but also in the speaking that we do *ourselves,*" says Heidegger, "there prevails Showing which causes to appear what is present, and to fade from appearance what is absent." What "showing" entails is that words give things to be thought and are not grafted to what already exists. Showing is an act that delivers things into being, and it therefore belongs to that postal technology that Heidegger (who would insist it is nothing technological) calls enownment, appropriation—*Ereignis.* It is enownment—neither an effect nor a cause nor even an event—that allows "all beings to be present in their own, in what is most appropriate for them," and gives them to signification. Heidegger calls *Ereignis* "the plainest and most gentle of all laws." But if it is a "law," the act of enownment is not a norm, an order or an ordinance—let alone a statute. It is a gift event that occurs, without occurring, at the limit of the metaphysical conception of being and time, and it *gathers* things and people into their own essence, "into the appropriateness of their nature and there holds them" (1971, 126–29).

It is clear by now that I do not endorse all that Heidegger proposes. The gift event that I have described here, using the antipotlatch law—a law against giving—as an uncircumventable example, was neither plain nor gentle. It delivered itself violently to the world, arriving in the disjunction—not the gathering—of two incompatible yet mechanical functions of the legal text. When it arrived, moreover, it ruptured—and did not unite—an ongoing continuum of events, for the potlatch that Canada banned did not correspond with the potlatches that were already under way on the northwest coast.

Heidegger might nevertheless agree that this textual gift had no author, was not the product of someone's intentions. It was an instrument that anyone could deploy in any number of racist undertakings. Instead of being a poor image of an original, the outlawed potlatch originated its own order of reality after the fact, and though its arrival in the world was purely aleatory, it made new oppressions possible. We have seen how it was used, and how it failed, to hasten the assimilation of the British Columbia First Nations into the Canadian body politic—part of a larger project to give Europe-in-Canada a feeling for its own whiteness and nationhood.

Assimilation had to fail, though, because the First Nations refused it and because it was based on an irony that it could not overcome. Its aim was to fold together the two sides of the limit dividing Canada from the First Nations, gathering them into a larger national totality. On the west coast of British Columbia the limit that whiteness traced between itself and its others took the form of the gift. If the fold was to be made, and assimilation to succeed, the distribution of property would have to be suppressed, but Europe-in-Canada had tried for years—in letters and in essays, in ethnography and in poetry—to set the coastal First Nations at an irreducible distance from itself. European observers placed the Kwakwaka'wakw in particular, the same people who bore the brunt of the potlatch prosecutions, at the farthest possible remove from Western European culture. What made them absolutely other to the European gaze was their apparent proximity to the gift and their alleged willingness to spend all.

As Albert Memmi ([1957] 1967) points out, the inscription of a limit dividing the colonizer from the colonized is one of the basic structures of colonial racism. Colonial logic works first to establish this limit as an "absolute fact," and once it is established, colonizers are free to exploit it for their own benefit (71). The inscription of a border between Europe-in-Canada and the First Nations of coastal British Columbia lent justification to the violence of European settlement, permitting it to be crudely interpreted as the victory of civilization over barbarity. Yet this mode of colonial racism has never ceased to be haunted by its internal contradiction. While Canadian colonialism has justified itself by marking an absolute limit between settler society and its aboriginal others, Canadian whiteness has at the same time thought itself as a transgression of that limit. The white nation—or, to be precise, the nation that desires to be white—frames its sense of itself, its self-consciousness, by repeating over and over to itself that it is about to swallow and to mourn an aboriginal other who has died. When the instant of death arrives, and even though that instant is endlessly deferred, the nation will be able to give itself a distinctive white Canadian subjectivity, but thanks to the irony that grounds it, the nation cannot realize its aim of folding others into itself because the limit that holds it apart from them is also what gives it a feeling for itself, the consciousness of its own nationhood. And somewhere in that self-consciousness, which knows that it is fundamentally incompatible with itself, the nation acknowledges that its strategies of self-justification are inadequate to their task, and it silently confesses that its existence is also a crime.

NOTES

# FOLDING

1. The phrase "totally other and yet the same" is a citation of Homi K. Bhabha citing Derrida's "Double Session" (1981, 241). Bhabha offers several indispensable analyses of the play of the other in the same within the frame of colonialism, for example, in "Of Mimicry and Man": "colonial mimicry is the desire for a reformed, recognizable Other, as *a subject of a difference that is almost the same but not quite*" (1994, 86).

2. Harry Assu of Cape Mudge on Quadra Island: "Nowadays our people here use the term Kwagiulth for all the Kwakwala-speaking tribes north to Smith Inlet. Beyond there the Heiltsuk language begins. Almost all our southern tribes are represented by the Kwakiutl District Council. The name Kwagiulth (or Kwakiutl) has been spelled in all sorts of ways by missionaries, government agents, and anthropologists. It's the name of the tribe at Fort Rupert near Port Hardy on Vancouver Island, but we all use that name." Assu notes, however, that "[e]ach tribe of the Kwagiulth Nation has its own name." For example, the community at Cape Mudge, in the roman alphabet, is the We-Wai-Kai band of the Lekwiltok tribe (16).

Joy Inglis adds the following comments in a footnote to this passage from *Assu of Cape Mudge:* "To get away from using the title of one band at Fort Rupert to stand for all bands of the Southern Kwagiulth, the word *Kwakwaka?wakw* was proposed by the U'Mista Cultural Society at Alert Bay. It is coming into increasing use by scholars and Native speakers to the north, but is not in use in the Lekwiltok area. It means 'speakers of the Kwakwala language' " (Assu 1989, 124).

3. Note that Sproat makes no mention of signing a treaty with the people of this community before expropriating their land. Ironically, it will later be his job to sort out the problems created by such acts of expropriation.

4. This passage from "Letter on Humanism" clarifies Heidegger's terms: "The thinking that is to come is no longer philosophy, because it thinks more originally than metaphysics—a name identical to philosophy" (242). "Metaphysics" is his name for Western European philosophy since Plato, while he reserves the name "thinking" for the work that comes after philosophy.

5. "But what 'is' above all is Being. Thinking accomplishes the relation of Being to the essence of man. It does not make or cause the relation. Thinking brings this relation to Being solely as some-

thing handed over to it from Being. *Such offering consists in the fact that in thinking Being comes to language. Language is the house of Being.* In its home man dwells. Those who think and those who create with words are the guardians of this home. Their guardianship accomplishes the manifestation of Being insofar as they bring the manifestation to language and maintain it in language through their speech" (Heidegger 1977, 193, emphasis added). For Heidegger, humanity inhabits a world of discourse: *logos* (202).

6. "Once," that is, in *Being and Time* (Heidegger [1927] 1962, 255).

## GIVING

1. In the "Annual Report on Indian Affairs for the Year Ending June 30 1872," Secretary of State Joseph Howe outlines the reasons for creating the British Columbia superintendency:

> In dealing with the new provinces of British Columbia and Manitoba, and the wide territories of the North West, it has become already apparent that Indian affairs cannot be managed by the application of *the old machinery* which has been found to work so well in the Canadas. In these vast countries no very extensive or valuable Reserves have been set apart for the Indians, no large funds are invested, the missionary labor (though zealous and self-devoted men have from the earliest times penetrated [!] into these regions) has been less in proportion to the mass of ignorance and pagan superstition to be encountered, and the distances from Ottawa are so formidable, that after a short experience of utter hopelessness of the task of carrying on Indian affairs *by correspondence* with this Department, I have felt it my duty to advise that Boards should be appointed, one at Victoria and another at Winnipeg, to whom should be largely entrusted the management of Indian affairs both in British Columbia and the North West. (Canada, *Sessional Papers,* 1873, no. 23, pp. 2–3, emphasis added)

A superintendent, rather than a board, was put in place in British Columbia. And the administration of "Indian affairs" continued to be carried on by "correspondence" despite the "utter hopelessness of the task"—giving rise to the postal literature discussed here.

2. To be precise, Powell was solely responsible for the administration of Indian affairs in the province when he was first appointed in 1872, but when a second superintendent, James Lenihan, was appointed in New Westminster in 1874, Powell became responsible for managing Canada's relations with the coastal First Nations. The new superintendent dealt with the First Nations of the interior. According to Robin Fisher, Powell was poorly qualified for his new job, and the appointment of the second superintendent only added to the problem since "Lenihan was, in the parlance of the day, going 'soft

in the head' " (181). In 1879 the dominion government wanted to establish a system of administration made up of one visiting Indian superintendent stationed in Victoria who would oversee the activities of several "sub-agents" located on the island and around the southern coast and interior of the province (*Sessional Papers*, 1881, no. 4, pp. 15–16). But by 1881 Powell was once again the only superintendent in the province.

3. The Douglas treaties were not directly modeled upon the Royal Proclamation. When he drew up his first treaty,

> Douglas had the chiefs [of "the Teechamitsa, a Songhees community occupying what is now Esquimault,"] indicate their approval at the foot of a blank sheet of paper; he then wrote to [Archibald] Barclay [the Hudson's Bay Company secretary] asking for a suitable text to place on the upper portion of the sheet. Barclay responded with a text virtually identical to that already used by the New Zealand Company in purchasing land from the Maori. Douglas himself then copied the text, with the necessary additions of names, dates, and amount of payment, onto the original sheet of paper. The same text was used for subsequent purchases from other Indian groups. Thus . . . it was New Zealand rather than Canada and the Royal Proclamation of 1763 that provided the immediate model for the Douglas transactions. (Tennant 1990, 18–19)

For a fuller account of Douglas's land purchases, Tennant refers his reader to an unpublished paper by James Hendrickson, "The Aboriginal Land Policy of Governor James Douglas, 1849–1864" (284).

4. Wilson Duff says that in the 1870s the land question gave rise to a three-way conflict between Canada, British Columbia, and the First Nations.

> While the two governments argued, the Indians became more and more agitated. By 1877 the situation in the interior was so tense that an Indian war seemed imminent. In Ottawa the Minister of the Interior thought the situation serious enough to warn the Provincial authorities by telegram that his government would side with the Indians in any trouble: "Indian rights to soil in British Columbia have never been extinguished. Should any difficulty occur, steps will be taken to maintain the Indian claims to all the country where rights have not been extinguished by treaty. Don't desire to raise the question at present but Local Government must instruct Commissioners to make reserves so large as to completely satisfy Indians." (Duff 1964, 67)

It would be misleading, however, to portray the federal government as the champion of the First Nations in nineteenth-century British Columbia. When the Conservative party returned to power in 1878, the superintendent general of Indian affairs allowed provincial officials to protect white interests by decreasing the size of reserves (Tennant 1990, 50–51).

5. Lawrence Vankoughnet, the deputy superintendent general of Indian affairs, reports in 1878 that Sproat had gone so far as to fire his surveyor and to hire "a non-professional, and consequently a cheaper man." Hence making an accurate survey and allotment of land was less important than saving "about $6 per diem or $180 per month in the expenses of the commission" (*Sessional Papers*, 1879, no. 7, pp. 16–17).

6. Settlers on Vancouver Island reacted to the meeting at Lytton with open hostility. A group of prominent whites—including William Duncan of Metlakatla and Alexander Anderson, who had recently served beside Sproat on the reserve commission—petitioned the premier of British Columbia that "to combine a number of half-civilised natives" would be "exceedingly dangerous to the peace of the province" (NA, vol. 3669, file 10,691, 25 September 1879). They had reason to be afraid: the white society's encroachment upon aboriginal lands and its refusal to recognize aboriginal title had almost led to war in the interior in 1877. In a letter forwarding the petition to Ottawa, a nervous Powell repeated that allowing the Nlaka'pamux to govern themselves might lead to conflict with white settlers—and he complained that Sproat had no business meddling in matters that belonged within the superintendent's jurisdiction (29 September 1879; also Fisher 1977, 178–79).

7. "The [Indian] act [of 1868] allowed the department [of Indian affairs] to impose a 'chief and council' structure, which, in spite of its name, was copied from the typical Canadian mayor and council structure and was intended to induce bands to copy the municipal style of local government and to adopt the white view that local government should be subordinate to central authorities. Despite the implication of some local autonomy, the act gave sweeping powers of regulation over reserves and bands to the federal minister of Indian affairs and his officials" (Tennant 1990, 45).

8. One of the complaints Blenkinsop makes in his report of 1874 (NA, vol. 3614, file 4105, 23 September 1874) is that the people of Barkley Sound ask the government for gifts while they are in his eyes giving their own property away. He claims that "were a proper disposal made of their immense gains they could furnish themselves with every comfort they could possibly wish for." Hence they violate the principle of classical utility.

9. In his contemporary study of "gift-exchange" (1979) Lewis Hyde extends the literary tradition that situates the gift, the potlatch, and the Kwakwaka'wakw at the limit dividing Western Europe from its beyond. And, as always, this gift limit is the site of a fold that endlessly overlaps Europe with a culture it defines as its absolute other. Basing his analysis on one book by Philip Drucker, Hyde condemns the potlatch as the illegitimate product of a union between the

Kwagiulth of Fort Rupert and a distinctively "European" economy. What seems to make the potlatch monstrous for Hyde is that it violates an unspoken prohibition on hybridity: "As first studied, the potlatch was the progeny of a European capitalism *mated* to an aboriginal gift economy, and with freakish results" (30, emphasis added). Writing in the 1970s, not the 1870s, Hyde extends a discursive pattern that singles out the Kwagiulth as Europe's absolute other and, in a troubling metaphor, villainizes the potlatch as the monster child of an interracial "mating," the "freakish" product of a miscegenation that transgresses the boundary between the "European" and the "aboriginal." Confronted with hybridity, Hyde, like the Sproat who narrates *Scenes*, longs for "the thorough savage in his isolated condition": "When American [*sic*] ethnographers first studied the potlatch at the end of the nineteenth century [a 'first' study that followed studies such as Sproat's], over a hundred years of trading with the whites had changed it to its roots. We must therefore look upon the literature we have about the potlatch with a wary eye—what is truly aboriginal and what is an accommodation to the new economy?" (28). Why "must" Hyde seek a "truly aboriginal" essence pure of any admixtures—and how can he claim to find it in texts that he considers contaminated? Such a move serves the overriding aim of his study, which is to use a pure theory of the pure gift to inscribe a clear limit between "art" and the marketplace of "European capitalism": "It is the assumption of this book," he says in his introduction, "that the work of art is a gift, not a commodity" (xi). Hence he vilifies the Kwagiulth in the interest of defending Western art from the very commercialism he finds in the potlatch. Ironically, however, to isolate even "the smudged image of earlier gift exchange" in Kwagiulth society, Hyde turns, inexplicably, to Boas's account of the sale of a copper—and never asks whether or not the copper is itself a mark of the hybridity that he finds so intolerable (31). See "Eating," note 5, especially the statement by Gloria Cranmer Webster.

10. Powell discusses what he perceives to be the "laxity" of women's morals in his report on the visits he made in the summer of 1879. Dated 26 August 1879, his report was sent to Ottawa almost exactly two months before Sproat's "Patlach" letter.

> The women have an exceedingly clear skin and pleasant contour, and were it not for the notorious laxity of their morals, would, no doubt, be the conservators of a fine race.
>
> As it is, most of the young women spend the greater part of their time at Victoria and the Pujet Sound [*sic*] ports, so that, in visiting any of their villages, they are rarely seen, and in some of the camps, very few, if any children.
>
> Indeed, the chief complaint made to me by some of the influential men of the tribe, was in regard to this matter, and expressing the hope, now that I could witness their condition,

that some regulation would be enforced, compelling their women to return home, and preventing these destructive pilgrimages in future. (*Sessional Papers*, 1880, no. 4, p. 126)

11. What is the relation between this text and Cole and Chaikin's history of the law against the potlatch, *An Iron Hand upon the People*? It is an anaclitic relationship: a relation of leaning. They have made my own textual analysis possible by translating archival documents into a historical narrative, but as de Man might say, the rhetorical mode of their narrative is that of the excuse. If the promise is "proleptic," says de Man, then the "excuse is belated and always occurs after the crime; since the crime is exposure, the excuse consists in recapitulating the exposure in the guise of concealment" (1979, 286). De Man notes too that there is a charge of pleasure to be won by reexposing a crime while pretending to cover it up.

How do Cole and Chaikin go about making excuses? Here is an example: at the end of chapter 2 they suggest that the antipotlatch law "was passed as reform legislation, intended to promote the health and the economic and social progress of British Columbia's Indians. . . . In many ways," they continue, "its supporters represented all that was best and most noble in Euro-Canadian society. The law was in the tradition of imperial reform—of William Wilberforce and Exeter Hall, of the Aboriginal Protection Society, of the abolition of slavery and the slave trade, and of the suppression of suttee in British India. That the proponents of the law prohibiting the potlatch and the tamananawas [*sic*] dance suffered from all the failings of this philanthropic and reform tradition should not blind their descendants to the fact that they also shared its virtues" (24). Sproat, Powell, Blenkinsop, Vankoughnet, and all their peers were therefore heroes, indeed a colonial "nobility" hounded by the same tragic flaw: they were too loyal to a certain "philanthropic and reform tradition." They were too good for their own good, and if you cannot see that, then you are "blind." Why then did they ignore all the voices that explicitly told them the law was wrong—including public opinion? Cole and Chaikin's portrait of the Noble Colonizer conforms to an old stereotype, one that is the object of an ironic commentary in Albert Memmi's *The Colonizer and the Colonized* ([1957] 1967).

> We sometimes enjoy picturing the colonizer as a tall man, bronzed by the sun, wearing Wellington boots, proudly leaning on a shovel—as he rivets his gaze far away on the horizon of his land. When not engaged in battles against nature, we think of him laboring selflessly for mankind, attending the sick, and spreading culture to the nonliterate. In other words, his pose is one of a *noble* adventurer, a righteous pioneer.
>
> I don't know whether this portrait ever did correspond to reality [maybe it *gave* reality to itself?] or whether it was limited to the engraving on colonial bank notes [or to the excuses of Canadian historians]. Today, the economic motives of colo-

nial undertakings are revealed by every historian of colonialism. The cultural and moral mission of a colonizer, even in
the beginning, is no longer tenable. (3, emphasis added)

Memmi insists that one does not go to a colony to help the colonized.
Rather, "[y]ou go to a colony because jobs are guaranteed [notably
in the Department of Indian Affairs], wages high, careers more rapid
and business more profitable" (4). One of the implicit goals of Cole
and Chaikin's book is to forestall precisely this criticism of Canada's
"noble pioneers"—to defend their ghosts, in advance, from a critique that has become inevitable.

12. Douglas Leighton (1983, 105) explains the relationship between the administrator and the politician.

Because his family was long acquainted with John A. Macdonald and because of his own sense of personal gratitude, Lawrence Vankoughnet made the prime minister his lifelong political hero. This became a particularly important element in
the administrative relationship of the two men after 1878 [the
year Macdonald put the Pacific scandal behind him and was
reelected as prime minister of a Conservative government],
when Macdonald was Vankoughnet's minister. The civil servant was always careful to defer to the wishes of the politician.
Macdonald found the arrangement convenient in another
way. He was notorious for paying scant attention to the day-
to-day operations of the government departments in his
charge. In Vankoughnet, he knew he had a loyal and consci-
entious deputy who could manage the Indian Department
with a minimum of supervision. Accordingly, Macdonald's in-
tervention was usually confined to problems with distinct political overtones.

13. Macdonald's (or is it Vankoughnet's?) comparison of the
"Aht" to the "Kwahkewlth" echoes a passage from Powell's report
for 1882 (162): "The West Coast or Aht Indians, are not much behind the Kwahkewlths in their love of holding potlaching [without
quotes this time] feasts, gambling, &c., &c. They are, however, much
more industrious and amenable to recognized authority."

14. Powell was an outspoken advocate of residential industrial
schooling for Native children in British Columbia, for example in
his annual report for 1882.

The present system of assisting Mission day schools is the
most economical, so far as mere outlay is concerned—in this
light it may be the best, but it quite fails, in my opinion, to
meet the requirements of the real object in view. [Powell's
concern for restricting expenditures deserves to be analyzed
"in light" of Bataille's commentary on the status of expenditure in bourgeois society.]
A glance at the Reports furnished from time to time, of

those that are not abandoned, prove, in my opinion, that, after all, the expenditure is large for the small amount of benefit conferred.

Indian school children are so irregular, that a large attendance is required to ensure a small average for the whole quarter, add to this, the opposing impressions and vicious allurements incident to the daily return of the child from school to uncivilized camp life, and the failure of the system to accomplish much in the way of education may be readily understood.

The only scheme for meeting the difficulty appears to me to be the establishment of two or three industrial boarding schools in the Province, where, separated from native customs and modes of living, children would have opportunities of putting in practice what they are taught in school. (*Sessional Papers*, 1883, no. 5, p. 167)

15. In "A Priest versus the Potlatch" (1982b, 75) Barry Gough confirms that "Hall's endeavours to convert the Fort Rupert Kwakiutl were virtually without reward, owing principally to the strengths of Kwakiutl society, most particularly the power of chiefs and, integrally related to this, the pervasive influence of potlatching."

16. On "the traditional conception of truth" see also Heidegger [1927] 1962, 257. Hegel describes the correspondence theory of truth as "the standard which consciousness itself sets up by which to measure what it knows. If we designate *knowledge* as the Notion, but the essence or the *True* as what exists, or the *object,* then the examination consists in seeing whether the Notion corresponds to the object" (1977, 53). But what consciousness really examines, while testing the agreement between notion and object, is itself: "For consciousness is, on the one hand, consciousness of the object, and on the other, consciousness of itself" (54).

17. In *Mémoires* (1989a, 112) Derrida offers a different account of what Heidegger and Austin say about the "meaning of a word."

18. In the "Letter on Humanism" (1977, 215) Heidegger links the idea of "destiny" to the gift of the *es gibt:* "This 'there is / it gives' rules as the destiny [*das Geschick*] of Being." Thus, "[t]he happening of history occurs essentially as the destiny of the truth of Being and from it. Being comes to destiny in that It, Being, gives itself. But thought in terms of such destiny this says: it gives itself and refuses itself simultaneously."

19. The overlapping of difference with sameness recurs in Boas's canonical ethnography "The Social Organization and the Secret Societies of the Kwakiutl Indians" (1897b). In the opening pages Boas affirms that "[t]he Pacific Coast of America between Juan de Fuca Strait and Yakutat Bay is inhabited by a great many Indian tribes *distinct* in physical characteristics and *distinct* in languages, but *one* in culture" (emphasis added). Ironically, as soon as he has said these

societies are "distinct" yet "one," he affirms that their homogeneity is an illusion generated by careless research: "While a hasty glance at these people and a comparison with other tribes emphasizes the uniformity of their culture, a closer investigation reveals many peculiarities of individual tribes which prove that their culture has developed slowly and from a number of distinct centers, each people adding something to the culture which we observe at the present day" (317). The tendency to reduce the "distinct" to the "one" is a standard feature of the rhetoric that describes "[t]he Indian Tribes of the North Pacific Coast" in the ethnography of the late nineteenth century and beyond.

20. "Here, we assume, is the essential nature of language. 'To say,' related to the Old Norse '*saga*,' means to show: to make appear, set free, that is, to offer and extend what we call World, lighting and concealing it. This lighting and hiding proffer of the world is the essential being of Saying" (Heidegger 1971, 93). Saying gives not only beings, but also their being-together: it gives world.

21. No doubt Clifford feared that the hostilities aroused by missionary work would harm relations between the First Nations and local settlers—and undermine the Hudson's Bay Company's ability to conduct its own, profitable business.

22. This theory of the textual gift, which is a theory of sending, of putting Being and beings in the mail, owes an incalculable debt to Derrida's fragmented commentary on Heidegger in "Envois" (1987, 1–256; see especially 64–67). Here Derrida relocates Heidegger's *es gibt*—which, in the "Letter on Humanism" at least, names "the destiny or destining of Being [*Das Schicken im Geschick des Seins*]"—within a consideration of the "post," "the postal," and "the post card" (65). What Derrida suggests, and what he says Heidegger would not entirely accept, is that the postal does not belong only to the modern epoch, the so-called machine age, in the history of the destining of Being. Postality is not a historically bound metaphor that substitutes itself for the entire history of the destining of Being. Rather, it is destining's most proper possibility. As soon as there is a sending, a send-off, says Derrida, "then the possibility of posts is always already there. . . . As soon as *there is*, as soon as it gives (*es gibt*), it destines, it tends" (64). The post is not a figure of speech that could be used, in a reductionist fashion, to describe destining in a given discourse. It is the possibility of rhetoric, of figurality, in general, for to use figurative language is to send one term in place of another: "If . . . I think the postal and the post card on the basis of the destinal of Being, as I think the house (of Being) on the basis of Being, of language, and not the inverse, etc., then the post is no longer a simple metaphor, and is even, as the site of all transferences and correspondences, the 'proper' possibility of every possible rhetoric. Would this satisfy Martin? Yes and no." No, because Heidegger would likely regard the attempt to think postality on the basis of destining (the *es gibt*) as a return to metaphysics. The concept of post-

ality implies a whole postal technology that, for Heidegger, belongs specifically to the modern epoch of a metaphysics that fails to interrogate its nonmetaphysical essence. Moreover, postality determines the sending of Being as "position" (posture, thesis, or theme), as the act of positing theses, and for Heidegger "position" belongs to metaphysics. Heidegger would therefore accuse Derrida "of constructing a metaphysics of the posts or of postality" (65).

For Derrida, however, the technology of the "posts" that underlies the destining of Being has a place both inside and outside the history of metaphysics. And since postality includes the possibility that whatever is sent will not arrive at its proper destination, since it is variously destined in order to be destined at all, one can no longer speak of a single metaphysics, nor of a single sending of Being, but only of multiple sendings that never end up in the same place. Because it is postal destining that puts metaphysics in the mail, it is always possible, and indeed necessary, that metaphysics will get lost and never arrive at itself. Metaphysics, understood as the history of the epochs of the destining of Being, the history of the ways in which Being gives history to itself, cannot be reduced to a homogeneous totality because it is forever deferred, forever on the way, in the mail, forever rendering itself different from itself: "as soon as there is [*es gibt*]," says Derrida, "there is *différance* (and this does not await language, especially human language, and the language of Being, only the mark and the divisible trait), and there is postal maneuvering, relays, delay, anticipation, destination, telecommunicating network, the possibility, and therefore the fatal necessity of going astray, etc." (66).

For two quite different accounts of "postal politics" see Bennington 1990 and Alloula 1986.

23. Formerly an officer in the militia, Reed joined the Ministry of the Interior in 1881 and served as an Indian agent and assistant Indian commissioner for the Northwest Territories before becoming the bureaucrat in charge of Indian affairs. "Certainly Reed, and sometimes his predecessor as deputy, L. Vankoughnet, could be inflexible and unwilling to consider the Indian viewpoint. Reed, nevertheless, had had at least two years' experience as an Indian agent. . . . [Yet h]e admitted in 1895 that he was 'necessarily out of touch, to a great extent, with the Indians' " (Hall 1983, 138–39).

24. On 29 February 1895 the *Province* had published an open letter on the potlatch from Tate to G. E. Courbould, a local member of parliament. It drew this response from William Dwyer of Cowichan.

I have seen a few potlatches and I must say that I have come to the conclusion that the same number of white people could not live together for a week or two and settle up their affairs in a more peaceable and orderly manner than the Indians of this coast do. The potlatches of the present day seem to take more the part of a country fair. Friends and relatives living far apart meet together—debts are paid and presents made, besides which boats, canoes, cattle are bought and sold, and store debts of deceased relatives are often provided for.

Visitors constantly remark about the orderly manner in which these gatherings are conducted, but of course they are not like Mr. Tate behind the scenes and do not see the "barbarous practices, drunkenness and immorality" which he does.

In conclusion I would say that I believe the majority of the people of this province are opposed to any forcible interference with the harmless customs of the natives, *knowing as all do that these customs are rapidly dying out.* (emphasis added)

25. Hall (1983, 138 n. 7) says of McLean: "McLean, grandson of a liberal MP at the time of Alexander Mackenzie, one John Farris, had been appointed to the department in October 1876, rising to the position of first-class clerk by 1896." Also, "Sifton had a high regard for his ability; but a perusal of McLean's correspondence suggested a man of short temper, concerned with picayune detail in day-to-day matters, and very impressed with his own importance. On more than one occasion he complained to the deputy that he was not being treated with due deference by other employees."

26. Hale was editor of the Committee for the Study of the Northwestern Tribes of Canada, and directed Boas's work for the BAAS, though Boas often felt that his directives did more to disrupt research than to help it (Rohner 1969, 81–82).

27. George Hunt was Boas's indispensable Kwagiulth informant and coauthor from the middle of the 1880s until Hunt's death in 1933. According to one estimate, he collected about two-thirds of Boas's material on Kwakwaka'wakw culture.

Drucker and Heizer (1967) note that Hunt was "adopted" rather than born into the social system of the Kwakwaka'wakw. "The son of the Scottish factor at the Hudson's Bay Company post at Fort Rupert and of a Tsimshian woman," he grew up among the Kwagiulth and "came to hold a chief's name and status and carried all the associated duties of his formal position—functioning in the potlatch and dancing as a Hamatsa in the Shaman's Society [*sic*] performances—because he was adopted by the hereditary holder of those rights" (25). Schulte-Tenckhoff (1986, 121) says that Hunt was the son of a Scottish father and a Tlingit mother, and that he was considered a stranger at Fort Rupert. While anthropologists are concerned with measuring Hunt's connection to whiteness, Charles Nowell (1941, 54–55) recalls simply that his older brother became wealthy while cooking for Hunt's father, who paid him in blankets.

Boas offers a glimpse into his method of conducting fieldwork when he recounts his first meeting with George Hunt in 1888. The following excerpts are from Boas's diary.

[12 June 1888] It may well be that my anthropological [anthropometric] observations will turn out to be the most valuable results of my trip. I am very glad about this. I now have photographs of three men, two Haida and one from west Vancouver, the last a splendid fellow. I am having them all photographed nude to the waist. . . . Not being able to get hold of any Indians [to serve as informants] this afternoon, I cleaned the first skeleton [which, as the agent of a cannibal culture, Boas had stolen from a graveyard about a week earlier] and packed it up. They take up more room than I thought, and I shall have to acquire larger boxes. Besides having scientific value these skeletons are worth money. . . . I had asked my Haida to come this evening, but he was so drunk that I had to send him away. So I took a walk to Beacon Hill [for the time being Boas is conducting his fieldwork in Victoria], from which one gets a beautiful view over San Juan de Fuca Strait. A Kwakiutl came this evening whom I had wanted very much, and so I am "fixed" for tomorrow. (Rohner 1969, 90)

The man Boas "thought" he wanted so badly was George Hunt. He met him after scanning the local jail for ethnographic data.

[13 June 1888] At least so I thought yesterday, but I have been very much disappointed. I went first to the jail, but after waiting half an hour I learned that no new Indians had been brought in. Then I went to my Tlingit lady and got along well for three hours, but then she began to mutter. My Kwakiutl, George Hunt, came at 1:45 to tell me that he had been called as an interpreter to a court sitting but would come to me at 4:00 p.m. He is an interpreter. I busied myself copying until four, but George Hunt did not appear. At eight I finally set out to look for him and was able to find his home after a long search, but he was not there. I must try to catch him tomorrow morning. The only way I can get people is to drag them in by the hair. (91)

Years later, Boas recalls what he achieved between 15 November and 6 December 1894, during his last trip for the BAAS. He was still making anthropometric measurements.

[17 November 1894] The day before yesterday I started to measure; I got twenty-five adults without any difficulty. I hope to get 100 altogether here, and for this I need George Hunt. His help is of the greatest value. (178)

No doubt Boas was often frustrated by his dependency on his research partner.

[22 November 1894] This morning I obtained a few more items concerning last night and also wrote down a few folktales. I wish I were away from here. George Hunt is so hard to get along with. He acts exactly as he did in Chicago [he had joined Boas there at the World's Columbian Exposition in 1893]. He is too lazy to think, and that makes it disagreeable for me. I cannot change this, though, and have to make the best of it. He left at noon with some excuse and returned only after several hours. He knows exactly how I depend on him. (183)

28. "And it is the baptising of the Indians; the giving away of blankets fastens a name on a child" (Boas 1925, 111).

29. "Finally, these total services and counter-services are committed to in a somewhat voluntary form by presents and gifts, although in the final analysis they are strictly compulsory, on pain of private or public warfare." Mauss's discussion of the gift never strays far from the potlatch of the Pacific Northwest. Here are the next two sentences: "We propose to call all this the *system of total services.* The purest type of such institutions seems to us to be characterized by the alliance of two phratries in Pacific or North American tribes in general, where rituals, marriages, inheritance of goods, legal ties and those of self-interest, the ranks of the military and priests—in short everything, is complementary and presumes co-operation between the two halves of the tribe" (1990, 5–6).

30. The concept of the "term," of difference and deferral, provides a way of mediating the conflict between Mauss and Derrida. Pierre Bourdieu argues that it is precisely the lapse of time that allows people who conduct symbolic exchanges to believe that what they are doing is giving each other gifts. Their transactions have the structure of exchange only in the eyes of an observer who neglects the lapse between gift and countergift. Such an observer occupies a timeless state unknown to the "agents" who actively participate in gift exchanges. In their perspective such transactions are everyday practices, an "art of living," and can never be a mere object of study. Hence, viewed from within its circle, the exchange of gifts is not a general system of rules that one follows—a system that says a gift is what never returns to sender—but a strategy one deploys at a particular time and for particular reasons. And it often fails.

> It is all a question of style, which means in this case timing and choice of occasion, for the same act—giving, giving in return, offering one's services, paying a visit, etc.—can have completely different meanings at different times, coming as it may at the right or wrong moment, while almost all important exchanges—gifts to the mother of a new-born child, or on the occasion of a wedding, etc.—have their own particular moments; the reason is that the lapse of time *separating* the gift from the counter-gift is what authorizes the deliberate oversight, the collectively maintained and approved self-deception without which symbolic exchange, a fake circulation of fake coin, could not operate. If the system is to work, the agents

must not be entirely unaware of the truth of their exchanges, which is made explicit in the anthropologist's model, while at the same time they must refuse to know and above all to recognize it. In short, everything takes place *as if* [emphasis added] agents' practice, and in particular their manipulation of *time,* were organized exclusively with a view to concealing from themselves and from others the truth of their practice, which the anthropologist and his models bring to light simply by substituting the timeless model for a scheme which works itself out only in and through time. (Bourdieu 1977, 6)

Bourdieu gives a curious twist here to the correspondence theory of truth. The truth about gift exchange, he says, is that it falsifies its own truth, while the anthropology of gift exchange is false because it identifies the truth while neglecting the truth about that truth: namely, that in true gift exchange the "agents" deliberately falsify the truth about the gift. Bourdieu's agents are, moreover, fetishists in the Freudian sense because they simultaneously know the truth and take strenuous measures to disavow it.

31. Why "holocaust" rather than "sacrifice" or "incineration"? Derrida (1986, 241) explains that "[t]he word *holocaust* that happens to translate *Opfer* is more appropriate to the text [Hegel's *Phenomenology of Spirit*] than the word of Hegel himself. In this sacrifice, all (*holos*) is burned (*caustos*), and the fire can go out only stoked."

Obviously "holocaust" also names the Nazi extermination of European Jews in the 1940s. The irruption of this name here makes it impossible to repress the knowledge that two of the writers whose works lay the foundations for my argument, Heidegger and de Man, openly affiliated themselves with National Socialism in the 1930s and 1940s. How can a text that tries to disable a particular mode of Canadian racism—one that is still in circulation, moreover—draw its theoretical resources from a philosopher and a critic who allied themselves, however briefly or clumsily, to one of the most violent and systematic racisms in history? How can I condemn these authors for their political decisions and still find value in their thought? I do not think it is possible to criticize Western European racisms from a region and a discourse situated beyond them. If I were to try to place my research somewhere beyond the wartime crimes of Heidegger and de Man, I would succeed only in folding my text together with everything I desire to exclude from it—which is precisely the result that my text predicts. My aim is to inhabit a certain folding, not to style myself as the only innocent white man on earth. Besides, the morality of bad conscience, with its masochistic (and therefore pleasurable) dialectic of innocence and guilt, good and evil, has nothing to do with radical politics. It is necessary to pursue a practice, not a sense of guilt, and guilt is no excuse for ignoring what most calls for thinking here, now.

In a way, then, my text endorses Walter Benjamin's declaration that "[t]here is no document of civilization which is not at the same time a document of barbarism" (1969, 256). Yet Benjamin cannot articulate this thesis without deploying two of the leading concepts of colonialism: "civilization" and "barbarism." What Benjamin also says is that you have to occupy the continuum of history, while the wreckage of the past piles up at your feet, in order to fracture it.

While I sometimes dream of purifying myself by renouncing Heidegger and de Man—thereby settling my bad conscience for good—the fact remains that to live in British Columbia is, already, to occupy a stolen land and to participate in a crime. Again, bad conscience.

## EATING

1. In the fall of 1903 DeBeck complained that the property owned by the family of George Hunt, Boas's informant, had become the center of potlatch activity at Fort Rupert (NA, vol. 3629, file 6244-2, DeBeck to Vowell, 30 October 1903).

2. DeBeck asked the department to send a detective to help him investigate the news report. Vowell dispatched Thomas Deasy, but by the time he arrived in Alert Bay, DeBeck had gone to the Koskimo Reservation alone, where he discovered that "a hamatsa" had been initiated but was unable to learn the details of the ceremony (NA, vol. 3629, file 6244-2, 23 January 1904). Meanwhile, Deasy was making his own inquiry into the potlatch in the vicinity of Alert Bay, and upon returning to Victoria he sent the *Daily Times* a long article describing a potlatch and "Cedar Bark Dance" held on Gilford Island. The article praises the Gilford Island people and contradicts the reports of whites who claim that the hamatsa dance involves acts of cannibalism. He suggests that the people be allowed to pursue their traditions in peace (*Daily Times*, 23 April 1904). An enraged DeBeck charged that Deasy was trying to incite public opinion against the suppression of the hamatsa-potlatch (see NA, vol. 3629, file 6244-2, letters between DeBeck, Deasy, and Vowell, 5, 10, 15, 17, 26, and 30 May 1904).

3. W. Arens argues in *The Man-Eating Myth* that there is simply no evidence that any human culture has ever practiced either ritual or gustatory cannibalism. Every culture, however, has been accused of it. Western European societies characteristically dismiss charges that they practice cannibalism while uncritically accepting undocumented claims that cannibals exist elsewhere. It invariably turns out that the cannibals in question ceased indulging in their grisly meals just before Western European observers arrived on the scene: hence Boas's opposition between "formerly" and "nowadays." What is most remarkable about the discourse on cannibalism is not that there is no reliable evidence for it, but that Western European anthropologists are willing to accept that it exists without bothering to check their data. Cole and Chaikin (see 1990, 23–24), for example, embrace the idea that the coastal First Nations practiced ritual cannibalism, yet by perpetuating the myth of cannibalism, the two historians

give themselves the rhetorical means to defend the framers of the law against the so-called "Tamanawas" from the charge of racism.

4. Martin was also provincial premier for three months in 1900.

5. Lewis Hyde's *Gift* perpetuates the discourse that styles the coastal First Nations as a vanishing race: "The American Indian tribes that have become famous for the potlatch—the Kwakiutl, Tlingit, Haida, and others—*once occupied* the Pacific coast of North America from Cape Mendocino in California to Prince William Sound in Alaska" (1979, 26, emphasis added). Hyde's text confirms that the discourse that intertwines gift, fold, and limit while affirming the death of potlatching cultures extends well beyond the potlatch papers under discussion here. Gloria Cranmer Webster calls for an end to this discourse: "The 'Kwakiutl' are one of the most described and, hence, most widely known ethnic groups in the world. Yet, increasingly, people write about us and, apparently, think about us in the past tense. We are told that Kwakiutl ritual, art, technology, and religion were colourful and complex. It is as if our culture were gone. But we Kwakwaka'wakw are very much alive, and we abide in our traditional lands. Our culture retains many aspects of the 'old ways' " (Galois 1994, 3). See "Giving," note 9.

6. Would Derrida "accept" this reading? Perhaps only "in part" (1989a, 35).

7. The government's own research points to the "obvious continuity" in Canada's Indian policy from 1830 until the present. See Canada, Department of Indian and Northern Affairs 1978, 191–93.

8. Section 94 of the Indian Act of 1876 denied the First Nations of British Columbia the "right" to enfranchisement because they were considered as yet unfit to be full citizens. They were protected from the legal mechanism of assimilation until 1892 (ibid., 69, 95–96).

9. "Canadians did not expect Indians to adapt to the modern world. Their only hope was to assimilate, to become White, to cease to be Indians. In this view, a modern Indian is a contradiction in terms: Whites could not imagine such a thing. Any Indian was by definition a traditional Indian, a relic of the past" (Francis 1992, 59).

10. Few aboriginal people—only 102 between confederation and 1918—gave up their special status and adopted the franchise. They knew the government was planning their demise. In 1920 Scott had the Indian Act amended to allow the government to enfranchise aboriginal people against their will. However, the new section 107 collapsed with Arthur Meighen's short-lived government (Meighen had been minister of the interior and superintendent general of Indian affairs before becoming prime minister). It was replaced in 1922 with less coercive legislation providing for voluntary enfranchisement. Provisions for compulsory enfranchisement were once again added to the act in 1933. See Titley 1986, 48–51, and Department of Indian and Northern Affairs 1978, 124–25.

When Scott proposed to "get rid of the Indian problem" in 1920 by enfranchising aboriginal people without their consent, he confessed that the goal of the new policy was to enable the political body of Canada to eat its aboriginal others. "Our object," he affirmed, "is to continue until there is not a single Indian in Canada that has not been absorbed into the body politic and there is no Indian Question, and no Indian Department" (Department of Indian and Northern Affairs 1978, 115; Titley 1986, 50). For Scott, Canada is a body, and the First Nations are its food. As long as they remain uneaten, Canada remains weak and impoverished because it must spend its wealth to support them; by dying, however, they will feed and nourish the new nation, allowing it to grow strong.

For the history of eugenics in Canada, see McLaren 1990.

11. To be precise, the report calls for the repeal of the first subsection of section 149 of the Indian Act. A second subsection had been added to the statute in June 1914. This amendment forbid "Indians" in Manitoba, Saskatchewan, Alberta, British Columbia, or the territories to attend dances outside their own reserves and to appear "in aboriginal costume" at "any show, exhibition, performance, stampede or pageant." It also prohibits whites from encouraging such behavior. It was intended to help suppress dancing throughout western Canada. See *Statutes of Canada, 1914*, chap. 35 (4–5 George V.), sec. 8. Subsection 2 was Scott's work (Titley 1986, 174–75).

249

BIBLIOGRAPHY

Abraham, Nicolas, and Maria Torok. [1976] 1986. *The Wolf Man's Magic Word: A Cryptonomy*. Trans. Nicolas Rand. Minneapolis: University of Minnesota Press.

———. 1994. *The Shell and the Kernel*. Vol 1. Trans. Nicholas T. Rand. Chicago: University of Chicago Press.

Adams, John W. 1973. *Gitksan Potlatch: Population Flux, Resource Ownership, and Reciprocity*. Toronto: Holt, Rinehart and Winston.

———. 1981. Recent Ethnology on the Northwest Coast. *Annual Review of Anthropology* 10:361–92.

Allen, R. A. 1956. The Potlatch and Social Equilibrium. *Davidson Journal of Anthropology* 2:43–54.

Alloula, Malek. 1986. *The Colonial Harem*. Trans. Myrna Godzich and Wlad Godzich. Minneapolis: University of Minnesota Press.

Ames, Kenneth M. 1981. The Evolution of Social Ranking on the Northwest Coast of North America. *American Antiquity* 46:789–805.

Amoss, P. 1978. *Coast Salish Spirit Dancing: The Survival of an Ancestral Religion*. Seattle: University of Washington Press.

Anderson, Benedict. 1983. *Imagined Communities: Reflections on the Origin and Spread of Nationalism*. London: Verso.

Archer, Christon I. 1980. Cannibalism in the Early History of the Northwest Coast: Enduring Myths and Neglected Realities. *Canadian Historical Review* 61, no. 4:453–79.

Arens, W. 1979. *The Man-Eating Myth: Anthropology and Anthropophagy*. Oxford: Oxford University Press.

Aristotle. 1954. *The Rhetoric and the Poetics of Aristotle*. Trans. W. Rhys Roberts and Ingram Bywater. New York: Modern Library.

Assu, Harry, with Joy Inglis. 1989. *Assu of Cape Mudge: Recollections of a Coastal Indian Chief*. Vancouver: University of British Columbia Press.

Austin, John L. 1961. *Philosophical Papers*. Ed. J. O. Urmson and G. J. Warnock. Oxford: Oxford University Press.

———. 1962. *How to Do Things with Words*. Oxford: Clarendon.

———. 1963. Performative-Constative. In *Philosophy and Ordinary Language*, ed. Charles E. Caton, 22–54. Urbana: University of Illinois Press.

Averkieva, J. [1941] 1966. *Slavery among the Indians of North America*. Trans. G. R. Elliot. Victoria: Victoria College.

Balibar, Etienne, and Immanuel Wallerstein. 1992. *Race, Nation, Class: Ambiguous Identities*. London: Verso.

Barbeau, Marius. 1911–12. Du potlatch en Colombie Brittanique.

*Bulletin de la Société Géographique du Québec* 5:275–97, 325–34; 6: 177–86.

———. [1958] 1973. *Medicine-Men on the Northwest Coast.* Ottawa: Department of Northern Affairs and Natural Resources, National Museums of Canada.

Barnett, H. G. 1938a. The Coast Salish of Canada. *American Anthropologist* 40:118–41.

———. 1938b. *The Nature and the Function of the Potlatch.* Eugene: University of Oregon Press.

———. 1955. *The Coast Salish of British Columbia.* Eugene: University of Oregon Press.

Bataille, Georges. 1985. The Notion of Expenditure. In *Visions of Excess: Selected Writings, 1927–1939,* ed. Allan Stoekl, trans. Allan Stoekl with Carl R. Lovitts and Donald M. Leslie Jr., 116–29. Minneapolis: University of Minnesota Press.

———. 1988. *The Accursed Share: An Essay on General Economy.* Trans. Robert Hurley. New York: Zone.

Benedict, Ruth. [1934] 1961. *Patterns of Culture.* Boston: Houghton Mifflin.

Benjamin, Walter. 1969. Theses on the Philosophy of History. In *Illuminations,* ed. Hannah Arendt, trans. Harry Zohn, 253–64. New York: Schocken.

Bennington, Geoff. 1990. Postal Politics and the Institution of the Nation. In *Nation and Narration,* ed. Homi K. Bhabha, 121–37. London: Routledge.

Benveniste, Émile. 1966a. Don et échange dans le vocabulaire indo-européen. In *Problèmes de linguistique générale,* 315–26. Paris: Gallimard.

———. 1966b. La philosophie analytique et le langage. In *Problèmes de linguistique générale,* 267–76. Paris: Gallimard.

Bhabha, Homi K. 1994. *The Location of Culture.* New York and London: Routledge.

———. ed. 1990. *Nation and Narration.* London: Routledge.

Blackman, Margaret B. 1977a. Blankets, Bracelets, Boas: The Potlatch in Photographs. *Anthropological Papers of the University of Alaska* 18, no. 2:53–67.

———. 1977b. Ethnohistoric Changes in the Haida Potlatch Complex. *Arctic Anthropology* 14, no. 1:39–53.

Blaser, Robin. 1993. *The Holy Forest.* Toronto: Coach House.

Boas, Franz. 1889. Letter to Horatio Hale, and Preliminary Notes on the Indians of British Columbia. In *Report of the British Association for the Advancement of Science, 1888,* 233–42. London: J. Murray.

———. 1890. First General Report on the Indians of British Columbia: Tlingit, Haida, Tsimshian, Kotonāqa. In *Report of the British Association for the Advancement of Science, 1889,* 801–99. London: J. Murray.

———. 1891. Second General Report on the Indians of British Columbia: Lku'ûngen, Nootka, Kwakiutl, Shushwap. With Horatio

Hale's "Introductory Remarks on the Ethnology of British Columbia." In *Report of the British Association for the Advancement of Science, 1890*, 553–715. London: J. Murray.

———. 1892. Third Report on the Indians of British Columbia: The Bilqula: Physical Characteristics of the Tribes of the North Pacific Coast. In *Report of the British Association for the Advancement of Science, 1891*, 408–49. London: J. Murray.

———. 1894. The Indian Tribes of the Lower Fraser River. In *Report of the British Association for the Advancement of Science, 1894*, 454–63. London: J. Murray.

———. 1895. Fifth Report on the Indians of British Columbia: Physical Characteristics of the Tribes of the North Pacific Coast, the Tinneh Tribe of the Nicola Valley, the Ts'Ets'ā'ut, the Nîsk·a', Linguistics of Nîsk·a' and Ts'Ets'ā'ut, and Vocabulary of the Tinneh Tribe of Washington. In *Report of the British Association for the Advancement of Science, 1895*, 523–92. London: J. Murray.

———. 1896. Sixth Report on the Indians of British Columbia: Notes on the Kwakiutl: The Houses of the Tsimshian and Nîsk·a'; The Growth of Indian Children from the Interior of British Columbia; Linguistic Notes on Kwakiutl and Nîsk·a'. In *Report of the British Association for the Advancement of Science, 1896*, 569–91. London: J. Murray.

———. 1897a. The Indian Potlatch. *Province* (Victoria), 6 March, xi.

———. 1897b. The Social Organization and the Secret Societies of the Kwakiutl Indians. Reprinted from *Report of the United States National Museum for 1895*, 311–738. Washington, DC: Government Printing Office.

———. 1899. Summary of the Work of the Committee in British Columbia. In *Report of the British Association for the Advancement of Science, 1898*, 667–82. London: J. Murray.

———. 1902. *Tsimshian Texts*. Bureau of American Ethnology Bulletin no. 27. Washington, DC: Government Printing Office.

———. 1912. Tamanos. In *Handbook of American Indians*, ed. Frederick W. Hodge, 681. Washington, DC: Government Printing Office.

———. 1925. *Contributions to the Ethnology of the Kwakiutl*. New York: Columbia University Press.

———. 1930. *The Religion of the Kwakiutl Indians*. Columbia University Contributions to Anthropology, vol. 10. New York: Columbia University Press.

———. 1940. *Race, Language, and Culture*. New York: Macmillan.

———. 1966. *Kwakiutl Ethnography*. Ed. Helen Codere. Chicago: University of Chicago Press.

Borden, C. 1975. *Origins and Development of Early Northwest Coast Culture to about 3000 B.C.* Mercury Series, Archaeological Survey of Canada Paper 45. Ottawa: National Museum of Man.

Borrows, John J. 1991. A Genealogy of Law: Inherent Sovereignty and First Nations Self-Government. Master of Law thesis, University of Toronto.

Bourdieu, Pierre. 1977. *Outline of a Theory of Practice*. Trans. Richard Nice. Cambridge: Cambridge University Press.

Bourinot, A. S., ed. 1979. *At the Mermaid Inn: Wilfred Campbell, Archibald Lampman, Duncan Campbell Scott in* The Globe. Toronto: University of Toronto Press.

British Columbia. Commission on Conditions of Indians of the North-West Coast. [1888] 1969. *Papers relating to the Commission Appointed to Enquire into the Condition of the Indians of the North-West Coast*. Toronto: Canadiana House.

British Columbia. Ministry of Native Affairs. 1990. *The Aboriginal Peoples of British Columbia: A Profile*. Victoria: Province of British Columbia, Ministry of Native Affairs.

Cail, R. E. [1954] 1974. *Land, Man, and the Law: The Disposal of Crown Lands in British Columbia, 1871–1913*. Vancouver: University of British Columbia Press.

Canada. Department of Indian and Northern Affairs. Treaties and Historical Research Centre. 1978. *The Historical Development of the Indian Act*. 2d ed. Ottawa: Queen's Printer.

———. 1981. *Indian Acts and Amendments, 1868–1950*. Ottawa: Queen's Printer.

Canada. Parliament. 1867–1950. *Sessional Papers*. Ottawa.

———. 1871. British Columbia Terms of Union. In *Revised Statutes of Canada, 1985: Appendices*. No. 10. Ottawa: Queen's Printer.

———. 1880. *Statutes of Canada, 1880*. Ottawa: Queen's Printer.

———. 1887. *Revised Statutes of Canada, 1886*. Ottawa: Queen's Printer.

———. 1895. *Statutes of Canada, 1895*. Ottawa: Queen's Printer.

———. 1914. *Statutes of Canada, 1914*. Ottawa: King's Printer.

———. 1918. *Statutes of Canada, 1918*. Ottawa: King's Printer.

———. 1985a. *Revised Statutes of Canada, 1985*. Ottawa: Queen's Printer.

———. 1985b. The Royal Proclamation, October 7, 1763. In *Revised Statutes of Canada, 1985: Appendices*. No. 1. Ottawa: Queen's Printer.

Canada. Parliament. House of Commons. 1867–1936. *Parliamentary Debates*. Ottawa: Queen's Printer.

Canada. Royal Commission on Indian Affairs. 1916. *Evidence Submitted to the Royal Commission on Indian Affairs for the Province of British Columbia*. Ottawa: King's Printer.

Carpenter, Carol Henderson. 1981. Sacred, Precious Things: Repatriation of Potlatch Art. *Artscanada* 12:64–70.

Chapman, F. A. R. 1965. *Fundamentals of Canadian Law*. Toronto: McGraw-Hill.

Clifford, James, and George Marcus, eds. 1986. *Writing Culture: The Poetics and Politics of Ethnography*. Berkeley: University of California Press.

Clutesi, George. 1969. *Potlatch*. Sidney, British Columbia: Gray's Publishing.

Codere, Helen. 1950. *Fighting with Property: A Study of Kwakiutl Potlatching and Warfare, 1792–1930*. Publications of the American Ethnological Society, no. 18. New York: J. J. Augustin.

———. 1956. The Amiable Side of Kwakiutl Life: The Potlatch and the Play Potlatch. *American Anthropologist* 58:334–51.

———. 1957. Kwakiutl Society: Rank without Class. *American Anthropologist* 59:473–86.

———. 1959. The Understanding of the Kwakiutl. In *The Anthropology of Franz Boas*, ed. W. Goldschmidt, 61–75. Menasha, WI: American Anthropological Association.

———. 1961. Kwakiutl. In *Perspectives on American Indian Culture Change*, ed. E. H. Spicer, 431–516. Chicago: University of Chicago Press.

Cole, Douglas, and Ira Chaikin. 1990. *An Iron Hand upon the People: The Law against the Potlatch on the Northwest Coast*. Vancouver: Douglas and McIntyre; Seattle: University of Washington Press.

Cornell, Drucilla. 1992. *The Philosophy of the Limit*. New York: Routledge.

Critchley, Simon. 1992a. The Problem of Closure in Derrida: Part 1. *Journal of the British Society for Phenomenology* 23, no. 1:3–19.

———. 1992b. The Problem of Closure in Derrida: Part 2. *Journal of the British Society for Phenomenology* 23, no. 2:127–45.

Curtis, E. S. [1913] 1970. *Salishan Tribes of the Coast*. Vol. 9 of *The North American Indian, Being a Series of Volumes Picturing and Describing the Indians of the United States, the Dominion of Canada, and Alaska*. New York: Johnson Reprint.

———. [1915] 1970. *The Kwakiutl*. Vol. 10 of *The North American Indian, Being a Series of Volumes Picturing and Describing the Indians of the United States, the Dominion of Canada, and Alaska*. New York: Johnson Reprint.

———. [1916] 1970. The Nootka. In *The North American Indian, Being a Series of Volumes Picturing and Describing the Indians of the United States, the Dominion of Canada, and Alaska*, 11:1–112. New York: Johnson Reprint.

Davy, G. 1922. *La foi jurée: La formation du lien contractuel*. Paris: F. Alcan.

Dawson, G. 1888. Notes and Observations on the Kwakiool People of the Northern Part of Vancouver Island and Adjacent Coasts. In *Proceedings and Transactions of the Royal Society of Canada for the Year 1887*, 63–98. Montreal: Dawson Brothers.

De Certeau, Michel. 1986. *Heterologies: Discourse on the Other*. Trans. Brian Massumi. Minneapolis: University of Minnesota Press.

———. 1988. *The Writing of History*. Trans. Tom Conley. New York: Columbia University Press.

Deleuze, Gilles. 1993. *The Fold: Leibniz and the Baroque*. Trans. Tom Conley. Minneapolis: University of Minnesota Press.

De Man, Paul. 1979. *Allegories of Reading: Figural Language in Rousseau, Nietzsche, Rilke, and Proust*. New Haven: Yale University Press.

———. 1982. Sign and Symbol in Hegel's *Aesthetics*. *Critical Inquiry* 8, no. 4:761–75.

———. 1983. *Blindness and Insight: Essays in the Rhetoric of Contemporary Criticism*. 2d ed. Minneapolis: University of Minnesota Press.

———. 1984. *The Rhetoric of Romanticism*. New York: Columbia University Press.

———. 1986. *The Resistance to Theory*. Minneapolis: University of Minnesota Press.

———. 1988. *Wartime Journalism, 1939–1943*. Ed. Werner Hamacher, Neil Hertz, and Thomas Keenan. Lincoln: University of Nebraska Press.

Derrida, Jacques. 1978. From Restricted to General Economy: A Hegelianism without Reserve. In *Writing and Difference*, trans. Alan Bass, 251–77. Chicago: University of Chicago Press. Originally published as *L'écriture et la différance*. Paris: Seuil, 1967.

———. 1981. The Double Session. In *Dissemination*, trans. Barbara Johnson, 173–285. Chicago: University of Chicago Press.

———. 1982. Différance. In *Margins of Philosophy*, trans. Alan Bass, 1–27. Chicago: University of Chicago Press. Originally published as *Marges de la philosophie*. Paris: Éditions de Minuit, 1972.

———. 1986. *Glas*. Trans. John P. Leavey Jr. and Richard Rand. Lincoln: University of Nebraska Press. Originally published Paris: Galilée, 1974.

———. 1987. *The Post Card: From Socrates to Freud and Beyond*. Trans. Alan Bass. Chicago: University of Chicago Press. Originally published as *La carte postale: De Socrate à Freud et au-delà*. Paris: Flammarion, 1980.

———. 1989a. *Mémoires: For Paul de Man*. Rev. ed. Trans. Cecile Lindsay, Jonathan Culler, Eduardo Cadava, and Peggy Kamuf. New York: Columbia University Press. Originally published as *Mémoires: Pour Paul de Man*, 1986. Paris: Galilée, 1988.

———. 1989b. Psyche: Inventions of the Other. In *Reading de Man Reading*, ed. Lindsay Waters and Wlad Godzich, 25–65. Minneapolis: University of Minnesota Press.

———. 1991. *Cinders*. Trans. Ned Lukacher. Lincoln: University of Nebraska Press.

———. 1992a. Donner la mort. In *L'ethique du don: Jacques Derrida et la pensée du don*, ed. Jean-Michel Rabaté and Michael Wetzel, 11–108. Paris: Métaillé-Transition.

———. 1992b. *Given Time: 1, Counterfeit Money*. Trans. Peggy Kamuf. Chicago: University of Chicago Press. Originally published as *Donner le temps: 1, La fausse monnaie*. Paris: Galilée, 1991.

Donald, Leland, and Donald H. Mitchell. 1975. Some Correlates of Local Group Rank among the Southern Kwakiutl. *Ethnology* 14: 325–46.

Dragland, S. L., ed. 1974. *Duncan Campbell Scott: A Book of Criticism.* Ottawa: Tecumseh.

———. 1994. *Floating Voice: Duncan Campbell Scott and the Literature of Treaty 9.* Concord, Ontario: Anansi.

Drucker, Philip. 1955. *Indians of the Northwest Coast.* Garden City, NJ: American Museum Service Books.

Drucker, Philip, and Robert F. Heizer. 1967. *To Make My Name Good: A Reexamination of the Southern Kwakiutl Potlatch.* Berkeley: University of California Press.

Duff, Wilson. 1964. *The Indian History of British Columbia.* Vol. 1, *The Impact of the White Man.* Anthropology in British Columbia, Memoir no. 5. Victoria: Provincial Museum of British Columbia.

Dundes, Alan. 1979. Heads or Tails: A Psychoanalytic Study of the Potlatch. *Journal of Psychological Anthropology* 2:395–424.

Fabian, Johannes. 1982. *Time and the Other: How Anthropology Makes Its Object.* New York: Columbia University Press.

Fanon, Frantz. 1961. *The Wretched of the Earth.* Trans. Constance Farrington. Preface by Jean-Paul Sartre. Harmondsworth: Penguin.

———. 1967. *Black Skin, White Masks.* Trans. Charles Lam Markmann. New York: Grove.

Felman, Shoshana. 1983. *The Literary Speech Act: Don Juan with J. L. Austin, or Seduction in Two Languages.* Trans. Catherine Porter. Ithaca: Cornell University Press.

Ferguson, Brian. 1983. Warfare and Redistributive Exchange on the Northwest Coast. In *The Development of Political Organization in Native North America,* ed. E. Tooker. Washington, DC: American Ethnological Society.

Fisher, Robin. 1977. *Contact and Conflict: Indian-European Relations in British Columbia, 1774–1890.* Vancouver: University of British Columbia Press.

Foucault, Michel. 1972. *The Archaeology of Knowledge.* Trans. A. M. Sheridan Smith. London: Tavistock.

———. 1977. *Discipline and Punish.* Trans. Alan Sheridan. New York: Vintage.

———. 1978. *History of Sexuality.* Vol. 1, *An Introduction.* Trans. Robert Hurley. New York: Vintage.

Francis, Daniel. 1992. *The Imaginary Indian: The Image of the Indian in Canadian Culture.* Vancouver: Arsenal Pulp Press.

Freud, Sigmund. [1913] 1957. *Totem and Taboo.* In *The Standard Edition of the Complete Psychological Works of Sigmund Freud,* trans. James Strachey, 13:vii–162. London: Hogarth.

———. [1914] 1957. On Narcissism: An Introduction. In *The Standard Edition of the Complete Psychological Works of Sigmund Freud,* trans. James Strachey, 14:73–102. London: Hogarth.

———. [1917] 1957. Mourning and Melancholia. In *The Standard Edition of the Complete Psychological Works of Sigmund Freud,* trans. James Strachey, 14:243–58. London: Hogarth.

————. [1923] 1957. The Ego and the Id. In *The Standard Edition of the Complete Psychological Works of Sigmund Freud*, trans. James Strachey, 19:12–66. London: Hogarth.

————. [1925] 1957. Negation. In *The Standard Edition of the Complete Psychological Works of Sigmund Freud*, trans. James Strachey, 19:235–39. London: Hogarth.

————. [1927] 1957. Fetishism. In *The Standard Edition of the Complete Psychological Works of Sigmund Freud*, trans. James Strachey, 21:147–57. London: Hogarth.

————. 1957. *The Standard Edition of the Complete Psychological Works of Sigmund Freud.* Trans. James Strachey. 24 vols. London: Hogarth.

Galois, Robert. 1994. *Kwakwaka'wakw Settlements, 1775–1920: A Geographical Analysis and Gazeteer*. With contributions by Jay Powell and Gloria Cranmer Webster. Vancouver: University of British Columbia Press; Seattle: University of Washington Press.

Gates, Henry Louis, ed. 1986. *"Race," Writing, and Difference*. Chicago: University of Chicago Press.

Goddard, P. E. 1924. *Indians of the Northwest Coast*. New York: Museum of Natural History.

Goldberg, David Theo, ed. 1990. *Anatomy of Racism*. Minneapolis: University of Minnesota Press.

Gormly, Mary. 1977. Early Culture Contact on the Northwest Coast, 1774–1795: Analysis of Spanish Source Material. *Northwest Anthropological Research Notes* 11:1–80.

Gough, Barry M. 1978. Official Uses of Violence against Northwest Coast Indians in Colonial British Columbia. In *Pacific Northwest Themes: Historical Essays in Honor of Keith A. Murray*, ed. James W. Scott. Bellingham, WA: Centre for Pacific Northwest Studies.

————. 1982a. The Indian Policies of Great Britain and the United States in the Pacific Northwest in the Mid–Nineteenth Century. *Canadian Journal of Native Studies* 2, no. 2:321–37.

————. 1982b. A Priest versus the Potlatch: The Reverend Alfred James Hall and the Fort Rupert Kwakiutl, 1878–1880. *Journal of the Canadian Church Historical Society* 24, no. 2:75–89.

Grant, John Webster. 1984. *Moon of Wintertime: Missionaries and the Indians of Canada in Encounter since 1534*. Toronto: University of Toronto Press.

Grant, S. D. 1983. Indian Affairs under Duncan Campbell Scott: The Plains Cree of Saskatchewan, 1913–1931. *Journal of Canadian Studies* 18:21–39.

Grumet, Robert Stephen. 1975. Changes in Coast Tsimshian Redistributive Activities in the Fort Simpson Region of British Columbia, 1788–1862. *Ethnohistory* 23:295–318.

Gunther, Erna. 1972. *Indian Life on the Northwest Coast of North America as Seen by the Early Explorers and Fur Traders during the Last Decades of the Eighteenth Century*. Chicago: University of Chicago Press.

Hall, David J. 1983. Clifford Sifton and Canadian Indian Administration, 1896–1905. In *As Long as the Sun Shines and the Water Flows:*

*A Reader in Canadian Native Studies*, ed. Ian A. L. Getty and Antoine S. Lussier, 120–44. Vancouver: University of British Columbia Press.

Halliday, William. 1935. *Potlatch and Totem, and the Recollections of an Indian Agent*. Toronto: J. M. Dent and Sons.

Halpin, Marjorie. 1984. Feast Names at Hartley Bay. In *The Tsimshian: Images of the Past, Views for the Present*, ed. Margaret Seguin, 57–64. Vancouver: University of British Columbia Press.

Hegel, G. W. F. 1956. *The Philosophy of History*. Trans. J. Sibree. New York: Dover.

———. 1977. *The Phenomenology of Spirit*. Trans. A. V. Miller. Oxford: Oxford University Press.

———. 1991. *Elements of the Philosophy of Right*. Ed. Allen W. Wood. Trans. H. B. Nisbet. Cambridge: Cambridge University Press.

Heidegger, Martin. [1927] 1962. *Being and Time*. Trans. John Macquarrie and Edward Robinson. London: SCM Press.

———. 1968. *What Is Called Thinking?* Trans. J. Glenn Gray. New York: Harper and Row.

———. 1969. *Identity and Difference*. Trans. Joan Stambaugh. New York: Harper and Row.

———. 1971. *On the Way to Language*. Trans. Peter D. Hertz. New York: Harper and Row. Originally published as *Unterwegs zur Sprache*, 1959. Pfullingen: Verlag Günter Neske, 1985.

———. 1972. *On Time and Being*. Trans. Joan Stambaugh. New York: Harper and Row.

———. 1977. Letter on Humanism. In *Basic Writings*, ed. David Farrell Krell, 193–242. San Francisco: HarperCollins. Originally published as "Brief über den Humanismus," in *Wegmarken*, 313–64. Frankfurt am Main: Vittorio Klostermann, 1976.

Hill-Tout, Charles. 1978. *The Salish People: The Local Contributions of Charles Hill-Tout*. Ed. Ralph Maud. Vancouver: Talonbooks.

Hou, Charles. 1973. *To Potlatch or Not to Potlatch: An In-Depth Study of Culture-Conflict between the B.C. Coastal Indian and the White-Man*. Vancouver: British Columbia Teacher's Federation.

Hutchinson, Allan C. 1992. Identity Crisis: The Politics of Interpretation. *New England Law Review* 26, no. 4:1173–1219.

Hyde, Lewis. 1979. *The Gift: Imagination and the Erotic Life of Property*. New York: Vintage.

Irigary, Luce. [1977] 1985. *This Sex Which Is Not One*. Trans. Catherine Porter with Carolyn Burke. Ithaca: Cornell University Press.

Jacobsen, J. A. 1977. *Alaskan Voyages, 1881–1883*. Chicago: University of Chicago Press.

Jensen, Doreen, and Cheryl Brooks, eds. 1991. *In Celebration of Our Survival: The First Nations of British Columbia*. Vancouver: University of British Columbia Press.

Jewitt, John R. 1807. *A Journal Kept at Nootka Sound. . . .* Boston: author.

Kan, Sergei. 1989. *Symbolic Immortality: The Tlingit Potlatch of the Nineteenth Century*. Washington, DC: Smithsonian Institution.

Kant, Immanuel. 1929. *Critique of Pure Reason*. Trans. Norman Kemp Smith. New York: St. Martin's.

Kobrinsky, Vernon. 1975. Dynamics of the Fort Rupert Class Struggle: Fighting with Property Vertically Revisited. In *Papers in Honour of Harry Hawthorne*, ed. V. Serl and H. Taylor, 32–59. Bellingham, WA: Western State College Press.

Kojève, Alexandre. 1969. *Introduction to the Reading of Hegel: Lectures on the* Phenomenology of Spirit. Ed. Allan Bloom. Trans. James H. Nichols Jr. Ithaca: Cornell University Press.

Krause, A. [1885] 1956. *The Tlingit Indians: Results of a Trip to the Northwest Coast of America and the Bering Straits*. Trans. E. Gunther. Seattle: University of Washington Press.

Lacoue-Labarthe, Philippe. 1990. *Heidegger, Art, and Politics: The Fiction of the Political*. Trans. Chris Turner. Oxford and Cambridge, MA: Basil Blackwell.

LaViolette, Forrest E. 1951. Missionaries and the Potlatch. *Queen's Quarterly* 58:237–51.

————. [1961] 1973. *The Struggle for Survival: Indian Cultures and the Protestant Ethic in British Columbia*. Toronto: University of Toronto Press.

Leighton, Douglas. 1983. A Victorian Civil Servant at Work: Lawrence Vankoughnet and the Canadian Indian Department, 1874–1893. In *As Long as the Sun Shines and the Water Flows: A Reader in Canadian Native Studies*, ed. Ian A. L. Getty and Antoine S. Lussier, 104–19. Vancouver: University of British Columbia Press.

Levinas, Emmanuel. [1961] 1979. *Totality and Infinity: An Essay on Exteriority*. Trans. Alfonso Lingis. The Hague: Martinus Nijhoff.

————. 1987. *Time and the Other*. Trans. Richard A. Cohen. Pittsburgh: Duquesne University Press.

Lévi-Strauss, Claude. 1949. *The Elementary Structures of Kinship*. Ed. Rodney Needham. Trans. Rodney Needham, James Harle Bell, and John Richard von Sturmer. Boston: Beacon, 1969.

————. 1982. *The Way of the Masks*. Trans. Sylvia Modleski. Vancouver: Douglas and McIntyre.

————. 1987. *Introduction to the Work of Marcel Mauss*. Trans. Felicity Baker. London: Routledge and Kegan Paul.

Locke, John. [1690] 1952. *The Second Treatise of Government*. Ed. Thomas P. Peardon. Indianapolis: Bobbs-Merrill.

Long, Frederick J. [c. 1909]. *Dictionary of the Chinook Language*. Seattle: Lowman and Hanford.

Lowe, Lisa. 1991. *Critical Terrains: French and British Orientalisms*. Ithaca: Cornell University Press.

Lyotard, Jean-François. 1990. *Heidegger and "the Jews."* Trans. Andreas Michel and Mark Robert. Minneapolis: University of Minnesota Press.

Macklem, Patrick. 1991. Of Texts and Democratic Narratives. *University of Toronto Law Journal* 41:114–45.

McLaren, Angus. 1990. *Our Own Master Race: Eugenics in Canada, 1885–1945.* Toronto: McClelland and Stewart.

Macleod, R. C. 1988. Royal Canadian Mounted Police. In *The Canadian Encyclopedia,* 2d ed. Edmonton: Hurtig.

McNab, David T. 1983. Herman Merivale and Colonial Office Indian Policy in the Mid–Nineteenth Century. In *As Long as the Sun Shines and the Water Flows: A Reader in Canadian Native Studies,* ed. Ian A. L. Getty and Antoine S. Lussier, 85–103. Vancouver: University of British Columbia Press.

Manganaro, Marc, ed. 1990. *Modernist Anthropology: From Fieldwork to Text.* Princeton: Princeton University Press.

Mauss, Marcel. 1969. Don, contrat, échange. In *Oeuvres,* 3:29–57. Paris: Éditions de Minuit.

———. 1990. *The Gift: The Form and Reason for Exchange in Archaic Societies.* Trans. W. D. Hall. London: Routledge. Published as "Essai sur le don," in *Sociologie et Anthropologie,* 143–279. Paris: Presses Universitaires de France, 1950.

Mauzé, Marie. 1986. Boas, les Kwagul, et le potlatch: Éléments pour une réévaluation. *L'Homme* 100:21–63.

Memmi, Albert. [1957] 1967. *The Colonizer and the Colonized.* Boston: Beacon Press.

Milloy, John S. 1983. The Early Indian Acts: Developmental Strategy and Constitutional Change. In *As Long as the Sun Shines and the Water Flows: A Reader in Canadian Native Studies,* ed. Ian A. L. Getty and Antoine S. Lussier, 56–64. Vancouver: University of British Columbia Press.

Mooney, Kathleen. 1978. The Effects of Rank and Wealth on Exchange among the Coast Salish. *Ethnology* 17:391–406.

Morrison, Toni. 1992. *Playing in the Dark: Whiteness and the Literary Imagination.* New York: Vintage.

Mueller-Vollmer, Kurt, ed. 1985. *The Hermeneutics Reader: Texts of the German Tradition from the Enlightenment to the Present.* New York: Continuum.

Murdock, George P. 1936. *Rank and Potlatch among the Haida.* Yale University Publications in Anthropology, vol. 13. New Haven: Yale University Press.

National Archives of Canada. 1878–1934. Record Group 10. Western (Black) Series. Ottawa.

Nietzsche, Friedrich. 1967. *On the Genealogy of Morals.* Trans. Walter Kaufmann. New York: Vintage.

Nowell, Charles James. 1941. *Smoke from Their Fires: The Life of a Kwakiutl Chief by Clellan S. Ford.* New Haven: Yale University Press.

Obeyesekere, Gananath. 1992. "British Cannibals": Contemplation of an Event in the Death and Resurrection of James Cook, Explorer. *Critical Inquiry* 18, no. 4:630–54.

Ott, Hugo. 1993. *Martin Heidegger: A Political Life*. Trans. Allan Blunden. New York: Basic Books.

Pearce, Roy Harvey. 1988. *Savagism and Civilization: A Study of the Indian and the American Mind*. Berkeley and Los Angeles: University of California Press.

Pearsall, Marion. 1949. Contributions of Early Explorers and Traders to the Ethnography of the Northwest. *Pacific Northwest Quarterly* 40:316–26.

Piddocke, Stuart. 1965. The Potlatch System of the Southern Kwakiutl. *Southwestern Journal of Anthropology* 21:244–64.

Powell, J. V. 1988. Chinook Jargon. In *The Canadian Encyclopedia*. 2d ed. Edmonton: Hurtig.

Reid, Susan. 1979. The Kwakiutl Maneater. *Anthropologica* 21:247–75.

Riches, David. 1984. Hunting, Herding, and Potlatching: Towards a Sociological Account of Prestige. *Man* 19:234–51.

Richman, Michèle H. 1982. *Reading Georges Bataille: Beyond the Gift*. Baltimore: Johns Hopkins University Press.

———. 1990. Anthropology and Modernism in France: From Durkheim to the *Collège de sociologie*. In *Modernist Anthropology: From Fieldwork to Text*, ed. Marc Manganaro, 183–214. Princeton: Princeton University Press.

Ringel, Gail. 1979. The Kwakiutl Potlatch: History, Economics, and Symbols. *Ethnohistory* 26:347–62.

Rohner, Robert P., ed. 1969. *The Ethnography of Franz Boas: Letters and Diaries of Franz Boas Written on the Northwest Coast from 1886 to 1931*. Chicago: University of Chicago Press.

Rosman, Abraham, and Paula G. Rubel. 1971. *Feasting with Mine Enemy: Rank and Exchange among Northwest Coast Societies*. New York: Columbia University Press.

———. 1972. The Potlatch: A Structural Analysis. *American Anthropologist* 74:658–71.

Ruyle, Eugene. 1973. Slavery, Surplus, and Stratification on the Northwest Coast: The Ethnoenergetics of an Incipient Stratification System. *Current Anthropology* 14:603–31.

Said, Edward. 1979. *Orientalism*. New York: Vintage.

Sapir, Edward. 1915. A Sketch of the Social Organisation of the Nass River Indians. *Museum Bulletin of the Canadian Department of Mines* 19:1–30.

———. 1955. *Native Accounts of Nootka Ethnography*. Research Centre in Anthropology, Folklore, and Linguistics, Research Publications, vol. 1. Bloomington: Indiana University Press.

———. 1966. The Social Organization of the West Coast Tribes. In *Indians of the Pacific Northwest*, ed. Tom McFeat, 28–48. Seattle: University of Washington Press.

Schulte-Tenckhoff, Isabelle. 1986. *Potlatch: Conquête et invention: Reflexion sur un concept anthropologique*. Lausanne: Éditions d'en Bas.

Scott, Duncan Campbell. 1926. *Poems*. Toronto: McClelland and Stewart.

———. 1929. *Three Songs of the Northwest Coast*. London: F. Harris.

———. 1931. *The Administration of Indian Affairs in Canada*. Ottawa: Canadian Institute of International Affairs.

———. 1935. *The Green Cloister: Later Poems*. Toronto: McClelland and Stewart.

———. 1947. *The Circle of Affection and Other Pieces in Prose and Verse*. Toronto: McClelland and Stewart.

———. 1968. *Poetry and Progress*. Toronto: Canadiana House.

———. 1985. *Powassan's Drum: Poems of Duncan Campbell Scott*. Ed. Raymond Souster and Douglas Lochhead. Ottawa: Tecumseh.

Searle, John. 1969. *Speech Acts: An Essay in the Philosophy of Language*. Cambridge: Cambridge University Press.

Seguin, Margaret. 1984. Lest There Be No Salmon: Symbols in Traditional Tsimshian Potlatch. In *The Tsimshian: Images of the Past: Views for the Present*, ed. Margaret Seguin, 110–33. Vancouver: University of British Columbia Press.

———. 1985. *Interpretive Contexts for Traditional and Current Coast Tsimshian Feasts*. National Museum of Man, Mercury Series, Canadian Ethnology Service Paper 98. Ottawa: National Museums of Canada.

———. ed. 1984. *The Tsimshian: Images of the Past: Views for the Present*. Vancouver: University of British Columbia Press.

Sewid-Smith, Daisy (My-yah-nelth). 1979. *Prosecution or Persecution*. [Cape Mudge, British Columbia]: Nu-yum-baleess Society.

Shaw, George C. 1909. *The Chinook Jargon and How to Use It: A Complete and Exhaustive Lexicon of the Oldest Trade Language of the American Continent*. Seattle: Rainier Printing.

Sioui, Georges E. 1992. *For an Amerindian Autohistory: An Essay on the Foundations of a Social Ethic*. Trans. Sheila Fischman. Montreal: McGill; Kingston: Queen's University Press.

Spivak, Gayatri Chakravorty. 1987. *In Other Worlds: Essays in Cultural Politics*. New York and London: Routledge.

———. 1989. Can the Subaltern Speak? In *Marxism and the Interpretation of Culture*, ed. Cary Nelson and Lawrence Grossberg, 271–313. Urbana: University of Illinois Press.

———. 1993. *Outside in the Teaching Machine*. New York and London: Routledge.

Spradley, James P., ed. 1969. *Guests Never Leave Hungry: The Autobiography of James Sewid, a Kwakiutl Indian*. Montreal: McGill; Kingston: Queen's University Press.

Sproat, Gilbert Malcolm. 1867. The West Coast Indians in Vancouver Island. *Transactions of the Ethnological Society of London for 1867*, 243–54.

———. 1868. *Scenes and Studies of Savage Life*. London: Smith, Elder and Co.

*b i b l i o g r a p h y*

————. 1873. *Canada and the Empire: A Speech.* London: Agent General for British Columbia.

————. 1875. *British Columbia: Information for Emigrants.* London: Agent General for British Columbia.

————. 1878. *Memorandum on Indian Reserves in the District of Yale.* Victoria: Colonist Steam Presses.

————. 1987. *The Nootka: Scenes and Studies of Savage Life.* Ed. Charles Lillard. Victoria: Sono Nis.

Steltzer, Ulli. 1984. *A Haida Potlatch.* Vancouver: Douglas and McIntyre.

Strathern, Marilyn. 1988. *The Gender of the Gift: Problems with Women and Problems with Society in Melanesia.* Berkeley: University of California Press.

Suttles, Wayne. 1987. *Coast Salish Essays.* Vancouver: Talonbooks; Seattle: University of Washington Press.

Tate, Charles Montgomery. 1889. *Chinook as Spoken by the Indians of Washington Territory, British Columbia, and Alaska: For the Use of Traders, Tourists, and Others Who Have Business Intercourse with the Indians.* Victoria: M. W. Waitt.

Teit, James A. 1930. *Salishan Tribes of the Western Plateaus.* Washington, DC: Government Printing Office.

Tennant, Paul. 1990. *Aboriginal Peoples and Politics: The Indian Land Question in British Columbia, 1849–1989.* Vancouver: University of British Columbia Press.

Thomas, Edward Harper. 1935. *Chinook: A History and Dictionary of the Northwest Coast Trade Jargon.* Portland, OR: Binsford and Mort.

Titley, Brian. 1986. *A Narrow Vision: Duncan Campbell Scott and the Administration of Indian Affairs in Canada.* Vancouver: University of British Columbia Press.

Tobias, John L. 1983. Protection, Civilization, Assimilation: An Outline History of Canada's Indian Policy. In *As Long as the Sun Shines and the Water Flows: A Reader in Canadian Native Studies,* ed. Ian A. L. Getty and Antoine S. Lussier, 39–55. Vancouver: University of British Columbia Press.

Upton, L. F. S. 1973. The Origins of Canadian Indian Policy. *Journal of Canadian Studies* 8, no. 4:51–61.

Vayda, Andrew Peter. 1961. A Reexamination of Northwest Coast Economic Systems. *Transactions of the New York Academy of Sciences* 23:618–24.

Visweswaran, Kamala. 1994. *Fictions of Feminist Ethnography.* Minneapolis: University of Minnesota Press.

Vizenor, Gerald. 1994. *Manifest Manners: Postindian Warriors of Survivance.* Hanover, NH: Wesleyan University Press.

Walens, Stanley. 1981. *Feasting with Cannibals: Metaphor and Morality in Nineteenth Century Kwakiutl Culture.* Princeton: Princeton University Press.

Weis, L. P. 1986. D. C. Scott's View of History and the Indian. *Canadian Literature* 111:27–39.

Wike, Joyce. 1984. A Reevaluation of Northwest Coast Cannibalism. In *The Tsimshian and Their Neighbours of the North Pacific Coast*, ed. Jay Miller and Carol M. Eastman, 239–54. Seattle: University of Washington Press.

*bibliography*

# INDEX

22–31; of thing, 94; and time, 121–27, 155–57; of women, 49; and word, 30, 94–99; and writing, 141. *See also* Being; Derrida, Jacques; event; exchange; Heidegger, Martin; legal text; name; narrative; thing; time; word

*The Globe,* 203

Gradual Civilization Act of 1857, 185

grammar, 121–27

Grant, Charles, 20

Grant, J. W., 182

Great Britain: Colonial Office, 2; colonies of, 2; limit of, 14. *See also* England

Green, A. E.: as Indian school inspector, 181; as missionary, 78, 89

Haisla First Nation, 179. *See also* First Nations of British Columbia

Hale, Horatio: and BAAS, 243n; opposition to law, 144

Hall, Alfred; missionary efforts, 65–66, 69, 240n; on prostitution, 132

Halliday, William May: attack on potlatch, 209–17; defense of potlatch, 186; fiction of potlatch, 217; on marriage and potlatch, 186–87; as photographer, 186, 192–99; *Potlatch and Totem,* 190–81, 200–2, 217; sale of regalia, 215; on waste of time, 217; on whiteness, 200–2

hamatsa: danced by James Knox, 215; defined by Boas (hā′-mats'a), 171–79; defined as cannibalism, 169–70; and theatre, 175–79. *See also* dances; tamanawas

Ha-mer-cee-luc. *See* He-ma-sak

Harris, Bob, 212

Harris, Ned, 188

Harris, R. W., 179

Hegel, G. W. F.: on circle, 103; *Phenomenology of Spirit,* 163; on truth, 240n

Heidegger, Martin: *Being and Time,* 103, 234n; the danger, 23–25; "Dialogue on Language," 23–

31; on dictionaries, 112; on gift, 29–31, 103–7, 240n; on history, 29–30, 162–63, 240n; "Letter on Humanism," 29–20, 162–63, 240–41n; on metaphysics, 25–30, 52; and National Socialism, 246–47n; "The Nature of Language," 28–30, 49–53, 94–97, 112; on saying, 27–28, 229–30, 241n; on showing, 230; on sign, 74; on time, 103–6; "Time and Being," 30, 98–99, 104–6; "The Way to Language," 229–30. *See also* Being, gift; *Ereignis;* event of appropriation; metaphysics; philosophy

He-ma-sak, 91

Heye, George, 215

Hill-Tout, Charles, 219

history: and destiny, 29–30; and gift, 162–65. *See also* gift; Heidegger, Martin; metaphysics

holocaust, 162, 246n

Howe, Joseph, 234n

Hudson's Bay Company, 2, 37, 40, 114, 241n

Hulbertson, Edward, 212

Hunt, George: and Boas, 144–45, 243–45n; *Contributions to the Ethnology of the Kwakiutl,* 147–48

Hyde, Lewis, *The Gift,* 236–37n, 248n

India, 20, 49, 238n

Indian Act, The: amended in 1951, 185, 228; and antipotlatch law, 83; as archive, 141; and colonial era, 185; and municipal councils, 236n; as promissory note, 201; and racial assimilation, 184–86; section 22, 170; section 114, 83–84, 117–21, 127; section 140, 228; section 149, 171

"Indian affairs," discourse on, 35–37

Indian agencies established, 61

Indian Branch: annual report for 1872, 35; closed, 61; criticized by Sproat, 43; and postal literature, 39; under Vankoughnet, 54. *See also* Department of Indian Affairs

274

*index*

*index*

technology, 24–25

Teit, James, 219

text: colonial, 5–6; defined by de Man, 121–27; in metaphysics, 26. *See also* gift; thing; time

thing: delivery of, 230; as textual gift, 28–30, 94–99, 123, 228; and word, 56, 94–99. *See also* gift; word

thinking, 27–28

Thomas, Edward Harper, *Chinook: A History and Dictionary of the Northwest Coast Trade Jargon*, 109, 111

time: as circle, 102–4; and ethnography, 178–79; and fetishism, 63; and gift, 50, 104–7, 245–46n; of legal text, 122–27; and nationalism, 205–8; of potlatch, 211; of promise, 125–26. *See also* Being; Derrida, Jacques; Heidegger, Martin; metaphysics

Tobias, John L., "Protection, Civilization, Assimilation," 184–86

Todd, Charles, 90

Todd, Murray, 229

translation, 24–25

trials for potlatching, 188–90, 211–14, 216

Trutch, Joseph, 42–42, 79

truth: as correspondence, 76–78; defined by Hegel, 240n; of gift, 246n; and law, 118

Tsimshian First Nation, 78, 179. *See also* First Nations of British Columbia

University of Toronto, 203

Uslick, Bill, 133–34, 180

Vancouver Island: colony founded, 2; as England's substitute, 12; and Japan, 10; political union with mainland, 2; treaties, 40–41

Vankoughnet, Lawrence: on Begbie's judgment, 112–13; as Macdonald's substitute, 61–65, 239n; order in council, 78–80; retirement, 129; on Sproat, 53–58, 236n; on tamanawas,

72–73. *See also* Department of Indian Affairs; fetishism

Victoria Memorial Museum, 215

Vizenor, Gerald, 15

Vowell, Arthur: ambivalence toward law, 138–39; on death of potlatch, 179–80; incident at Salmon River, 134–35; policy of non-enforcement, 129, 131, 135; resignation, 187

Walker, Frank, 221–22

waste: and property, 21, 45, 130, 132; of time, 131, 169; and war, 209–10; of women, 132. *See also* gift; expenditure; potlatch

West, the: closure of, 8; history of, 29–30; undecidability of, 22–23. *See also* Canada; Europe; Europe-in-Canada; whiteness

Westness, 23. *See also* Europeanness; whiteness

White, Thomas, 90

Wilson, Peter, 213

Wilson, Robert, 213

whiteness: and assimilation, 200–9, 230–31, 248n; of British Columbia, 2–3; as cannibalism, 202; and death, 190–91, 200–2; and fetishism, 64; and fold, 16–17; versus gift, 191; and industry, 68; as light, 19, 48; at limit, 8; and memory, 182–84, 190–91, 200–2; as mourning, 201–2, 204–8; and poetry, 224–25; versus potlatch, 82; as promise, 201, 204–5; and tamanawas, 72. *See also* Europe; Europeanness; Europe-in-Canada; mourning; nationalism; Westness

Woodsworth, J. S., 229

word: as gift-event, 95–99, 230; as prosthesis, 56; and thing, 30–31, 56, 63, 86, 94–99, 230; for the unknown, 53. *See also* gift; thing

zones of text, 5–6